"*The Book of Boundaries* is the rare book that manages to be practical, thoughtful, readable, and even *funny*. If you've struggled to identify and establish healthy boundaries—with family, in romance, at work, or in life—Melissa Urban shows the way forward with clarity, vulnerability, and humor."

—GRETCHEN RUBIN, *New York Times* bestselling author of *The Happiness Project* and *The Four Tendencies*

"I always tell my therapy patients that boundaries create trust, comfort, and safety in a relationship, but many people struggle with how to effectively communicate what they need. In *The Book of Boundaries,* Melissa Urban helps you identify your boundary needs, offers actionable scripts, and shares proven tips based on a decade of experience helping people live more freely by holding their limits with confidence."

—LORI GOTTLIEB, *New York Times* bestselling author of *Maybe You Should Talk To Someone*

"*The Book of Boundaries* is funny, direct, and smart, bringing you actionable tools and science-backed strategies for setting boundaries, using language that feels kind, natural, and empowering. Urban's straightforward scripts and practical tips make it easy to identify your limits and communicate them with confidence, so you can start putting yourself first and create a life that feels bigger, freer, and more authentically *you*."

—MEL ROBBINS, *New York Times* bestselling author of *The 5 Second Rule*

"Helpful as hell and lovingly direct, Melissa Urban is the boundaries big sister we all so desperately need. Through her insightful advice and easy-to-follow scripts, Urban teaches you how to stand up for yourself without walling yourself off from the people you love."

—TARA SCHUSTER, author of *Buy Yourself the F*cking Lilies*

"Healthy boundaries are good for your relationships, your business, and your finances. *The Book of Boundaries* shows you how to stand up for yourself, say no, and communicate your needs in a way that leaves you feeling confident and empowered. Through her stories, personal experiences, and research, Melissa Urban gives you the tools, affirmations, and language you need to reclaim your time, energy, and health."

—TIFFANY ALICHE, *New York Times*
bestselling author of *Get Good with Money*

"Melissa Urban has written the playbook for creating connection, protecting our peace, and expanding our lives. At once insightful, personal, funny, and direct, *The Book of Boundaries* should be required reading for anyone who has relationships with other humans."

—ELLEN VORA, MD, psychiatrist and bestselling
author of *The Anatomy of Anxiety*

"If you're a people-pleaser, can't say no, or constantly put other people's comfort ahead of your own, you need Melissa Urban and *The Book of Boundaries*. Through her entertaining stories, years of research, and personal experience, Urban helps you identify your needs, gives you just the right words to communicate them effectively, and empowers you to transform your relationships, self-esteem, and confidence."

—SARA KUBURIC, existential therapist, author
of *It's On Me,* and creator of @millennial.therapist

"Urban's encouraging tone and detailed 'scripts,' which provide examples of what one might say in common situations to establish boundaries, make for an empathetic and pragmatic outing. This helpful manual is a boon for those unsure of how to set limits."

—*Publishers Weekly*

The
Book of
Boundaries

The Book of Boundaries

Set the Limits That Will Set You Free

MELISSA URBAN

THE DIAL PRESS

New York

2023 Dial Press Trade Paperback Edition

Copyright © 2022 by Melissa Urban
Bonus chapter copyright © 2023 by Melissa Urban

LIBRARY OF CONGRESS CATALOGING-IN-PUBLICATION DATA
Names: Urban, Melissa, author.
Title: The book of boundaries: set the limits that will set you free / Melissa Urban.
Description: New York: The Dial Press, [2022] |
Identifiers: LCCN 2022037169 (print) | LCCN 2022037170 (ebook) |
ISBN 9780593448724 (trade paperback) | ISBN 9780593448717 (ebook)
Subjects: LCSH: Boundaries (Psychology) | Self-protective behavior. |
Assertiveness (Psychology)
Classification: LCC BF697.5.S45 U73 2022 (print) | LCC BF697.5.S45 (ebook) |
DDC 158.2—dc23/eng/20220829
LC record available at https://lccn.loc.gov/2022037169
LC ebook record available at https://lccn.loc.gov/2022037170

Printed in the United States of America on acid-free paper

randomhousebooks.com

9 8 7 6 5 4 3 2 1

Book design by Debbie Glasserman

FOR MY HUSBAND AND MY SISTER,
WHO ARE ALWAYS ON MY TEAM

Contents

Author's Note   ix

Introduction: How I Became the "Boundary Lady"   3

PART ONE | BOUNDARY BEGINNINGS   **23**

  1. **A Crash Course on Boundaries**   25

  2. **How to Use This Book**   48

PART TWO | YOUR BOUNDARY PRACTICE   **57**

  3. **The Real Work/Life Balance:** Setting
Boundaries in the Workplace   59

  4. **When the Drama Is Your Mama:** Setting
Boundaries with Parents and In-Laws,
Grandparents, and Other Family Members   94

  5. **Relationships We (Mostly) Choose:** Setting
Boundaries with Friends and Neighbors   134

  6. **Love, Marriage, Sex, and Dishes:** Setting
Boundaries in Romantic Relationships   165

  7. **When You Can't Just Walk Away:**
Setting Boundaries with Co-Parents   211

8. **Clearing the Table:** Setting Boundaries Around
   Food, Alcohol, and Table Talk   227

9. **Handle with Care:** Setting Boundaries Around
   Sensitive Subjects   259

10. **Gifts to Future You:** Setting and Holding
    Boundaries with Yourself   291

PART THREE | **BOUNDARY BENEFITS**   **317**

11. **Gifts to the World:** How to Hold Your
    Boundaries, and Everyone Else's   319

12. **The Magic of Boundaries**   342

BONUS CHAPTER   **349**

 Mom Prefers to Pee Alone: Setting
   Boundaries with Children   351

Acknowledgments   361

Notes   365

Author's Note

In the last decade, I've talked to thousands of people about their boundary issues. The stories you'll read in this book came from those conversations. A few stories have been told without alteration, using real names and circumstances, always with that person's blessing. In most cases, I've changed names and other details as needed to protect people's privacy. In still others, I've merged multiple conversations into one cohesive story. Always, I have tried to capture the full depth and breadth of the many issues—and opportunities—that arise when we set boundaries.

When it comes to gendered terms (like "wife" or "hers"), I've preserved what was sent to me by my readers. If you see a specific gendered term, that story was told to me using those terms or pronouns. In the scripts or stories in this book, there are instances where I've merged multiple narratives into one. In those cases, I've used the gender-neutral pronouns "they/them" and gender-neutral terms like "partner" or "manager."

Finally, a dynamic I must recognize and state from the outset: Setting a boundary is an expression of power and a privilege. (And if you've never thought about it like that, it's probably because, like me, you have a lot of unearned privilege.) Because I am white, straight, able-bodied, financially secure, and thin, I am afforded a certain degree of power in our society. Those privileges and that power mean I can speak a boundary with relative confidence, and generally expect others to respect my wishes. People who belong to historically marginalized groups—whether people of color, disabled, plus-sized, or LGTBQ+—don't have the same privilege, the same power, or the same relationship to boundaries that I do. Without that privilege, you're likely more fearful of setting a boundary and the truth is, others are less likely to respect it. (That's how systems of oppression work.)

I have to be conscientious of this power disparity in my work, but awareness has value only if it leads to changed behavior and sustained action. This recognition is just one small step, and an acknowledgment that I will not accurately capture everyone's lived experiences in this book.

I am grateful to each and every person who has so generously shared such intimate details of their life with me. And if we've never spoken, I hope that you will see your own stories reflected in those I tell here, and that they will give you the confidence you need to set the limits that will set you free.

The
Book of
Boundaries

How I Became the "Boundary Lady"

In certain circles, I am known as the "Boundary Lady."

To be fair, I am known as many things. I am a CEO, a wife, and a mother. I am a bestselling author, an avid hiker, and a voracious reader. But when it comes to boundaries, specifically, many of my readers' spouses know me only as "that boundary lady on Instagram."

If you were to look at me today, this label would make total sense. Personality-wise, let's just say I am not a people pleaser. To even the casual observer, I appear assertive, independent, and self-confident; both comfortable with conflict and direct about expressing my needs. That behavior, especially coming from a woman, sometimes evokes an accusation of selfishness, and a few others I won't mention here, but you can probably imagine what they are.

I'm not selfish, though, or any of those other descriptions you just envisioned. What I am is someone who takes her mental health, energetic capacity, and worth seriously, and does what needs to be done to protect them. This can look like:

- **In business:** "Thank you for thinking of me. This project doesn't feel like a good fit, so I'm going to pass."

- **With my parents:** "I know you're trying to help, but it's my job to make the rules for my son. I'll let you know if I want your input."
- **In friendships:** "Oh, let me stop you—please don't share stories about what my ex is up to. I really don't want to hear about it."
- **With my husband:** "I could use some alone time, so I'm going into the other room to read."

Reading these statements may make you uncomfortable, but they're all firmly in my wheelhouse, and I use them often as a means of strengthening my relationships, bolstering my energy, and preserving my mental health. And I don't apologize for setting these kinds of limits, because when I'm expressing my needs in a direct and polite manner, there is nothing to apologize for.

I am also the co-founder of the Whole30 program, which means I've led millions of people through successful habit change and dramatic transformations. You say no a lot when you're on the Whole30, and many people find that idea daunting at best. For the past thirteen years, I've taught my community how to set boundaries around their health and habits, and how to deal with pushback and peer pressure. (Are you ready to embrace "no thank you" as a complete sentence? We'll get there.)

Once people realized I was good at helping them say no to pizza and wine, they started asking me how to say no to their pushy co-worker, toxic mother-in-law, and nosy neighbor. I was getting so many questions from people about how to set boundaries that I did a deep dive into all the boundary-related work I could find. I read every book, article, and research paper I could dig up from therapists, psychiatrists, sociologists, addiction specialists, medical doctors, and business leaders, in a quest to discover what makes good boundaries and how they're established.

Through that research, my own self-work, and listening to the needs of my community, I developed my own methodology and language around boundary-setting. Four years ago, I began running "Help me set a boundary" Q&As in my online community and in my newsletter, which has given me the opportunity to hear thousands of your stories and to fine-tune my approach and advice. (Side note: Y'all's in-laws really do behave badly.)

All of this is to say I wear my "Boundary Lady" badge with pride, especially knowing how far I've come to earn it. I wasn't always like this.

My journey with boundaries starts twenty-two years ago, when I was at one of my lowest points and was basically a boundary disaster. The list of "things that I am" also includes "recovering drug addict"—and it took many years of struggling in desperation before I realized that boundaries were the thing that would literally save my life.

I know that sounds dramatic, and I am *also* a repeat offender of using the word "literally" to mean "anything but literally," but in this instance, it's the truth. I came from a home that modeled avoidance instead of healthy conflict, and after a traumatic experience in my teens, I spent the better part of a decade hiding my emotions, trying not to make anyone uncomfortable, and never saying no. Standing up for myself wasn't a skill I was taught, and confrontation made me incredibly anxious. I desperately needed boundaries, but I didn't feel worthy or capable of setting them.

Then one night twenty-two years ago, while sitting next to a keg of Natty Light, I set a boundary in a desperate act of self-preservation . . . and it changed the entire trajectory of my life. That experience encouraged me to set more boundaries—with friends, family, co-workers, even myself. The more boundaries I set, the more expansive my life became, which led to Whole30, my business, and this book.

The point is, I *learned* how to set boundaries. The hard way, sure, but I did learn. And if I did, you can, too.

WHAT ARE BOUNDARIES, AND WHY DO WE NEED THEM?

Before we dive into that story, let's establish a working definition of what I mean when I say "boundaries." I'm sure you've heard the term, but you probably have only a squishy idea of what boundaries are. I suspect the word itself makes you a little uncomfortable, or perhaps even triggers feelings of guilt. Maybe you think boundaries are mean. Maybe you think they're selfish or uncaring. Maybe you think they're about trying to control other people.

Maybe you've been told all of those things by the people who benefit the most from you having none.

I define boundaries as clear limits you establish around the ways you allow people to engage with you, so that you can keep yourself and your relationships safe and healthy. The dictionary says a boundary is "a line that marks the limits of an area," and that's a good way to think about it. Picture yourself standing in the middle of a field. Now draw an imaginary circle around you—that's a boundary. Anything you allow inside the circle is acceptable to you, because it's safe, healthy, and feels good. Anything unacceptable, you keep outside the circle, because it makes you feel unsafe, unhealthy, or generally not good. You can set a limit when it comes to other people, certain conversation topics or behaviors, or your own actions—and you're always in charge of where those limits lie, and enforcing them.

Boundaries mark the limits of behaviors that are acceptable to you, where words or actions beyond that limit cause you harm or make you feel unsafe.

Boundaries are not used to tell other people what they can and cannot do. That *would* be controlling. Boundaries are established to help you plan and communicate your *response* to what other people say or do. In a healthy boundary practice, you'll notice how other people's behavior impacts you, communicate your healthy limit in relation to that behavior, then consider what you are willing to do to enforce that limit. So you can't tell Uncle Joe to quit smoking—that's controlling. But you can notice that cigarette smoke makes you cough and smells bad, communicate to Uncle Joe, "We don't allow smoking inside the house," and not invite Uncle Joe inside if he won't respect that limit. You set a boundary not to shame Uncle Joe or change his lifestyle or health, but to protect your own.

See the difference?

There are many reasons you might want to set a boundary, which means boundary-setting will sound different for each situation. Sometimes you set a gentle boundary around frustrating but minor issues, like a neighbor who keeps inviting themselves on your morning walk. Other times, you set firm boundaries around behaviors that cause real harm, like when your mom criticizes your weight over lunch, or your parents tell you they've booked a flight to see the new baby without asking. (I cannot *imagine,* but people tell me this happens.) Boundaries can sound like "I can walk with you on Saturday, but during the week I need my alone time," or "I'm going to leave the table if you keep talking about my weight," or "We aren't ready for visitors, so we'll let you know when you can come."

There are a lot of misconceptions about boundaries, and to make it worse, no one teaches us about them. They're rarely modeled at home, not taught in school, and likely not part of your professional development at work. In fact, most of what you know about boundaries probably came from a therapist on social media, if you happen to be on that side of TikTok. The truth is, setting boundaries is an essential life skill, like time management and budgeting. Unfortunately, as my credit report from 2001 would prove, many of us realize only during times of crisis that these skills are lacking, and we're forced to pick them up under less-than-ideal circumstances.

All of this is both terrible and excellent news.

Terrible, because this truly magical tool with the ability to transform every area of your life has been at your disposal all this time and *you didn't even know it*. Excellent, because I'm about to give you a boundary crash course, and it's going to change everything.

THE BOUNDARY THAT SAVED MY LIFE

In my case, the first boundary I ever set happened twenty-two years ago, and it went like this: "If you offer me drugs again, we can't be friends. Not even if I say I'm better, not even if I ask you for them, not even if I get really mad at you for saying no." (I told you it was dramatic.)

I wish I could say this boundary was thoughtfully planned and eloquently communicated, but it was basically an accident. I word-vomited all over my best friend in a moment of intense fear. But what a happy accident it was, because those upchucked words led me to the discovery that *boundaries* were the key to expanding my life exponentially; helping me release anxiety, self-doubt, and resentment; and firmly establishing the kind of physical and emotional security, bomb-proof self-confidence, and deeply satisfying relationships I'd been craving my whole life. *Now* it's time for that story:

Hi, my name is Melissa, and I am a drug addict. I've been in recovery for twenty-two years, but identifying as an addict still serves me, reminding me how hard I've worked to build the life I have now, and what I would give (and the limits I would set) to never find myself in that dark place again.

I had a pretty idyllic childhood. I grew up with two parents who stayed together until I was in college, and a tight-knit group of aunts, uncles, and cousins who loved spending time together. Nobody in my family drank or did drugs. My mom stayed home with me and my sister while my dad worked outside the home, sometimes two jobs. I was always described as a "good kid," earning straight A's, rarely getting in trouble, studying hard, and preferring books to social gatherings.

At sixteen, all of that changed following an incident of sexual abuse by someone in my extended family. My mood, grades, and behavior took a sharp turn as I hid the abuse from my parents and tried to pretend it never happened. When I finally did tell them, they didn't know how to handle it. They decided not to tell anyone for fear it would shatter the family peace, so we all just went on as if it hadn't happened. I spent the next few years seeing my abuser at holiday gatherings, pretending everything was fine. It did a number on my teenage brain.

I searched for ways to numb and escape from my family dynamics and the trauma we all refused to address. I ran through the gamut of Afterschool Special topics. Drinking alcohol didn't work, controlling my eating didn't work, shoplifting didn't work, dating an abusive guy didn't work. These self-destructive behaviors didn't take me as far away as I wanted to go; nothing felt all-consuming enough.

Then I found drugs, and it was like the heavens parted and the angels sang—except the angels were a German death-metal band and I was in the mosh pit.

It started with pot my senior year of high school and morphed into far more serious drugs in college. (The phrase "that escalated quickly" comes to mind.) I was using cocaine, heroin, meth, and any prescription narcotic I could get my hands on. I was known for never saying no. I mixed drugs I should never have mixed and overdosed at least once, coming to on the floor at a party where a friend casually mentioned I had "stopped breathing there for a minute." I told myself I was just having fun. I told myself I was making up for my nerdy, studious childhood. I told myself I could stop anytime, I just didn't *want to*.

My life slowly unraveled, and everyone started to notice except me.

In my junior year of college, I began stealing from my roommates and dealing pot as a way to subsidize my habit. I skipped nearly all my classes. My roommates discovered I was selling drugs from our apartment and told me I had to move out or they would tell their parents.

Looking back, that was probably the first real boundary anyone had set with me around my drug use. Setting boundaries is a hard and uncomfortable process, and it was easier for people to ignore my behavior or to quietly ghost me than it was to enact the limits necessary to preserve our relationship. My freshman roommate didn't say, "I can't live with you if you keep behaving like this," she just found new roommates. My old friends didn't say, "We can't keep going out with you if you're going to get this blitzed," they just stopped calling. My sister didn't say, "Your drug use is freaking me out, I think we need to talk," she just avoided me unless she needed a ride home. I don't blame any of them; I didn't make it easy for anyone to even try to have a conversation about how my behavior was affecting them.

My roommates tried, though . . . so I dropped out of school and moved in with my dad and his new wife, where I swore things would be different. I was very good at compensating and I was relatively functional for a while, until I wasn't. I met a new boyfriend who enabled my use, and I began calling in sick to work. My parents started to notice, so I found a new therapist to get them off my back. I mostly used my appointments to drug-seek.

When my boyfriend was arrested, I moved again, to go live with my mom and her new husband. I swore things would be different. I didn't have a job or a plan. I was stealing from my parents and dealing from their condo. My guests were, in a word, shady. One day my stepdad said to my mom, "I think your daughter is on drugs."

I moved out immediately, got a new job, and found my own apartment. I swore things would be different. I started selling heroin and fell behind on my rent. My landlord said I had a month to catch up, or he would have to evict me. He looked sorry when he said it.

My drug use was starting to feel out of control. I did more drugs to shove that feeling down.

When I think back to this time, I can't help but feel compassion for the young woman I was then, doing the best I could to save my own life with whatever tools I had at my disposal. But through the lens of boundaries, it's obvious how my desire to numb and run away, and the lack of any healthy limits to protect my physical and mental health, turned into a full-blown drug addiction. And that made my life smaller and smaller, until I almost disappeared.

Four years into my addiction, I met a man named Nate. He drank, but only socially. He smoked pot, but only recreationally. He had a good job and was ambitious. We moved in together. I swore things would be different . . . and for a little while they were. I stopped dealing and partying. I did fewer drugs. But at that point, I needed them to simply exist, so I used to maintain a quiet baseline. Nate never knew me any other way, so he didn't yet suspect I had a problem. I went to work, we hung out with friends, he met my family. They liked this one.

But my drug use once again began to creep. Nate noticed that the way I used drugs wasn't at all casual. Before, I had always been able to curb my use when I really needed to. This time, I couldn't. I behaved erratically in front of family and friends. Nate and I fought constantly, and I began staying out late. I hated myself for my drug use and for what I was doing to my relationship, but that shame and self-loathing led me to use even more. I saw no way out.

Nate gave me a long handwritten letter, telling me how he was at the end of his emotional capacity, how much he loved me, and how hard it was to be with me like this. He didn't explicitly say he would leave unless I got help, but the meaning was clear. I cried, made an appointment with my therapist, and swore things would be different. Again.

Nothing changed.

Nate did his best to continue to set boundaries with me. In that moment I hated him for it, but looking back, his boundaries saved us both. He started by protecting his space and preserving his mental health. "If you can't discuss this calmly, I'll leave until you can." "Please text if you're going to stay out late." "I'll keep working on it with you, but please keep going to therapy." I recognize now that he was trying his best to keep our relationship alive, a goal I was making impossible. At the time, I resented the inquiries, the pressure, the reminders that what I was doing was hurting him. I now see he was using these boundaries to protect himself—from me.

Finally, Nate confronted me. "I can't do this anymore," he said. "I can't stay and watch you self-destruct, and it's clear that I can't help you. I'd like to call a rehab facility and take you there tonight. If you're not ready to do that right now, I have to leave."

To this day, I still refer to Nate as "my favorite ex-boyfriend." His boundaries, and eventually his ultimatum when I failed to respect them, were a turning point, one that would ultimately lead to my recovery and a fuller life than I ever could have imagined.

In that moment, however, I was equal parts furious and terrified. In the face of that ultimatum, perhaps because I knew what would happen if I let him walk out the door, I found the strength to say two words out loud: "I'll go."

I spent several weeks at an inpatient facility, then many more in outpatient therapy, group sessions, and meetings. I went on antidepressants, started to work with a new therapist, returned to my job, and began rebuilding relationships with family and friends. Nate and I tried to make it work but broke up shortly after I came home. We lived together in friendship for another few months. He was one of the good ones.

For a whole year, I was free from all drugs and alcohol. And here is where we return again to boundaries, because twelve months into my recovery, I discovered I had none, and it almost cost me my life. Up until this point, the only boundaries I had experienced were when my college roommates and Nate set them with me. (And to be honest, I didn't recognize them as boundaries at the time.) I still had not set any boundaries *myself*—or with anyone else—around my fledgling recovery. I didn't even recognize that I needed them, and that was exactly the problem.

In that year after coming home from rehab, I maintained my life exactly the same as it had always been, minus the drugs. My friends were the same, my routines were the same, my clothes, music, and eating habits were the same. I went to the same places with the same people who were doing the same things they had always done, and everyone (including me) expected me to show up mostly the same as well. So I did.

When I look back on that time now, it's clear why I relapsed. I had set just one shaky boundary with myself around my drug use, relationships, and mental health: I said I wouldn't use. Except I did *nothing* to support that. My entire recovery hinged on me saying to me, "Hey, that highly addictive behavior that you relied on for everything from love to comfort to distraction to avoidance for the last five years of your life? Let's not do that anymore." I spent a year building a recovery house of cards, but instead of shoring up my structure with concrete and rebar, I crossed my fingers and prayed the winds would stay calm. The trouble is, it was windy every damn day.

I had friends who still used and still offered me drugs, thinking I was better now, as if recovery from heroin addiction is like recovering from the flu. When they held up a joint as if to say, "Do you mind?" I insisted it didn't bother me. It did, a lot, but I white-knuckled my way through it. I accepted rides to parties without asking, "Who will be there, what's the vibe, maybe I should drive myself?" I went to office happy hours and quietly sipped water, praying no one pressured me to have "just one." I had little emotional support, and my family didn't really want to talk about *any* of it—not my drug use, not my recovery, and certainly not the trauma that triggered it all.

You know how Oxford picks a "word of the year," one that reflects the ethos, mood, or preoccupations of that particular time period? My word that year was "*fine*." As in, "No, I'm fine," or "I don't mind, it's fine," or "I'll be there, it's fine." It was easiest for everyone, including myself, if we all just accepted this narrative: I once had a problem, and now I am fine. The truth was, I was scared every single day, relying on nothing but willpower, inconvenience, luck, and the occasional NA meeting to maintain my sobriety. I didn't know how to enact boundaries to keep myself safe, and even when I could have ("Actually, I do mind, please go outside"), I stayed quiet.

I was afraid that setting boundaries would strip me of my friends, my family's tentative trust, my self-image, and my social life. I can see now that it was the *lack* of boundaries that made me lonely, insecure, and anxious, and ultimately led to my relapse. I was so focused on making sure everyone else was comfortable that I stopped asking myself, "What do *I* need in this moment?" The result was that I was free from drugs, yet my life was smaller than it had ever been.

I somehow made it to the one-year mark, walking onto the stage at an AA meeting to collect my chip. A few weeks later, I found myself in the bathroom at a party with my head bent over the sink, snorting up a line of white powder. I remember looking into the mirror, a bitter taste dripping down the back of my throat, and wondering, "What even was that?" To this day, I don't know.

From the outside, it looked like a wild swing, but my relapse was the eye of the hurricane that had been bearing down on my house of cards for a very long time. The truth was, my willpower and luck were bound to run out. I found myself in the wrong place with the wrong people, at a party I didn't say no to, faced with a line on the sink that I didn't turn down, with zero friends who knew enough to say, "Hey, all of this is a terrible idea."

I had no boundaries, and I relapsed hard.

Something they don't tell you about relapses is that your experience gets just as bad as it was before you quit, but way faster the second time around. The good news is that after a few weeks, I *was* able to seek help on my own, drawing on my terror that this time I really would die. I called the rehab facility and checked myself back into outpatient therapy. I attended group sessions for a few weeks, committed to continued weekly psychotherapy, and went back into the world to reestablish my recovery for the second time.

I needed this time to be different, but I didn't know how to make that happen. The word "boundaries" wasn't in my language yet. I was in this weird space where I knew what I used to do didn't work, but I had no clue how to do anything differently. So I mostly did nothing . . . and of course quickly found myself in yet another precarious situation. Except this time, out of sheer desperation, an honest-to-God boundary *tumbled* out of me.

My friend James and I had been invited to a party, and I had tentatively accepted the invitation. (This is the part where you scream at the horror movie, "What are you doing? Don't go in there!") James had a bottle of Sam Adams, and I was drinking tap water out of a red plastic Solo cup. James had been a close friend for years, and he was supportive of my recovery, in the way you can be supportive of something you don't really understand. He asked if I wanted a beer. I told him no, I was fine.

There was that pesky word again—"fine." How many times had I robotically said that word when I felt anything but? It's what we say when we're trying not to disturb the peace, make anyone uncomfortable, or call attention to an offense or harm. It's what we say most often when someone crosses a boundary we've set, or a boundary we've yet to set but know we need.

I was not, in fact, fine.

I had a sinking feeling in the pit of my stomach and was growing more anxious with every minute. What was I even doing here? My friends didn't know I had relapsed, how tenuous my hold on recovery really was, or how very much I couldn't afford to be in this situation. I was anything but confident in my willpower or luck. This could be the drugs in the bathroom all over again—all it would take was one unexpected offer, one split second of hesitation, and everything I'd worked so hard for would again be lost.

I had an immediate sense of urgency—I had to do something NOW. If I wanted to stay safe, if I wanted to not drink and not use drugs, I had to tell James what was happening inside my brain at this very minute. With no preamble, I started talking, fast and far too loud.

"I need you to know that I'm not okay," I said. "I'm here, but I don't feel good. It's not okay for me to be around alcohol or drugs right now. I'm at this party, and I should not be. I need to go home."

He stared at me for a second, blinked once, then nodded. "Oh, wow, okay. Uh . . . I'm sorry? I didn't know."

I wasn't done. I had to keep going if I wanted things to be different. I had to say it all.

"Also," I continued, "I need to say some things if I'm going to stay clean. I don't care what you do in your own life, but I can't see you doing drugs, not even pot. You can't smoke in front of me anymore, and neither can anyone else. If that's in the plans, then don't invite me. You can't offer me any, ever. No matter what I say or how hard I try to convince you that it's okay. Not even as a joke. If you don't agree to this, I can't hang out with you. I will never be able to use drugs again. And I never want to, even if someday I try to convince you otherwise. I need to be able to trust you with this if we're going to stay friends."

I said all of this in one breath, as if not to break the spell I was attempting to cast.

I certainly didn't plan on having one of the most important conversations of my life in the shadow of a beer pong table. But as I sat there clutching my water, I knew I had to speak up. I had to do more than just try not to use drugs. I had to set myself up for success, creating buffers between myself and drugs, recruiting friends to act as bodyguards, and making sure I didn't put myself into those kinds of situations ever again. If I didn't set these boundaries now, I might lose my nerve, and down the line, that could mean losing my recovery. I couldn't afford to do that. I didn't think I'd make it back a third time.

James could have laughed and called me dramatic. He could have blown me off, told me to find my own way home, or insisted we at least finish out the night. I half expected him to, but he didn't. He looked scared, to be honest. He nodded his head and quietly said, "Oh. Okay." He asked some follow-up questions: "Can I drink in front of you? Do you think you'll ever drink again? Are you clean right now?" I answered (yes; I don't know, but not for a long time; yes). "Okay," he said again, as if that was the end of it. We said goodbye to our friends and drove home.

In a way, that was the end of it. I remember feeling an immediate sense of relief and a bubble of happiness. James was one of the most important people in my life, and we had drifted apart because I wasn't able to communicate my needs. I didn't want to lose him as a friend, but now that I had set these boundaries, I trusted him to keep his word, and I trusted myself around him, too. I knew he would do what he could to protect my recovery, and that alone felt like it opened up a world of possibility for our friendship.

It was also the beginning of a whole new life. I had been worried about hurting my relationship with James, but communicating clearly what I needed and how he could support me only deepened our friendship. It also gave me the courage to have the same conversation with my other close friends. Most of them agreed to hold these same boundaries for me. Some demonstrated they could not, and I had to let them go. It hurt in the moment, but then I would ask myself, "Is this person really my friend if they can't do the bare minimum to keep me safe?"

It turns out boundaries were what I'd been missing all along.

I began establishing lines that mark the limits of an area for my own protection—the very definition of a boundary. "This is the limit of behavior that is acceptable to me. If you're willing to respect those limits, our friendship can be rich and fulfilling, full of trust and mutual respect. If you can't, I'll find myself anxious around you, dreading our interactions, and subconsciously avoiding you. That kind of relationship is unacceptable to me, and I'll remove myself from it." (I'm sure you have people in your life who bring about one of those responses, don't you? We'll get there.)

Getting clear on what I needed for my own health and safety only strengthened my commitment to stand up for myself and my recovery—and if people were unable to respect those limits (either because they were unwilling or because they struggled with their own issues), my boundaries gave me the clarity I needed to let the relationship go.

I went on a boundary-setting spree, committing to regular and truthful therapy sessions, saying no to invitations that felt sketchy, and telling people flat-out, "If you want to smoke, that's cool, I'll just take off." I told a few key members of my family, "I can't pretend my addiction didn't happen. That hurts me. Can you listen if I need to talk?" I started talking to one close friend about my trauma, gaining another ally in my recovery and healing. But I didn't stop there.

I changed the way I dressed, throwing away my Cypress Hill tee and the baseball hat with the pot leaf. I stopped listening to music that reminded me of partying—it would be years before I'd voluntarily play another Portishead album. I got a new job, moved into a new apartment, started going to the gym every morning, and made new health-conscious friends.

I began setting boundaries with *myself* that I would behave in all things like a healthy person with healthy habits. That became the mantra that would guide my life for the next few years. "Would a healthy person with healthy habits carpool to this cookout, not knowing who else will be there? Nope; drive yourself. Would a healthy person with healthy habits go out to dinner with her new running group, but order a sparkling water with lime? Yes, they would; go have fun."

I began to see how setting boundaries actually *expanded* my life, instead of shrinking it. I went out more with friends, because I trusted them to respect my limits and knew they had my back if something unexpected came up. I loved my new job, because I established limits there, too. ("I don't drink, but I'll totally come watch the Red Sox game.") My house felt like a clean slate after clearing out the junk that reminded me of my drug days. The more I talked about my recovery and how I was feeling, the easier it was to make real progress in therapy.

Most important, all of the boundaries I set meant my recovery was no longer a house of cards. I had a solid foundation now, with layers of insulation between me and my drug use, such that if one blew away, I had many others to keep me safe. I was going to bed early, learning to cook, buying new clothes, going to the gym, meeting up with friends who respected my goals, excelling at work, decorating my apartment, and spending quality time with my family . . . all because of *boundaries*.

Because of the guardrails I placed around my recovery, health, and safety, I felt freer than ever, and my life was bigger than I had ever imagined. I think back to how many situations I avoided, how many people I felt anxious around, how isolated I felt, and how often I moved through life unsure and scared before I discovered boundaries. The irony is, the very thing I thought would make my life smaller was the key to expanding it beyond my wildest dreams. My relationships were stronger, my mental health was better, my career was flourishing, and my self-confidence was at an all-time high *because* I had plainly communicated the limits of acceptable behavior in every area of my life, even with myself. I knew what they were. My people knew what they were. Expectations were clear, agreements were made, trust and respect were established, and everyone thrived—especially me.

THE LIFE-CHANGING POWER OF BOUNDARIES

Once I saw the transformative power of boundaries in my own life, I began to notice where other people could benefit from boundaries, and through my work eventually began helping them find the words to express their needs. Over the years, I have helped employees establish boundaries with bosses who email after hours, new mothers establish boundaries around receiving unsolicited advice, and thousands of people gracefully say no to alcohol in social settings. People I have helped report that establishing these boundaries, communicating them clearly, and enforcing them consistently has led them to better mental health, improved self-confidence, and more fulfilling relationships.

You don't have to be in serious danger to benefit from setting and holding a boundary—in fact, setting boundaries around the little things you overlook, brush off, or grudgingly tolerate can make the biggest impact on your life. Think about how many times a day you just "let it go" at work, at home, or with family and friends. Each one of those instances adds up to resentment, anger, frustration, and exhaustion. Like me before I found boundaries, you're probably so used to staying quiet so no one will be inconvenienced or uncomfortable that you don't even realize how often you're letting others run you over.

Imagine how you'd feel if you *didn't* have to stress over your mom talking about your weight, your in-laws surprising you with a visit, or your boss texting you during your vacation. Really sit with that. How much more enjoyable, comfortable, and free would your life be if you knew your needs would be respected? Now imagine the only thing standing between you and that version of you is one or two sentences, spoken clearly and kindly.

I'm going to help you set those boundaries.

I know it's scary. I know it's uncomfortable. I know it's hard. *But so is what you're doing now.* Avoiding certain people, dreading specific conversation topics, feeling anxious before social events (or just staying home), getting angry at hypothetical interactions, over-committing your time and energy, prioritizing other people's feelings over your own, and letting everyone sip your cup dry—that's *hard.* Maybe not "spiraling into addiction" hard, but certainly "crying in an empty bathtub with a box of Gluten-Free Oreos at 10 P.M." hard.

I set my first boundary out of necessity, as a matter of life or death. Your boundaries may not feel that consequential, but I bet you can relate to the idea that your life is shrinking without them. You can keep allowing everyone to set their own limits for you, gradually taking up so much space that your life becomes small and flat. Or you can have an expansive, rich, deep, joyous life;

one with far less friction, a life that you get to create on your own terms. The difference between the two is . . . *boundaries*.

This book will help you make your life as big as possible through the magic of setting and holding boundaries. You'll learn to identify the signals that tell you a boundary is needed. You'll learn my "minimum dose, maximum effect" method of setting boundaries in language that is both natural and appropriate for the setting. You'll learn how to hold a boundary; what to do if people respond poorly; and how to establish consequences if your needs are not respected. More than that, you'll come to believe that you are worthy of creating that safe space for yourself and reclaiming your rightful power, which you've been ceding to others for far too long. All that stands between you and feelings of ease, confidence, capacity, and *freedom* are a few carefully selected words, spoken with kindness from a place of self-care. I'll show you how. (They don't call me the Boundary Lady for nothing.)

PART ONE

Boundary Beginnings

CHAPTER 1

A Crash Course on Boundaries

Not long ago, I received a direct message from Charley, who follows me on Instagram. She was dreading an upcoming visit with her mom and sent me an SOS the day before her trip. "Tomorrow, I'm seeing my mom for the first time since gaining twenty pounds," she wrote. "My weight (and hers) has always been a favorite topic for her, even though I hate talking about it. Her comments cut straight to my self-esteem and aren't helpful, though I assume she intends them to be. We already have a strained relationship because of this, but I have missed her over the past year. I'd just love a good, fun visit instead of one that leaves me feeling insecure."

This kind of dread should ring an alert inside your brain: *Ding, ding, ding—boundary needed!* If a boundary is a line that marks the limits of an area—in this case, your area of comfort, safety, and mental health—then feeling anxious, nervous, or avoidant of a certain person or conversation topic is a sure sign that your limits are being overrun, and that a boundary is necessary.

Unfortunately, most of us ignore those alerts in favor of, well, less healthy responses. You show up for the visit prepared for battle, exploding in anger at the first casual comment. You cancel last minute without reason, leaving your loved one feeling confused and hurt. Or you sell yourself out, joking about your weight first to take away the other person's power to hurt you.

You've allowed anxiety, hurt feelings, and resentment to invade your relationships because you haven't known how to make the relationship function better. But now you know boundaries are the solution—and the very first step is *knowing when you need one*.

> The three steps of boundaries:
> 1. Identify the need for a boundary.
> 2. Set the boundary using clear, kind language.
> 3. Hold the boundary.

STEP 1: IDENTIFY THE NEED FOR A BOUNDARY

Last year while I was visiting with my parents, they surprised me with a "discussion" about the way I was choosing to co-parent with my son's father. Though they were coming from a good place, they overstepped in a major way by inserting their strong opinions into my parenting, and the rest of the visit was awkward and uncomfortable. In the months that followed, my parents invited us to come see them several different times, but I kept finding reasons to say we couldn't make it—I was busy with work, my son had a playdate, the weather wasn't great. Of course, the real reason I was avoiding them was that I didn't want them to spring the parenting conversation on me again. At one point, my new husband gently asked, "So, are you just gonna never see them again, or . . ."

I found this annoyingly perceptive. Obviously, I wanted to see my parents again, but I also wanted them to respect my right to make my own decisions about my own child. I needed to set a boundary.

The next time we visited, as soon as we arrived, I said, "Hey,

I'm not talking about my son's dad with you anymore. I'm his mom, and I am not asking for your feedback around co-parenting." To be honest, it seemed like my parents knew this was coming. They said they understood and would respect my request. I was then able to relax and enjoy our time together, sharing family updates without fear they'd make the same kinds of "suggestions" again.

This is the perfect example of how boundaries can make a relationship better. I'd dreaded seeing my parents solely because of anxiety around this one conversation topic—then I realized I could just tell them it wasn't a conversation I was willing to have. Immediately, a weight was lifted. I was able to fully enjoy being with them, and my parents knew exactly where my limits were.

A BOUNDARY IS ABOUT YOUR BEHAVIOR, NOT THEIRS

I may not like the idea of my parents questioning my decisions, but I can't make them stop thinking independent thoughts, or talking about my parenting amongst themselves. What I can do is set a limit around the way I receive those thoughts. The boundary isn't "Don't question my decisions," because that isn't under my control. Instead I say, "I won't accept your opinions on my decisions," because that focuses on my behavior, not theirs. We'll dive into this more on page 36.

I bet you can think of at least twelve scenarios just like this in your own life right now. Feeling dread or anxiety around the idea of spending time with someone is the loudest sign that a boundary is needed. Maybe you want to avoid seeing someone because they offer unsolicited advice on your weight, your relationship (or lack thereof), or your baby-making status. Maybe they bring conflict and drama wherever they go, always gossiping, complaining, or fixating on negative news. Maybe they guilt-trip you every time you tell them no. Maybe every time you interact, you leave feeling taken advantage of.

Think about the relationships in your life—familial, professional, or even friendships. Are there any relationships you feel conflicted about right now? These could even be relationships with people you really like, admire, and want to keep in your life—but the thought of interacting with them brings an impending sense of foreboding, anxiety, or dread. That pit-of-your-stomach feeling is a key indicator that there is some aspect of your relationship that would be smoothed over or repaired with a boundary (or six).

Sometimes, though, the signs that a boundary is needed can be subtle. Let's talk about energy leakage.

HAS ANYONE SEEN MY ENERGY?

Energy leakage: It sounds pretty woo, but I bet you know what it feels like. Every interaction you have, whether it's meeting your mom for lunch, replying to a social media comment, or just thinking about your ex, is an energetic exchange. Sometimes those exchanges leave you feeling invigorated, positive, and restored. But we all know what it feels like to leave the restaurant, close Instagram, or stop looking through those old photos and feel . . . depleted. Anxious. Overwhelmed. Frustrated. This is energy leakage: where your interactions are consuming more energy than they're giving back.

You may not even realize it's happening, but this is why you feel depressed after conversations with that co-worker who is always unhappy, in the middle of drama, or gossiping. It's why you feel exhausted after even a short visit with your critical in-laws. It's why you hit "decline" every time you see that one friend's name pop up on your cellphone. In these interactions, your energy is getting sucked in only one direction: *out*. That feeling is a sure sign that your relationship is missing a boundary.

SIGNS YOU MIGHT NEED A BOUNDARY

- You feel dread or anxiety around a conversation topic.
- You consistently avoid certain people.
- You regularly receive unsolicited opinions or commentary.
- You feel like the relationship is one-sided.
- You agree to everything just so things can "go smoothly."
- You're told, directly or indirectly, that their feelings are more important than yours.
- You feel drained in their presence or after they leave.
- You are regularly sucked into their conflict or drama.
- You feel negative or anxious after spending time with them.
- You've considered "taking a break" from them.

Energy leakage also happens outside of relationships with other people—sometimes it's self-inflicted. You might notice your energy is quickly depleted when you drink alcohol, shop online out of boredom or anxiety, make up fights or stressful scenarios inside your head, compare yourself relentlessly to others on social media, watch the news, or stay up late zoning out on Netflix. If you find your solo endeavors leave you feeling angry, drained, or just plain depressed, it's the perfect place to set a boundary with yourself—a loving limit *from* you *to* you, designed to keep you safe and healthy. (We'll talk more about self-boundaries in Chapter 10.)

BOUNDARIES AREN'T MEAN

A woman named Nancy recently sent me a message on social media: "I take a walk by myself every morning, for my own mental health. Lately, my elderly neighbor has been inviting herself along, waiting for me to come outside, then joining me. She's very nice, and it's clear she likes the company, but this is the only alone time I get in my day. How can I say no to her without feeling mean?"

I get where Nancy is coming from. We (especially women) are often told that it's selfish to put our own feelings and needs first. This is a common objection to boundaries: that setting them feels cold or punitive, like you're building a wall between people and creating division. But remember, boundaries aren't walls, they're *fences*. And good fences make for good neighbors.

Boundaries allow those who care about us to support us in the way we want to be supported. They provide a clear line between the helpful and the harmful, so people don't have to try to read our minds. They let us engage in relationships fully and openly, knowing we've clearly expressed our limits and made it easier for others to respect our needs. In fact, the best way to preserve a relationship often includes setting boundaries within it.

Nancy liked her neighbor and wanted to have a good relationship with her. If this neighbor kept crashing her morning walks, Nancy was going to become resentful, then angry, and perhaps even lash out one morning out of sheer frustration. Setting a boundary here would be an act of *kindness,* allowing Nancy to care for her neighbor without putting her own needs on hold to do so.

I asked Nancy how many mornings she might be willing to spend in her neighbor's company—from zero days to every morning of the week. She replied that she'd enjoy walking with her once a week on the weekend, so I sent Nancy a script for her to use the following day: "Good morning! Hey, I'm going to start walking by myself again during the week. This is the only alone time I get, and I really need it for my mental health. Would you like to join me on Saturday morning when things are less busy?"

Nancy loved the suggestion. This allowed them both to get what they wanted—some quality time when they're both feeling relaxed, and the alone time Nancy needed to recharge during the busy work week.

You're not being mean when you set boundaries, you're being *kind*—to yourself and your relationships. But that doesn't mean they're not uncomfortable. Any conflict can be uncomfortable—if your burger comes out rare instead of medium-well, I'm betting at least some of you would just eat it rather than speak up. Setting boundaries can be uncomfortable because when we set a boundary, we're expressing a limit that hasn't yet been established (while perhaps pointing out someone else's inconsiderate behavior) and asking if the other person is willing to make an adjustment for the good of the relationship.

If that just made you throw up in your mouth a little bit, you're not alone. My research shows that the main reason people don't set boundaries where they need them is that it's so damn *uncomfortable*. I won't try to pretend otherwise—I feel it, too. It's not always easy for me to say no to an esteemed work colleague, to ask my husband for alone time, or to tell my parents, "I won't discuss this with you further." Speaking up in the moment, advocating for yourself, and asking for what you need *is* uncomfortable. But what's both uncomfortable *and* damaging is reaffirming the story that someone else's feelings are more important or worthy than your own—which is what you do every time you swallow your healthy boundary in an effort to keep the peace.

The truth is, when someone oversteps your limit, *there is no comfortable solution*. But one path is paved with short-term discomfort that leads to major long-term improvements in your health and happiness . . . and the other path is just an endless circle that leaves you feeling unworthy, anxious, angry, and resentful.

One of those sucks way more. And for those of you stuck on

the sucky path, I have to ask . . . how's that been working out for you, really? How has it felt to honor everyone's needs but your own? To sell yourself out to keep other people happy? To take on too much whenever people demand it? To spend all that energy on people, conversations, or behaviors that never give you anything back? Said with so much love: I bet the reason you're reading this book is that it's not going very well at all. What I'm giving you here is a better way—one that leads to more fulfilling relationships, improved self-confidence, better health, and more time and energy for the things that are important to you. It may be uncomfortable, but I guarantee it will be worth it. *Boundaries* are how we care, stay supportive, and give to those we love without sacrificing our own health and happiness in the process.

STEP 2: SET THE BOUNDARY USING CLEAR, KIND LANGUAGE

Remember Charley, who was dreading seeing her mom because she knew her mom would comment on her weight? Charley recognized the need for a boundary, but she didn't know exactly what to say. So Charley asked me, "Can you give me some words to set a boundary that I don't want to talk about my weight, or her weight? My mom will see any boundary I set as a personal attack on her, so I want to summarize my feelings without sounding overly harsh."

Here's something that may sound obvious, but isn't: In order to set a boundary, you have to *actually set the boundary.* You can't hint, suggest, or otherwise behave in a manner that is designed to get others to guess where your limit is. People aren't mind readers. If you need to set a limit around your own comfort, safety, or mental health, you'll have to spell it out.

I know that's the scary part. But it's also the *kind* part.

If you were going to tattoo one boundary-related phrase somewhere on your body, it should be "Clear is kind." (If you do this somewhere other than your butt cheek, please DM me a picture.) In fact, you'll hear this phrase over and over again in this book. It comes from Brené Brown's *Dare to Lead: Brave Work. Tough Conversations. Whole Hearts:* "Clear is kind. Unclear is unkind."

Brené describes picking up this saying from a twelve-step meeting—something else we have in common—but in her book, she applies it to a professional environment. She writes, "Feeding people half-truths or bullshit to make them feel better (which is almost always about making ourselves feel more comfortable) is unkind. Not getting clear with a colleague about your expectations because it feels too hard, yet holding them accountable or blaming them for not delivering, is unkind . . . Clear is kind."

I love Brené's work, and this idea now forms one of the central tenets of my boundary practice and teachings. When it comes to boundaries, clear *is* kind! Showing people exactly where your limit is and how they can help you preserve it is kind. By comparison, leaving them to guess, wonder, or face your disappointment and frustration if they unknowingly get it wrong is quite unkind.

So if clear is kind, then the ideal boundary is *direct*. Not squishy. Not passive-aggressive. Not up for interpretation. You'll find hundreds of examples in this book, but I want you to think about one thing when you're considering the words you'll use to set your next boundary: "When I'm done talking, will they know exactly where my limit is, and how to avoid crossing it?" If the answer is yes, congratulations, you've set a clear, kind boundary! If the answer is, "I hope so, like, it should be obvious, right?" then we're not quite there.

Squishy boundary: eye roll, deep sigh, ignoring the question, or making a joke about it.

Clear boundary: "I'd rather not talk about our bodies or weight today, thanks."

ALERT—BOUNDARY INCOMING!

One of the most challenging parts of setting a boundary is getting from "Whoa, that person just did something that was not okay" to expressing the clear, kind limit you need to set. This is where the boundary alert comes in—a brief word, noise, or gesture that bridges the gap between a boundary crossing and your reply. Boundary alerts give you a quick way to signal to your conversation partner that they've overstepped a boundary and that the energy of this conversation is about to shift, and buy you a moment to compose yourself before you state your boundary. You'll see alerts like these used often in the scripts included later in this book:

- "Wow."
- "Huh."
- "Oof."
- "OH, um . . ."
- Putting up your hands

- Making a displeased face
- Raising one eyebrow
- "Ooh, nope."
- "Ouch."
- "Really?"

In practice, using a boundary alert looks like "Wow, I am not going to answer that" after an especially insensitive question, or "OH, um . . . I actually don't plan on looking at my email at all during my vacation" after a coworker's request, or putting up your hands and saying, "I'm not a hugger, thanks" when approached by a stranger at a wedding. (Trust, if I could raise just one eyebrow, I'd use that one *all the time*.) It's important to note that a boundary alert doesn't replace the need for a clearly set boundary—it just bridges the distance between the violation and your response.

IT'S NOT TOO LATE

Another common challenge with setting boundaries is not being able to grasp the full gravity of the misstep in the moment, or feeling such shock at a statement or action that you're unable to quickly respond to it. It's the second-most-common cited reason for not setting a boundary, and it's happened to me, too. I can remember multiple occasions in my old job where a co-worker made a highly inappropriate and sexist joke in front of me, and I just froze. Internally, I was thinking, "What just happened? This person is a vice president. What am I supposed to do?" In the meantime, the conversation kept rolling along, and by the time I got my feet underneath me, the moment had passed and it felt awkward to speak up.

Had I blurted out "WOW" in that moment, perhaps conversation would have stopped and I could have said, "John, I cannot let that slide." (Not the most eloquent boundary, but better than nothing.) But even if you freeze in the moment and say nothing, it's never too late to establish and communicate a boundary for future interactions. Here are a few strategies for doing so, even if the moment has passed:

CIRCLE BACK. Ask the person to return to that part of the conversation once you can clearly state the issue and share your boundary from here on out. That might be five minutes from now, an hour from now, or the next day. (Don't let too much time pass, though, or your conversation partner is likely to have forgotten the details of what felt like an "ordinary discussion" to them.)

EXPLAIN WHAT HAPPENED FROM YOUR PERSPECTIVE. "Yesterday, you made this joke about women climbing the corporate ladder. It felt really icky to me, and I want you to know I didn't find it funny or appropriate."

FOCUS ON WHAT'S HAPPENING NOW. If your conversation partner says something like, "Well, you should have said so," tell the truth. "Honestly, I was just shocked in the moment, and wasn't sure how to reply. I've had a minute to think about it, though, and it's important that I share."

COMMUNICATE YOUR NEW LIMIT PROACTIVELY. "From now on, I'm going to start calling out inappropriate behavior on the spot, no matter who's in the room. You have a lot of women reporting to you. Please do better."

With practice, you'll be able to spot boundary violations faster, and can develop a few go-to phrases for calling them out or buying yourself time to evaluate the situation as it occurs. Even if your initial statement is less than clear, like, "Wait, that's not okay," or "Hold on, I need to back up for a second," it's still a step in the right direction toward finding your voice and setting the right limits for yourself when you need them, even if the limit itself is communicated after the fact.

CLEAR, KIND LANGUAGE STARTS (AND ENDS) WITH YOU

An important idea you should use to direct your boundary language is that a healthy boundary always comes from the *self*. Remember, you're not telling Uncle Joe he can't smoke, you're saying *you* don't allow smoking in your house. Boundaries aren't about controlling the other person, they're about the limits you put in place around *yourself* to stay healthy and safe. In the case of my parents, they can talk smack about my ex-husband to each other all they want, but they now know not to bring it up with me. Nancy's neighbor is free to keep walking the same route, but she knows to let Nancy walk alone unless it's Saturday. You aren't attempting to control what *other people* do; you're expressing what *your* limits are.

A boundary doesn't tell someone else what to do, it tells them what you will do.

This might seem confusing, because in the boundary scripts throughout this book, you will see a lot of requests: "Would you please take that cigarette outside?" "Could you confirm for this weekend before I buy tickets?" "Can we hold off on that vent session? I need an hour of downtime first." But remember, each of those requests will be centered around *your* healthy limit. Here are three things to keep in mind:

- Boundaries come from a desire to establish and preserve *your* limit.
- People are not mind readers, so you need a way to communicate that limit.
- If someone continues to overstep, *you* will take the action you need to hold the boundary.

In the example where Uncle Joe lights a cigarette inside your house, your boundary is, "I don't allow smoking inside to protect my health, and because I don't like the smell." But Uncle Joe might not know that, so you need to make your boundary clear. What you might say is, "Oh, please take that cigarette outside before you light it. We don't smoke inside the house." You're not trying to persuade Uncle Joe to quit smoking—that would be controlling, not a boundary. You're not telling him not to smoke in his own house, or anyone else's house—that's not your boundary to set. You're only using your request to draw a limit around *your* house, and your health.

If Uncle Joe balks at going outside, you might reinforce the boundary by saying, "Then please put the cigarette out. I said I don't allow smoking inside the house." Yes, this requires Uncle Joe's cooperation, but the focus is still on reinforcing *your* limit. If Uncle Joe refuses to do either (rude), then you might no longer allow him to visit—an action *you* take to enforce the consequences of *your* boundary.

TELL ME MORE? (AND WHY YOU MIGHT NOT WANT TO)

A clear, kind boundary doesn't require you to overexplain or make excuses for your needs. Nancy might be tempted to say, "My walks are the only alone time I get each morning, and my life is so busy and chaotic right now, work is a mess and my kids are at a tough age, I feel bad asking but . . ." as a means of softening the blow. But this approach can be problematic. First and most important, it's not necessary to share the context of your boundary—your limit is your limit. Repeat after me:

People don't need to understand or agree with my boundary to respect it.

I'll emphasize this here because women have been conditioned to see selflessness as a virtue, and to require a damn good reason (and often approval) to ask for anything for ourselves. It can feel deeply uncomfortable to state our boundary and let it stand without overexplaining, making excuses, or justifying our desires—so that is exactly what I'm asking you to practice, as a means of reminding yourself that you are worthy of having and meeting your own needs. Every time I acknowledge and honor my own needs without asking for "permission" first, I think of it as giving a quiet middle finger to the patriarchy.

In addition, adding context to your boundary may actually backfire. By explaining, you've made it possible for your conversation partner to disagree with your reasoning, therefore canceling the need for a boundary in their minds. Imagine Nancy overexplaining, and her neighbor saying, "Life can't be *that* hard—it's just a walk, and we don't even have to talk." Overexplaining can shift the focus to your reasoning and not the boundary itself, requiring you to justify further (when all you had to say is, "Oh, I can't walk with you today—have a great day").

Sharing the detailed (and perhaps overly exaggerated) reason for your boundary can backfire in other ways, too. Let's say two weeks later, your neighbor sees your family outside and asks if your work is any less busy. Your helpful spouse answers, "Yes, things are great! She finally got an assistant and work is so much more manageable. It's nice to see her more relaxed." Cue the neighbor, popping in for a morning walk the very next day, because surely you don't *need* the alone time now that things have settled down.

Overexplaining is a natural response when you feel uncomfortable or when you've been taught to get approval from others before claiming something for yourself. The problem is, providing unnecessary context or attempting to justify your needs gives the impression that your boundary isn't that strong, which means people will be more likely to try to plead, guilt, reason, or pressure you out of it. Setting a boundary *without* explaining, justifying, or excusing is a truly boss move, indicating that you've given this plenty of thought, you're crystal clear on what you need, and you're comfortable advocating for yourself. Plus, if you truly believe setting healthy boundaries is an act of kindness, then there is no "blow" to soften.

DEALING WITH THE "WHYS"

Just as you do not need to share your reasons for establishing a boundary, you also do not have to answer when people ask, "Why?" People set boundaries for all sorts of reasons, some deeply personal. If you don't want to share, you can simply say, "It's just what I need right now," "I'd rather not share further," or "It's a sensitive topic." (You'll see more examples of this type of language in the boundary scripts, particularly in Chapter 9.)

Going back to Charley and her mom: They were close and had an otherwise great relationship, and Charley wanted to share from the heart how this boundary would improve their time together and support her mental health. I advised her to use this script for a text message as a starting point: "Hi Mom, I can't wait to see you tomorrow! One thing I wanted to bring up before our visit . . . the pandemic has me feeling really insecure about my body. I'm sure you'll notice some changes when you see me, but any conversation about it, no matter how well meaning, would trigger negative thoughts and distract me all day. I really want to enjoy my time with you, so I'm asking that we don't talk about our weight or how our bodies look."

Charley loved that language, telling me that it "perfectly sums up my feelings without sounding harsh or accusatory." See? Clear *is* kind.

STEP 3: HOLD THE BOUNDARY, ENFORCING CONSEQUENCES IF NECESSARY

The first rule of parenting that I learned was to never set a consequence I'm not willing to enforce. ("No iPad for a week" hurts me just as much as it hurts my nine-year-old, and he knows it.) The same goes for a boundary; in order for it to be effective, it has to be enforceable, and you have to be *willing* to enforce it. That means that even after the scary, uncomfortable practice of setting the boundary, you're still not quite there. You must now *hold* that boundary.

The ideal boundary usually includes a component we've only touched upon: the consequence. This is the step you'll take to hold that boundary, should your conversation partner prove unable or unwilling to respect it. Usually, I leave the consequence unsaid the first time I set a boundary. This helps me to avoid coming off as unnecessarily harsh. (Nancy telling her elderly neighbor "I'll be walking alone during the week now . . . and if you try to join me, I will SPRINT in the other direction until I lose you" would not fall into the "kind" category.) I may even leave it unsaid the second time, in the spirit of good faith that my conversation partner might have simply forgotten.

However, should my boundary continue to be dismissed or disrespected, it's time for a restatement *plus* a clear consequence. In the case of Nancy's neighbor, she might restate her boundary by saying, "I've mentioned I won't be walking with you during the week," but share a consequence if her neighbor continues to try to invite herself along. She might say, "If we can't come to an understanding about this, I'll start taking my morning walks elsewhere," or "I'm going to start leaving in the morning without stopping to say hello, so please don't take it personally."

If we're being super picky, the consequence technically *is* the boundary—the concrete establishment of the limit, in the form of the action you're going to take to keep yourself safe and healthy. In Nancy's case, that might be driving to the park to walk, leaving for her walk at a different time each morning, or starting her walk with a brisk jog to the end of the block. But jumping straight to the consequence doesn't leave a lot of room for connection, which isn't good for the relationship, and doesn't give the other person an opportunity to help you meet your needs. That's why most of the time, you'll share your limit in the form of a request first. You're saying, "Here is this limit that I have recognized. I'd love for you to help me preserve it—are you willing?" That's a much kinder approach than saying nothing, then sneaking out the back door so your neighbor doesn't see you.

When someone refuses to honor your boundary time and time again, it puts you in a really tight spot. You're faced with a difficult choice: Rescind the boundary (which will cause you harm, hurt the relationship, and set a nasty precedent) or employ the consequence, which will likely be painful for you both, and may change the relationship permanently. After multiple boundary violations (and reminders), Charley may tell her mom, "I've asked you again and again to stop commenting on my weight. If you can't respect that, I'll need to take some time off from visits. Conversations about my body do a number on my mental health. I won't keep subjecting myself to that." But before she goes there, she needs to ask herself, "Will I really not visit? Am I willing to distance myself for a while? Can I really follow through?"

There are no easy answers here, especially when it's family who continually disregards your boundaries. But I have to ask, how good is the relationship if the other person won't do the bare minimum to keep you healthy and safe? Is it worth repeatedly falling on your sword when the other person isn't willing to do something relatively small to demonstrate their respect and care? How much of yourself are you willing to give up?

TACTICS FOR HOLDING YOUR BOUNDARIES

Here are some strategies you can use in the moment to hold a boundary you've set with someone else:

RESTATE THE BOUNDARY. It seems redundant, but try to use the same language every time you talk about your boundary, whether in person, in writing (like via text or email), or over the phone. If Charley's mom casually brings up her weight over lunch, Charley could say, "Remember, it's important for my mental health right now that we don't discuss our bodies or weight." This reinforces that respecting this boundary is good for Charley and their relationship.

ADD INFORMATION AS NEEDED. If necessary in the moment, be even more specific about what is and isn't within your limits, and give examples. Charley might add, "When I asked that we not talk about our bodies, that includes other people's bodies, too, even Kim Kardashian's. Let's not talk about *anyone's* body, okay?"

EXPLAIN THE CONSEQUENCES. If your limits continue to be disrespected, it's time to share what you are willing to do to keep yourself safe and healthy. Charley would say, "Mom, you keep bringing up my weight, though I've asked you not to. If you can't honor this simple request, I'm going to cut our visit short."

ENFORCE AS NEEDED. If your boundaries still aren't being respected in a way that works for you, it's time to enforce the boundary by taking action. Charley might set even more limits around interactions with her mom (like communicating only via email or text and not visiting in person), or she might have to make the hard decision to employ the ultimate consequence— cutting off communications (at least temporarily) as a last-ditch effort to preserve her own health and safety.

We'll talk more about navigating boundary resistance and other challenges in Chapter 11, but in Charley's case, a boundary was needed, the script was rehearsed and executed, and (as they often do) it went *beautifully*. Charley sent me a follow-up a few days later, saying, "Yesterday was one of the best visits with my mom in a long time. She honored my request 100 percent, and I felt so supported and understood. THANK YOU."

FLEXIBLE, NOT RIGID

Relationships aren't set in stone, and neither are healthy boundaries. If your context changes and behaviors that used to be triggering or painful just aren't any longer, you can and should communicate that change to anyone you've set a boundary with. In fact, *any* context can change a boundary dynamic, which is why it's important to continue to ask yourself if a boundary is still needed, and if so, is *that* boundary still needed? It's also important not to be overly rigid with your boundaries. You may tell your office, "I won't answer work texts after hours," but if your boss texts that your building is on fire, you should probably reply. Healthy boundaries need to serve your highest self (the "you" at your best), so if you recognize for whatever reason that the limit you set is no longer in your best interest, even if it's just in that moment, please do adjust as needed.

RESTING GUILT FACE

We've already spent plenty of time talking about why boundaries are mission critical for your mental health, happiness, and relationships, but if I asked you to word-associate for "boundary" right now, I'm sure many of you would still reply, "Ick." Boundaries just make us feel . . . bad. Scared. Anxious. *Guilty*. Whether those feelings come from you or others, they almost certainly will come up when you start actively working with boundaries, so let's break it down.

First, these icky feelings may be calling from . . . *inside the house*. We often automatically feel anxious or guilty about setting a boundary, sometimes before the words are even spoken. We may not be comfortable sticking up for ourselves, and some of us have a deep belief that we're not worthy of setting limits around how others treat us. If boundaries haven't been modeled for us, we're likely to grow up passive and people-pleasing at all costs. Women, especially, have been conditioned to put our own well-being dead last and make ourselves small so as not to inconvenience others. (Refer back to my Year of Fine, when I never once said, "Actually, I do mind.")

WHEN GUILT COMES KNOCKING

These "boundary feel-bads" are referred to in psychology as "unearned guilt." It's not productive guilt, which is an important social regulator and helps us right a wrong when we're actually at fault. Unearned guilt is a learned means of self-punishment that tells you to feel bad for putting your feelings ahead of others', standing up for yourself, or "making" other people feel uncomfortable. We've learned this from a dozen different sources: the people-pleasing we've done with our parents, teachers, and other authority figures; the responsibility we felt for friends' or family members' feelings; societal pressures from the patriarchy, sexism, and mass marketing; or from the abuse, trauma, or neglect we've experienced. The good news is that if this is learned behavior, it can be *un*learned, and that's exactly what we're here to do.

Unearned guilt can arise when you set or hold a boundary, but you can preempt it first by acknowledging the feeling. "Hey, guilt, I see you trying to barge in. You *can* be helpful, but I don't need you here." Then remind yourself why you're establishing this clear, kind boundary. "I'm setting a limit to keep myself safe and healthy. I deserve that in this relationship, and anyone else in my life should want that for me, too. My boundary will be clear and kind. I have nothing to feel guilty for—I'm doing nothing wrong." It can also be helpful to imagine you are giving advice to someone else with the same problem. If your best friend was struggling when people talked about her weight, would you back *her* up in setting a boundary? Imagining it's your best friend can help you see that your boundary is reasonable, too, and there's no need to feel bad about establishing it.

People can also feel guilty or nervous because they're anticipating a horrible reaction to their boundary—whether that's justified or not. I remember wanting to have a tough conversation with my mom, and nervously laying it out for my sister. "She's not going to like it," I muttered anxiously. "She's gonna get all quiet and do her lemon face. I might as well just put up with it." My sister interrupted me: "Hey, that hasn't even happened, and you don't know that it will. Give her the benefit of the doubt, and if it doesn't go well, deal with it then." Fast-forward to a few days later, when I nervously stated my boundary and my mom said, "Oh, okay, that's fine." My sister got to say "I told you so" and I never forgot the lesson.

Combat proactive guilt by reminding yourself of what you've learned about clear, kind boundaries: They're designed to make the relationship better and to keep you safe and healthy. Your needs are just as important as anyone else's. Don't rehearse disaster—it's more likely than not that the person will be happy to accommodate your needs because they care about you. Repeat as often as needed and remember that practice makes all of this easier.

BIG T, LITTLE T

Trauma can play a big part in how you feel about setting healthy limits on your own behalf. When someone has a history with trauma, they can carry those experiences with them into present-day boundary conversations. If they felt they didn't have the right or power to stand up for themselves (or if it was dangerous to do so), they may have a hard time contextualizing *you* standing up for yourself. And if you have a history with trauma, setting a boundary may feel especially terrifying, and lead to an immediate sense of guilt or fear. You may find, as I did, that talking to a therapist or counselor can help you work through that trauma and reclaim your power. Setting boundaries will also help to reinforce your worth and value, and keep you safe as you do your own work to heal.

By now, you should feel eager and excited about creating some healthy boundaries in your own life (or at least not quite so terrified at the very idea). But there's one important piece missing . . . what *specifically* should you say? Much like Charley, you probably know the point you want to get across, but you're struggling with the clear, kind language—not too short or harsh, but not so wishy-washy that it won't hold up. In the next chapter, you'll learn more about the unique way I categorize boundaries, how my "Green/Yellow/Red" boundary levels came about, and how to make sure your boundary conversations come out sounding natural and conversational. Then you'll move on to Part Two, which is devoted to providing you with the exact scripts you'll need to go on a boundary-setting Rumspringa in every area of your life.

CHAPTER 2

How to Use This Book

Before we dig into the actual language you'll use to tell your boss that you will not be answering emails while on vacation (ahem), let's talk about how I've structured this book.

Many experts categorize boundaries by the area of your life the boundary will support, like physical, emotional, or financial. To be honest, I've always found that framework challenging to navigate. For instance, a woman named Paige recently messaged me to ask how to talk to her husband about his recent "surprise" purchase of an expensive home gym, which was taking up valuable real estate in their small home. At first, it sounded like she needed a physical boundary (please don't crowd our shared space), but on another level, she was asking about establishing an emotional boundary (please treat me as a valued partner) *and* a financial boundary (please don't spend our money without discussing it with me).

In my approach to boundaries, I prefer to simplify them into *relationship* categories. In this case, Paige needed to set a boundary with her romantic partner. Her husband's decisions weren't just affecting their finances or the free space in their home, they were having a negative impact on their *relationship*. She needed to set a limit around when she'd like to be consulted on decisions that impact them both, and communicating that limit (and seeing it honored) would strengthen their marriage, not just their bank account or floor plan.

In this book, I've identified eight specific relationship categories in which you are most likely to need boundaries. They encompass all of the relationships you're likely to have in your life—parents and in-laws, friends and neighbors, bosses and romantic partners—but this doesn't just mean relationships with other people. Sometimes the relationship we need to support is with ourselves, ensuring our own physical well-being and mental health are safe and protected. When it comes to topics like the foods we eat or the beverages we drink (or don't drink); the way others address our bodies, health, or appearance; and how we navigate deeply personal issues like having a child or grieving the death of a loved one, setting boundaries here will teach *you* to stick up for *you,* and become your own protector, caretaker, and advocate.

Even within my relationship-based framework, there will be some crossover, like when you need to set a boundary with your mom about diet talk over dinner, or with a co-worker who constantly gives you unsolicited health advice. You'll find language in every chapter that will apply to a multitude of situations, and you may find the words you need for your next boundary conversation in an unexpected place within this book. As you move through the chapters, my unique framework will help you quickly identify where a boundary is needed, communicate your limit effectively, and strengthen *all* of your relationships.

HOW DO YOU SAY THAT?

Early in my boundary research, one of the things that frustrated me was that the experts rarely talked about exactly *how* to set the boundary. I'd read pages and pages of valuable boundary information, then get to the end and ask, "But how do you SAY IT?" When my Whole30 community began asking me how to say no to alcohol, their persistent mother-in-law, or that extra work project, I vowed to give them the exact words they needed for the moment. I'd write back, "Try, 'No thanks, I'm not drinking right now,' " or " 'We love seeing you, but if you don't call before stopping by, we may not be able to visit,' " or "Just say, 'If I take that on, Project A won't be done on time—do I have your permission to deliver Project A next week?' " I'd often hear back that they used my script with great success.

Over the years, I also began sharing more of my own boundaries word for word. People loved having examples of clear, kind language appropriate for any situation or setting, allowing them to catalog a growing list of potential boundary responses. Those simple scripts turned into the framework for the boundary chapters in this book. You'll not only read lots of tips, strategies, and guidance for having successful boundary conversations, I tell you *exactly what to say*. The scripts contain scenarios submitted by my community and gathered from my own life over the years, and a variety of responses you can copy and paste to address them. Eventually, you'll naturally develop your own boundary language and won't need specific scripts for most situations, but until then, I won't leave you hanging.

THE ORIGINS OF "GREEN, YELLOW, RED"

In the chapters that follow, I offer scripts organized into three categories: Green, Yellow, and Red. For decades, I've been using a color-coded system to evaluate situations that may require a boundary, but I first explained it in 2011, when I wrote an article about boundaries and alcohol for the Whole30 blog. To illustrate the concept, I shared a story about attending a wedding early in my recovery. At this wedding, another guest (who happened to be dating my ex-boyfriend) was peer-pressuring me relentlessly to drink, and I found myself having to flex my boundary muscles to stay sober and avoid conflict.

I arrived at the event alone and was standing by the bar when this woman, who I had only met once before, approached me. She noticed I was sipping water, and it seemed to really bother her that I wasn't indulging. She said hello, then immediately launched into, "Why aren't you drinking tonight?" She didn't know I was in recovery, and I wasn't comfortable sharing, so I just said I was good with water and that I liked her dress, thinking that would be the end of it.

It wasn't.

Later we found ourselves in a group together, and she "jokingly" asked why I was being such a prude. At that point, I realized she was already pretty tipsy (as was most everybody), and this situation was starting to feel like a threat to my recovery. I didn't think I'd give in, but I didn't feel safe, and it didn't feel healthy for me to continue to engage with her. For whatever reason, my mind flashed to the Homeland Security Advisory System—you know, their "threat level" colors—and I began mentally evaluating where I thought we were.

Threat Level Green? Oof, we're past that already. I tried to laugh and change the subject an hour ago, but that didn't work. We're clearly at Threat Level Yellow now—she's getting pretty drunk, and emboldened by the presence of her friends.

In the moment, I said something dismissive like, "I just don't feel like drinking tonight," and left to talk to someone else. But I was on higher alert now, anticipating this wouldn't be the end of it.

Sure enough, a few minutes later, the woman approached me again—this time with my ex in tow (who at least had the decency to look embarrassed) and two shots in hand, insisting I do one with her. *This is Threat Level Red, Melissa,* I thought to myself.

If she doesn't chill out, I'm going to have to leave. I don't want to feel pressured to share my recovery status with a room full of strangers—or worse, take a drink I don't want. I again declined, threw a pointed look at my ex, and walked away.

I did my best to avoid the woman for the next hour or so, but the more everyone drank, the more she seemed to fixate on me, and I began feeling very alone in that room. By 10 P.M., she was seriously hammered and I was at "Threat Level Fuchsia"—which Homeland Security does not recognize but anyone who's been in front of their ex's current girlfriend after multiple tequila shots surely does. At that point, I knew there was only one thing I could do to keep myself safe: I grabbed my coat and walked out the door.

That experience is still so vivid in my head, not just because I went home and cried, but because the "threat level" system I used then carried into all of my boundary conversations going forward. Through that experience, I recognized that different levels of threat—to your relationship with that person, your mental health, or your safety—require different levels of boundary response. Just like you don't use a flamethrower to kill a mosquito, I didn't need to walk out of my friend's wedding after the first hint of peer pressure. The threat at that point wasn't severe, so setting a gentle boundary and changing the subject felt appropriate. But several hours later, the threat to my health and safety (and my relationship with the bride and groom) was *real*. If I didn't set the strongest boundary possible, I was afraid something irreparable was going to happen—I'd either blow up at this woman and start a fight, or give in and have a drink.

The three-part color-coded system you'll find throughout this book—Green, Yellow, and Red—was born from that experience, and represents the level of *threat* that stems from the boundary-crossing you're facing. The threat could be to your own health or safety, as it was for me at the wedding. If someone continues this behavior, is your mental health going to suffer? Are your health commitments at risk? Is it putting you in the way of physical or emotional harm?

The threat could also be to your relationship. If this behavior continues, is the good relationship you have with this person in jeopardy? Are you already feeling avoidant, anxious, or annoyed before you even interact? How close are you to exploding with resentment, frustration, or anger; saying something you can't take back; or cutting off the relationship altogether?

If that threat is minimal at this point—their behavior is not okay, but it's the first time it's happened, or it's not hugely harmful—you're still in Green territory, and the language you use to establish or reinforce the boundary should acknowledge that. But if the threat to your relationship is imminent—as in, "If you mention my weight one more time, I'm walking out the door"— you're in the Red, and your boundary language and the consequences should reflect that, too.

GREEN: Low risk, and the gentlest language. Assumes the other person wasn't aware they were overstepping and wants to respect your limits. Your boundary language is clear, generous, and very kind. Leaves any potential consequences unsaid in the spirit of good faith.

YELLOW: Elevated risk, and firmer language. Used as a follow-up if your Green boundary isn't respected, or if historical interactions with this person indicate the threat is higher. Your boundary language is just as clear, but more firm. Yellow may also include an intended consequence, if appropriate.

RED: Severe risk, and your most direct language. At this point, your health, safety, and/or the relationship are in jeopardy, and your language must reflect the severity of the situation. It's still kind, but this is their last reminder, and makes it clear that you *are* prepared to hold your limits. State the consequence plainly here and be ready to enforce it.

MINIMUM DOSE, MAXIMUM EFFECT

The best boundary uses the *minimum dose* for *maximum effect*. This is a physics principle first credited to Greek scientist and mathematician Archimedes, but it has been popularized in the modern fitness industry. It asks the question:

What is the smallest action you can take to produce the desired effect?

The principle allows you to leverage your efforts to get the most bang for your buck—and prevents you from the negative consequences of thinking more is always better. So if your chicken nuggets are hot after one minute in the microwave, don't cook them for two. If sets of five squats make you stronger, you don't have to do ten. And when it comes to boundaries, how softly can you tread while still effectively establishing your limit?

That's where my boundary color-coding system comes in. If you start every boundary conversation with the firmest and most direct language, sure, the boundaries you set will be effective, but you'll create more conflict than necessary, and probably burn some bridges along the way. Ideally, you'll head into these conversations assuming the best, starting with Green and only escalating to Yellow or Red if you need to. If your Green boundary is successful, congratulations! You've spoken in the gentlest language possible (which your conversation partner certainly appreciates) *and* your limits have been acknowledged and respected.

However, take the concept of threat seriously. If you find that repeating your Green boundaries just isn't working and the offending behavior continues to escalate, what's a kinder response: saying nothing and ignoring the other person for a while, or speaking a Yellow- or Red-level boundary clearly and setting the stern but necessary limit that could save the relationship?

For each boundary situation in this book, you'll find all three options—Green, Yellow, and Red—with language corresponding to the threat level. These scripts are meant just to get you started, although plenty of people have spoken them verbatim and found them highly effective. If you're nervous about an encounter and want a script, you'll find one in this book. If you just want inspiration for what a Yellow-level boundary could sound like, use the options I provide to find the language that works for you.

PRACTICE MAKES PROGRESS

One last piece of advice: Practice makes boundaries feel and sound far more natural, which means you'll come across as more confident, and the boundary is more likely to be taken seriously. I read every single one of these boundary conversations out loud to myself several times while writing this book. If anything sounded stilted, unnatural, or overly scripted when I spoke it aloud, I rewrote it until it sounded right. While I encourage you to adopt the specific language and words that feel the most natural for you, once you land on what you want to say, *practice*. Tell the mirror, "No thank you, I'm not drinking right now." Tell your dog, "Wow, that's a rather personal question. Let's move on." Tell your shower wall, "I've already left the office. Slack me tomorrow morning and I'll help."

Say it out loud until it feels easy and confident, so your brain and body get used to the idea that *this* is your space, and you have every right to protect it with clear, kind boundaries.

And with that, I think we're ready to build some fences.

PART TWO

Your Boundary Practice

The Real Work/ Life Balance

Setting Boundaries in the Workplace

My sister, Kelly, was on her first real vacation in over a year. She was standing on her paddleboard, gazing out over the peaceful turquoise waters off the shore of Barbados, when she heard someone yelling her name. She turned to see her sister-in-law, Kara, running down the beach, waving her arms and calling for her. Kelly frantically started to paddle back—was someone hurt? Was there bad news from home? She finally landed on the shore and gasped out, "WHAT'S WRONG?!" To which Kara replied, "Matthew is on the phone for you."

Matthew, as in Kelly's *boss*. He had weaseled the name of Kelly's hotel from a reluctant co-worker, called her room, and persuaded Kara to track her down. On her vacation. In the ocean. For something that was absolutely *not* an emergency.

I'd gasp in disbelief, too, had I not already heard so many equally appalling stories from countless people who have asked me to help them establish boundaries at work. Turns out *Horrible Bosses* isn't just a movie title.

Boundaries at work have been a trending topic since March of 2020, when COVID forced work, home, kids, school, and leisure to run together like that time I washed an entire hamper full of clothes with a stray red crayon. I have worked from home for the past twelve years, and I learned a decade ago that if I didn't set boundaries around what was "work time" and what was "home time," I'd literally never leave the "office." (See: me in 2010 responding to emails from bed at 11 P.M.) Still, during COVID, when I was running Zoom calls from the cleanest corner of my bedroom while managing my kid's Zoom classes in the dining room *plus* cooking, cleaning, doing laundry, and entertaining a bored seven-year-old, even my expert-level boundary skills were put to the test.

PEOPLE WILL TAKE AS MUCH AS YOU WILL GIVE

Whether you're working from home or going into an office, serving customers or managing a job site, have a boss or are your own boss, the biggest lesson I learned when I first entered the workforce is that *people will take as much as you are willing to give.* That's not a judgment; it's just human nature. I first discovered this in the earliest days of Whole30, when we were trying to grow the program, and I was the only one manning email and our Facebook page. If a question came in at 9 P.M., I felt like I *had* to answer it. If a workshop request came in on a Sunday morning, I'd stop my workout, brunch, or errands to reply. If someone sent in a question for the blog, I'd stay up until midnight writing the answer. I was running myself ragged trying to be in ten places at once, feeling reactive instead of proactive, and fast approaching burnout . . . until a friend and fellow entrepreneur said to me, "Melissa, people will take as much as you are willing to give. You have to set some limits." This brings us to one of my principal tenets of boundaries:

It's not your job to guess my boundaries,
it's up to me to set and hold them.

This applies to every relationship category, but is often over-looked at work, especially if you work for someone else. We tend to assume our boss's expectations, workplace culture, or job demands all supersede our personal need for (and right to) healthy boundaries—but those assumptions are wrong. Yes, you accepted the job. Yes, they pay you for your work. But you have every right to demand a healthy, safe, respectful work environment, and that almost always involves setting boundaries.

The thing is, your company is not likely to proactively establish healthy boundaries for you. It's rare that a manager says to an employee, "I notice you haven't taken a vacation in a year—make sure you use the time off you've earned, and I promise we won't bother you at all while you're out." The truth is, if left unchecked, your company, managers, co-workers, and clients will hungrily absorb *all* of your time, energy, space, and attention. This doesn't make them evil, it's just the way the world works; everyone is under pressure to do more, produce more, and make more money. (It's called capitalism, sweetie.) Which is why *you* need to create strong, healthy boundaries in the workplace.

The trouble is, work boundaries are extra hard because of power dynamics; company culture; and the cold, hard truth of workplace consequences.

FIGHT THE POWER

Anytime you have a power dynamic, whether it's parent/kid, teacher/student, or boss/employee, it makes setting and holding boundaries exponentially more difficult. If you are the kid, student, or employee, hierarchy dictates that you're *supposed* to take orders. If your boss asks you to work late, pick up a shift on the weekend, or cover for their long lunch, they may see it as insubordination if you say no. And because of the power dynamics in play, it makes questions like "Can you come in on your day off?" "I know I said I needed it next week but can you get it to me tomorrow?" and "Will you go on a date with me?" a mine-field. (Yes, managers still ask their employees out, and yes, it's as problematic and gross as it sounds.) While these power dynamics don't give anyone the authority to take advantage of you, the line gets blurry when the person on the receiving end of your bound-ary outranks you, and you really need the job.

It's not just the hierarchical structure that plays into office power dynamics. What if you need to set the boundary with your boss's golf buddy—who happens to be your co-worker? Or the colleague who your boss is not-so-secretly sleeping with? (I have *stories*.) Even if you do not report directly to these people, even if they have less experience or tenure than you, if the boss just likes them better, you need to tread cautiously. (This workplace is starting to look like an episode of *Big Brother,* isn't it?)

Compounding these power dynamics is the reality that the sys-tems of oppression pervasive in our society—sexism, racism, ho-mophobia, and ableism, for example—are also present in the workplace. If you're a woman, a person of color, LGBTQ+, or disabled, there is yet another workplace power dynamic to break through, beyond the basic structure of your team. For example, I recently heard from a Black woman named Victoria, who was working for a tech company and found herself navigating what she called the "bro culture" of her workplace. Victoria struggled to meet gender-based expectations as she climbed the ranks from customer service to product manager; she felt like she *had* to laugh at the sexist jokes, take notes in meetings, and play down her accomplishments, even when she crushed a goal. When she tried to set healthy boundaries, she was often labeled "angry" or "aggressive," both common stereotypes of Black women in our country.

Victoria told me, "What was worse was that I began to inter-nalize the misogynoir of my workplace. I discouraged my female teammates from calling out bad behavior, speaking too directly, or setting healthy boundaries around their time, while the male coders could be as offensive, brash, or demanding as they wanted, and no one blinked an eye." After learning more about boundaries, using some of my scripts, and asking her co-workers hard questions like, "But *is* it aggressive to ask that you not talk over me in meetings?" Victoria said her work environment improved. Colleagues began respecting her opinions, and even joking with her, "Let's ask Victoria—you know she'll give it to us straight." She also began encouraging her direct reports to discuss boundary challenges with her, so she could offer them support when they needed to set a boundary with others. "It's not always easy and change can be slow," she reported, "but I feel so much better about the behavior I'm modeling for my team, and it's given me a new sense of self-confidence at work."

As someone with just about as much privilege as you can have without being a straight, cis white man, I'm still learning how to effectively ally for others, especially in the workplace. Sharing my tools for setting boundaries is one way for me to do that work, and being aware of these factors of intersectionality is a necessary first step for *all* of us as we try to create positive, rewarding workplace environments for everyone.

SPOT THE RED FLAGS

You may have to swim against office culture if you prefer to not be flagged down for a nonurgent issue while in the middle of the ocean during your vacation. To help gauge what you're up against, look at the way management models various behaviors around time off, sick time, after-hours emails, and integrity. If the exec team is still Slacking and emailing from their Mexican villas or while out sick with the flu, it's going to be much harder for you to set a boundary around your time off. That kind of culture comes from the top down, and even though your company might *say* it values employees' work/life balance, the actions of those in charge speak louder than their words.

In Kelly's case, her first red flag came during her job interview, when her soon-to-be-boss said, "Work starts at 8 A.M., but most people are here by 7:00 or 7:30." Kelly tried setting her first boundary before she was even hired, saying, "I work out in the morning so I won't be in that early, but I'll always be here by 8:00," but she didn't spot this as a warning sign. Just one year later, she said, "I should have known that the time demands at that office would be completely unsustainable. I often had to come in early *and* stay late, and forget about needing to leave early for a doctor's appointment." Her boss hinted strongly at their office culture right from the start, but that didn't even scratch the surface of how little her employer respected reasonable, healthy boundaries.

JOB-HUNTING?

Had Kelly known then what she knows now, she would have dug further into their office culture before accepting the position. In your next job hunt, one question you can ask around workplace culture (which speaks to how they might handle boundaries) is, "Does the company consider their employees 'family'? Why or why not?" While it may sound promising to hear "We treat our people like family," the *Harvard Business Review* considers it a *major* red flag. When a business uses the family metaphor, it creates an even more unbalanced power dynamic where your boss isn't just your boss—they're also your parent, demanding loyalty, respect, and obedience instead of teamwork, trust, and a fair exchange of value. Employees often feel obliged to protect the "family" at any cost—including working unreasonable hours, behaving unethically, and not reporting their "brothers and sisters" for wrongdoing. The "family" narrative leaves employees feeling disempowered, burned out—and incapable of setting healthy boundaries. A "no" answer to this question isn't a guarantee of healthy workplace culture, but an employer should be able to demonstrate a culture of respect, camaraderie, and teamwork without using the "f-word."

I bet you can identify areas in your own job that would benefit from a boundary or three, but it's important to know what you're up against in terms of office culture. Maybe your boss has been taking what you've been historically willing to give, but setting a simple boundary or two would be quickly acknowledged and respected. Or maybe your entire organization appears to be a "boundary-free zone," and you've got your work cut out for you. Either way, it benefits you to know what you're walking into. Here are some areas of office culture to pay attention to:

- Are you, your co-workers, or your managers regularly expected to work extra hours, nights, or weekends (with or without pay)?
- Are other people regularly sending or replying to work emails or texts at night, on the weekends, or during sick days or vacations?
- Do meetings regularly run long, or start late while awaiting the arrival of the CEO or department manager?
- Are you and others *always* running at or over capacity with your workload, goals, and deadlines?
- Do co-workers or managers over-share personal details, touch without consent, ask personal questions, or otherwise overstep the line of professionalism?
- Does the team or office culture overlook or tolerate sexual harassment, off-color jokes, homophobia, racism, sexism, or any other ism in the workplace?

- Are you or co-workers regularly "othered" at work for healthy boundaries (like leaving on time or not drinking at business lunches)?
- Are you or your department often asked to tell white lies to clients or customers, fake or "massage" the data, or otherwise compromise your integrity?
- Do clients often cancel last minute, change the scope or time-line of projects, or expect you or your team to work extra hours for free?

These questions speak to the array of workplace boundary violations I've observed after spending more than a decade in corporate America, another twelve years running my own busi-ness, and helping thousands of people with their boundary ques-tions. It's likely you'll notice at least a few areas in your current job that would benefit from improving some of these dynamics with a boundary. But it's unlikely you'll be able to solve all of your workplace issues at once, so apply the principle of triage here. If you could solve *one* problem with a healthy boundary, which would carry the most weight and have the biggest impact on your health and happiness at work? Start there.

Setting just one boundary at work will go a long way toward improving your work environment and building your confidence to set others. You'll also create some momentum within yourself and for your co-workers. Once you set a boundary in one area and see how impactful it can be, it will motivate you to set others—and once your co-workers see you were able to hold a boundary around your vacation time, weekends, or workload, it will encourage them to do the same, which can lead to a culture shift within your entire organization.

To help you on this journey, I've grouped the most common workplace boundary needs into four categories: work time, per-sonal time, ethical dilemmas, and personal space and energy.

WORK TIME: These are issues around how you spend your time while you're on the clock, including the number of tasks on your plate, project management and deadlines, and how your time is valued during the workday. Think Zoom calls that continually run long, a boss consistently adding more work to your plate, or clients who regularly no-show.

PERSONAL TIME: This is where work bleeds into personal time, like when you're on vacation, out sick, or relaxing at home after hours. It could be weekend texts from co-workers, pressure to "pitch in" and stay late, or fielding calls from your boss while you're paddleboarding in Barbados.

ETHICAL DILEMMAS: These are tasks, requests, or pressures that make you feel icky and compromise your integrity. It's being asked to tell customers little white lies, feeling like you have to laugh when your boss tells a sexist joke, or being pressured to drink with clients while out to lunch.

PERSONAL SPACE AND ENERGY: These are situations in which your time, personal space, mental health, or privacy are being intruded upon in the workplace. It's co-workers who can't take a hint when you're too busy to chat, bosses making inappropriate physical contact, and supervisors who micromanage every task.

Before we get to the scripts, though, let's talk about the very real challenges of setting a boundary at work when your mortgage, student loan, car payment, and desire to continue eating food regularly *really* need you to keep that paycheck coming.

BOUNDARIES ARE HARD (BUT THERE IS GOOD NEWS)

The first thing I want you to be prepared for when setting boundaries in the workplace is the specific kind of pushback you may receive. Here are some of the phrases that various bosses have said to me when I've tried to set a healthy work boundary:

- "Be a team player."
- "But Elaine has kids, and you don't, so . . ."
- "You already said you don't have plans."
- "Everyone is pitching in right now."
- "Are you saying you won't do it?"
- "I thought you were a go-getter."
- "How important *is* this job to you?"
- "You're too sensitive."
- "Don't bring your personal issues into work."

I heard this last one after I asked for an extra fifteen minutes on my lunch hour once a week to meet with my therapist. My boss at the time was a real peach.

In addition to gaslighting and passive-aggressive jabs, your boss, colleagues, or clients may also respond in a plain old aggressive manner. In Kelly's situation, even after she returned from Barbados and had a frank, professional conversation with her boss about respecting her vacation time in the future, he continued to text and call her during camping trips, sick days, and even *her honeymoon* (RED FLAG). Furthermore, every time she tried to set *any* sort of reasonable boundary, she was made an example of to her colleagues, labeled as unprofessional, and told she was a bad role model for not being "company-first."

Thank goodness most of our work environments aren't that toxic. Still, it's common for management to feel like you're rocking the boat when you start setting healthy boundaries, and to fight just a little to preserve the status quo. Remember, *people will take as much as you are willing to give,* and if you've been giving more than is right, establishing a boundary to set a new precedent may feel like you're taking something away from them.

You don't have to play into that narrative. You have a responsibility to ensure your relationship with work is healthy and sustainable. You want work to be a "place" (whether it's remote or in-person) where you can perform your best, stay motivated to succeed, retain high morale, and feel valued and respected. And the best way to make that happen is with *boundaries*.

Now the hardest part: Even if you do set healthy boundaries at work, as Kelly consistently tried to do, *enforcing* them is an even bigger challenge, and occasionally begs the question: Can you afford to lose this job? Even if you set clear, professional boundaries, if you and management continue to disagree on how to handle paid time off, working hours, your workload, or reasonable self-care initiatives, your only options might be to appeal to Human Resources, change departments or locations, band together with co-workers to exert some pressure, or quietly start looking for a new job.

Yes, I could give you a pep talk about how no paycheck is worth sacrificing your physical or mental health, but that reeks of privilege, and I'm not gonna do it. Quitting isn't an option for many people, which means you may have to start asking yourself, "Where am I willing to compromise my boundaries just to keep my paycheck?" There aren't always easy answers to this question.

The good news (finally, Melissa, *give me some good news*) is twofold: First, when you advocate for yourself by trying to establish boundaries at work, you'll learn a lot about what really matters to you and what you're actually looking for in a corporate culture. After years of fighting her company's culture and getting physically sick from the stress, Kelly decided she'd *finally* had enough—and she quit. (I hope you're cheering with me!) She quickly found another position, and what immediately sold her on her new employer was that all of the boundaries she'd been advocating for at her old job (work/life balance, respectful language, professional conduct, and self-care initiatives) were baked into the culture of the new company. She's been working there happily for the last eight years, although, incredibly, her old boss continues to ask her for favors to this day. I can't even.

The second piece of good news is that I have *many* tips and scripts to help you establish clear, kind, professionally appropriate boundaries at work right away. And just in case you need extra motivation and encouragement, here's your new office mantra:

> *Healthy workplace boundaries are good*
> *for everyone's bottom line.*

Boundaries help you perform your best when you're on the clock, and they help you recharge effectively when you're not. They improve your mental and physical health; create a culture of respect and trust; keep morale, motivation, and loyalty high; and prevent good employees (like you) from burning out— because burnout is very, very real even if you're doing a job you love. When employees are feeling energized, respected, and valued, it has a positive impact on their productivity, creativity, and the results they achieve for the business.

Remember that the next time you're tempted to feel guilty for setting a boundary at work—you're a true team player *because* you're helping to create a workplace culture in which everyone thrives.

WORK BOUNDARIES AND PREP TIPS

Before we launch into the scripts for each of our work boundary categories, let me offer some tips designed to better prepare you for some of the challenges you may face setting and holding boundaries at work.

DO SOME LIGHT READING. Your company handbook and official HR policies should be your first resource when looking to support healthy workplace boundaries. Know how many paid days off you're entitled to; whether there are laws protecting break and lunch times; the rules around overtime and working nights or weekends; employee codes of conduct; and the process for reporting issues. You can use these policies as the foundation for at least some of your boundaries, so you've got backup if your boss tries to pressure you to work from home on your "sick day" or Roger won't stop telling off-color jokes in the break room.

LOOK FOR THE DIAMOND IN THE ROUGH. Ask around and see if any manager, shift leader, captain, foreman, director, or C-suite exec actually *does* take time off. Who's not answering emails or phone calls from vacation? Who has a strongly worded out-of-office reply? Who actually stays home when they're sick? If you can identify anyone else in your company espousing the kind of boundaries you want to set, seek them out and say, "Teach me your ways." These folks can offer tips for navigating the workplace culture and talking to your boss, and they can be powerful allies if you decide to raise the issue with management.

ASK YOUR TEAMMATES ABOUT THEIR EXPERIENCES. Share your struggles around work time, personal time, ethics, or personal space. If your co-workers all feel pressured to work while sick, laugh at sexist jokes, or answer emails on vacation, talk about it. There is strength in numbers, and if you all go to management with the same clear, kind boundary (especially if those boundaries are grounded in your company's written policies), you'll be a far more powerful voice.

INVOLVE MANAGEMENT IN THE PROCESS. Explain your healthy limit, then invite your boss or co-workers to work with you to find a way to uphold that limit together. You'll get better buy-in if they have a say in the process, and they may find a solution you hadn't thought of. Compromise where you can, but not so much that your limit is erased.

AUTOMATE AS MUCH AS POSSIBLE. If you work in an office, a good out-of-office message and voicemail greeting (see page 81) can set a boundary for you. Designate a co-worker as backup ahead of time, so everyone knows who to go to while you're out. Block off an hour on your calendar for scheduling, invoices, or creative tasks. Physically leave your workplace to eat lunch. Have a clear cancellation policy on your website, and keep a card on file to charge clients who no-show. Turn your Slack notifications off after 6 P.M., and delete the email app from your phone during vacations. Leave the job site at the end of the day without announcing it, avoiding the "wait, before you leave, could you . . ." drama. Automated responses, establishing clear habits, and smart use of technology can provide boundary-setting support *and* help you hold a boundary you've already established.

DOCUMENT, DOCUMENT, DOCUMENT. Get everything in writing, so your objections, requests, and responses can be referenced later. Take notes, including dates, times, who was present, and what was said or done when boundaries are disrespected by co-workers, managers, or clients. Take screenshots of after-hours texts or emails, save away messages to make it clear you left specific instructions in your absence, and cc your boss and/or Human Resources on issues that violate company policy. If nothing else, this written record can help you clearly see patterns and prove you've been standing up for yourself in an appropriate and professional way. And if over time your boundaries still aren't being respected, this information will help should you need to make a case for requesting a transfer or explain why you're resigning.

SCRIPTS FOR SETTING BOUNDARIES
AROUND WORK TIME

Work time boundaries are meant to help you operate efficiently and effectively when you're on the clock. Time management is especially challenging when you're working on multiple projects or priorities while juggling meetings, customers, emails, inventory, or just trying to eat lunch somewhere other than your desk or car. Added pressures from your boss, co-workers, or clients make you feel like you're running around putting out fires all day, and an overly full schedule or workload can impact your performance, bonus, or promotion potential.

Setting boundaries around your work time will help you better manage your priorities, meet deadlines and expectations, and demonstrate that you respect everyone's time and capacity at work—especially your own.

> **How can I say no to a boss who keeps putting things on my plate when I'm already over capacity? I hate saying no, but if I take on one more thing, nothing will get done on time or to the right standards, and I'm already approaching burnout.**
>
> **GREEN:** "I can add this to my workload if you can approve other tasks coming off my plate or being pushed to the back burner." Share a list of tasks, who is supervising, the percent completed, and deadlines if applicable.
>
> **YELLOW:** "Normally I'd step in to help, but I have zero bandwidth right now with X, Y, and Z on my plate."
>
> **RED:** (in writing) "I am at the breaking point with my current workload. I can't take on anything new right now or it will negatively impact my performance and results, not to mention my mental health. Let's set up a time to discuss possible solutions."

Keep track of your workload, tasks assigned by others, and requests that your manager may not be aware you're working on. Ask your boss for help prioritizing your projects and share any suggestions you may have for delegation, scope reduction, or streamlined processes. As recommended, document all conversations related to your workload, just in case.

Former consulting clients are still hitting me up for favors, long after our contract is over. Sometimes they're quick one-offs, but sometimes one question leads to lots of follow-ups. How do I say no? Should I say no?

GREEN: "I can send you a few quick thoughts by the end of the week, but that's all I have capacity for."

YELLOW: "Unfortunately, I can't help unless you want to establish a new contract."

RED: "I cannot. Our time together is up, and I've got other projects now."

Remember, boundaries should be flexible when it serves you. Determine how big the ask is, whether this client is a relationship worth maintaining, and if you have the capacity to give them a little time. If you do throw them a freebie, though, keep a close eye on how hard they're trying to move your fence posts and know when to say "enough."

My boss imposes ridiculous deadlines on my entire team. We tell him it's going to take at least a week to get the project done, and he insists he needs it in two days. This stresses my whole team out, but when I try to stand up for them, my boss gets angry at me. Help me find a better way?

GREEN: "If you want this in two days, my team will have to drop everything else we're working on and focus solely on this. Will you authorize that, as well as our overtime?" Or "We could do this in two days, but only if you cut half the features. Your call."

YELLOW: "This cannot be done to the scope you've outlined in just two days. If you want this built right, my team needs the full week."

RED: "We cannot complete this project to spec in two days, and I'd be happy to explain to upper management why."

There's an old project-management adage: You can have it fast, you can have it cheap, you can have it right . . . pick two. "I'm happy to explain" is a nice way of saying, "If you messed up the project plan, I'm not taking the fall for that."

I work in an open floorplan, and it seems like people are always stopping by to chat when I'm knee-deep in a spreadsheet and really need to focus. I don't want to be rude, so how can I nicely say, "Please don't distract me right now?"

GREEN: "Ooh! I'm right in the middle of this just now, can I swing by later / meet you in the break room at three / grab you for lunch?"

YELLOW: (waiting a beat, then removing your headphones) "Oh, I throw my headphones in when I really need to focus. Let me come find you later."

RED: Make a sign for the back of your chair/outer cube wall that says "Do Not Disturb," and let your boss and co-workers know it's intended to help you stay focused during the busiest times of your day. (Just don't leave it up all day, as that would be unreasonable.)

I also hate being interrupted when I'm working, which was problematic when I worked in a large office and had many direct reports. So I tried something new, and started proactively chatting people up in the break room or by the copier when I had free time. Being sociable on my terms made my co-workers less likely to label me rude or standoffish, and made it easier to set boundaries around my cubicle.

I'm self-employed, and my income depends on clients reliably showing up to appointments. However, my twenty-four-hour cancellation policy is often ignored, and I've found it hard to enforce. How do I respond to someone who cancels last minute, then gets mad when I try to charge them?

GREEN: Send every new and existing client an agreement that includes a detailed cancellation policy and fees. Require that clients give you an active credit card to keep on file, along with notification that their card will be charged in accordance with your policies. If they don't agree to any of these terms, release them as clients. (You'll do yourself a favor.)

YELLOW: "Thanks for letting me know. Since you're canceling within twenty-four hours, I'll charge your card 50 percent, per your client agreement."

RED: Charge their card per your policy, and notify them that if they have one more no-show, you will no longer accept appointment requests from them.

As an entrepreneur, it can be tempting to let clients walk all over you because you need the work. Your best bet is to have the boundaries in place from the start and to treat any flexibility on your part as a "favor" you're doing for them. This gives you the space to hold firm to the boundary if they continue to disregard

it, or if your business grows and you no longer need to compro-
mise to make the rent.

I'm constantly in Zooms/meetings that run long (often because
they don't start on time). I'm not in charge of these meetings,
but nobody likes feeling that their time is being disrespected.
How could I speak up politely?

GREEN: (before the meeting) "We only have an hour for today's
meeting, so if someone could distribute the agenda ahead of
time, that would be helpful."

YELLOW: (five minutes before the meeting is scheduled to end) "I
see we only have five minutes left, Bill. Are there final action
items we need to cover?"

RED: "I have a hard stop now. I'll look for next steps via email."
Leave the meeting.

Here, the Red boundary is the consequence—essentially "I am
taking control of my time." You can help this process along by
asking that someone create an agenda before the meeting (or
creating one yourself), not letting the team stray too far off topic,
and reminding everyone when time is almost up.

SCRIPTS FOR SETTING BOUNDARIES AROUND PERSONAL TIME

The boundaries you establish around your personal time are just
as important as the limits you set while you're in the office. In
order for you to perform your best, your personal time must effectively help you unwind, recharge, and recover from the stress
of the workplace. This is especially true if you're out sick, in-
jured, grieving, or on vacation—especially if paid time off is lim-

ited. Creating a culture of care and respect is hugely important for employee morale, mental health, and retention. If your company isn't already world-class at respecting employees' time off, you'll have to advocate for yourself and others through your own boundary-setting.

Setting boundaries around your personal time will help you truly relax when you're out of the office, knowing you and your team share the same expectations and priorities. They'll also help you show up at work refreshed and ready to perform at your peak—which should be readily apparent in your performance metrics, reviews, and attitude.

> **Co-workers keep pulling me into tasks as I'm leaving for the night. I don't have kids (and most of my co-workers do), so it's hard to say no, but my downtime in the evening is valuable, too. Help?**
>
> **GREEN:** "I can't stay tonight, but I'll help you tomorrow morning."
>
> **YELLOW:** "I can't, I'm on my way out. Brad is here until close tonight, maybe ask him?"
>
> **RED:** "Can't tonight!" as you walk out the door.
>
> *Let's please normalize Netflix, takeout, and decompressing counting as "plans." It's great to pitch in where you can, but if you're being taken advantage of because you don't have kids or you live alone, set some boundaries for your mental health.*

> **I'm out sick today but people are still calling and texting me with questions. Technically I feel well enough to text, but I get sick days for a reason, and I'd recover much better if I could just rest. How do I respond when this happens?**

GREEN: Set an email "out of office" message and leave the same message on your voicemail. Answer texts with, "I'm home sick today and can't help. Try asking Russ."

YELLOW: "I'm out sick today. I'll be turning my phone off now so I can rest." (Set your phone to DND or simply stop answering calls and texts.)

RED: (in an email to your boss) "I am out sick today, but I keep getting work calls and texts. I need to prioritize my health and won't be responding to work requests. I'd appreciate talking about this when I get back so we can make a plan to help others avoid this in the future. I'm sure you agree that employees shouldn't have to experience additional stress when they're already sick."

If you can get your boss or HR in your corner, this can be a huge win for your whole team. When you return to work, try something like, "I know how much you care about our team's physical and mental health. Can we recirculate some best practices for sick or vacation days?"

Management is constantly pressuring us to come in on our (already limited) days off, to cover for a sick team member, help during a promotion, or attend an important meeting. When I tell them I need my days off, they'll say, "Be a team player and come in anyway." I sometimes do, but I can't keep giving in like that! What should I say?

GREEN: "I'll help the team catch up on Friday, but I cannot come in tomorrow."

YELLOW: "Days off are necessary for my mental health and my family life. I don't like being pressured to give that up. I can't help tomorrow."

RED: "I will not be coming in tomorrow."

If this happens often, connect with your co-workers and management to discuss how you might adjust staffing needs, scheduling, or covering shifts or tasks in a way that allows you all to get the rest (or extra income) you need.

I'm constantly expected to reply to emails while on vacation—and I haven't had a single vacation yet where I wasn't pulled into some work thing. I've got my next trip planned, and this time needs to be different. SOS!

GREEN: (to your boss and team the week before) "I'm out next week and won't be on email or Slack during my trip. Ashley is covering my invoice approvals; you can ask Liilu any other questions."

YELLOW: (to your boss, team, and key clients) "Reminder: I'm out next week and deeply committed to this vacation. I won't be on email and I'm turning off Slack notifications. I've assigned coverage for X, Y, and Z projects and don't anticipate anything coming up. Only text me if *The Kelly Clarkson Show* calls, because Kelly Clarkson is a national treasure. But I'm serious. Don't text me."

RED: Set an away message: "I'm on *vacation* vacation from Monday the 11th through Friday the 15th. I will not be looking at email or Slack during this time. I'll be back in the office on Monday the 18th with a fresh tan and an overflowing in-box, so thanks in advance for your patience with my response. If you need someone while I am out, email Liilu at headquarters@whole30.com."

These are all my actual away messages. Feel free to steal any of them, including the Kelly Clarkson part. What's unusual in this situation is that I'm advising you to employ all three boundaries in a row, timed appropriately around your trip. What you're doing is automating the boundary such that nobody expects you to check in, and you can feel confident turning off notifications and setting your phone to Do Not Disturb for the rest of your trip.

DOS AND DON'TS FOR CRAFTING THE PERFECT AWAY MESSAGE

Sure, you can stick with, "I'll be out this week with limited access to email," but there's a better way.

- **DON'T say you'll have "limited access to email."** First, you're lying; your phone will be within five feet of you at all times. More important, that opens the door to "I may be able to check in here and there." Do not check your email when you're on vacation. Just don't do it.
- **DON'T say "I'll reply when I'm back in the office on Monday."** Chances are your in-box will be overflowing, and if people expect an immediate response, you may end up with tons of "Did you get my email?" emails on top of the original emails.
- **DO communicate clearly.** "I'll be out of the office from [this date] to [this date] and I won't be checking email, Slack, voicemail, etc." Boom, there's some truth-telling in action.
- **DO use your voice.** If you want to inject some humor or personality, go for it! Just make sure your language around "don't text me" is still crystal clear.
- **DO give people a way to achieve their task without you.** Share a list of whom to contact in your place, link to a form prospective clients can fill out, or offer your customer-service line.
- **DO make it clear you'll be replying to emails as you have capacity.** "Thanks in advance for your patience" is a nice way to set that expectation.

My boss texts me at night (on my personal phone) about work. I get why he'd send late-night emails, but texts about normal business stuff feel invasive. How can I gently provide this feedback?

GREEN: Assuming this is not an emergency, answer the text, but add, "Going forward, if it's after hours, can you please not text unless it's an emergency? Slack or email is best after 6 P.M., so I can address it the next morning. Thanks."

YELLOW: Don't reply to the text. The following morning, say in person, "Hey, I got your text last night during my family time. Next time, please send an email so it doesn't disturb my personal time. Let's talk about those purchase orders . . ."

RED: Don't reply to non-emergency texts at all. Reply via email the next business day, repeating the request that your boss not text you about work-related issues after hours. Loop in HR if your home time is not being respected.

If your company culture values employees' mental health and work/life balance (or says it does), you should gently remind your boss that after-hours texts don't model the kind of behavior he's encouraging. Tell him how much the entire team would appreciate him scheduling emails for the next business day so he can document his late-night thoughts without disturbing anyone's family time.

SCRIPTS FOR SETTING BOUNDARIES AROUND ETHICAL DILEMMAS

Everyone wants to show up at their jobs as their best selves, feeling good about their work, impact, and contributions. But every time you give a piece of your integrity away, whether it's lying to a client, covering up for your boss, or tolerating inappropriate workplace behavior, it makes you feel smaller, less confident, and less authentic. For work to be a healthy, sustainable environment, you have to feel as though your values aren't up for debate—and that the company, your boss, or your clients won't ask you to choose between your integrity and your job.

Establishing boundaries around what you will and will not accept when it comes to your moral code and values demonstrates your loyalty and integrity to the company, and functions as an act of self-care. When you set a boundary here, you affirm that you are worthy of protecting yourself and your belief systems, and you can be proud that you stood up for what is right.

> **I'm in sales and my boss says I have to drink when we're out with clients, to make them feel comfortable. Sometimes I don't want to, but I don't know how to respond to the pressure, so I usually give in. What could I say?**
>
> **GREEN:** (before the outing) "Hey, I'm not drinking tonight. I'll order soda water and lime and won't make a big deal out of it—just giving you a heads-up."
>
> **YELLOW:** "I don't feel comfortable with the idea that I *have* to drink during sales dinners. I'm a great salesperson, and I'm even more persuasive when I'm sober. I won't be drinking tonight."
>
> **RED:** "It sounds like you're suggesting my performance depends on my alcohol consumption, and that violates at least three HR policies. I hope you don't ever again pressure anyone on your team to drink."
>
> *I pray it doesn't get to Red, because that work environment has some big problems. Sobriety as a choice is on the rise, and more people are talking about why they're choosing not to drink. Maybe your stand will help a client feel more comfortable doing the same—and that could translate into closing the deal.*

One person on my team is always taking super long lunches or running midday errands and asking me to cover for them with our boss. It puts me in an awkward position, and frankly, I feel taken advantage of. How can I politely push back here, so I don't end up in trouble?

GREEN: "If anyone asks, I can say you must be running late, but that's all I feel comfortable saying."

YELLOW: "I will not continue to cover for you, and it's unfair of you to keep asking."

RED: "I won't lie for you anymore."

Prepare for a rough reaction, especially if they get caught—but remember, this isn't your business or your problem, and your co-worker is an adult who can manage their own time. You can't set a boundary that your colleague stop taking long lunches—only that you won't continue to cover or lie for them if (when) they get caught.

My boss sometimes asks me to do questionable things (like lying to clients). This feels deeply wrong and I hate that I'm put in this position, but I also don't know how to say no to my boss. There must be a nice way of saying, "This feels sleazy."

GREEN: "I'm not comfortable with that. My clients/customers trust me, and they deserve to hear the truth. I'll focus on what we are doing to keep things on track for them."

YELLOW: "That still doesn't feel good to me. I'd like to check with Perla first and see what she thinks." (Reference a colleague or someone in HR.)

RED: Share your concerns in writing, creating a paper trail. "Today you asked me to [blank]. I'm not comfortable with that, and don't believe it's in the best interest of the client/customer/ company. I would rather not be involved at this stage. Thank you for respecting that."

This is a sucky situation, especially if you have a relationship with your customers or clients. Ask for advice outside of your organization, see if other co-workers feel the same way about your boss's requests, and document the heck out of it, just in case.

How do I respond to inappropriate remarks in the workplace? I've been a party to snide comments about women "sleeping their way to the top," blatantly sexist jokes, racist microaggressions directed at others . . . I want to speak up, but I often freeze. How can I interrupt this dynamic?

GREEN: "Oof, Roger—maybe you don't realize how poorly what you just said came across. Do you want to try again?"

YELLOW: "No, no—what you just said is not okay, and I will not let it slide."

RED: "Wow, Roger. That's legitimately inappropriate/slanderous/sexist/racist, and in violation of about twelve different company policies. I can't stay silent when I hear things like that."

Notice the use of Boundary Alerts here, to buy you a moment to shift the tone and steel your confidence. Green gives your colleague the benefit of the doubt, believing that they want to do better. It's possible they started their career in a time or at a workplace that was more tolerant of this kind of behavior, and they need reminders to make the necessary adjustments here and now. Mentioning company policy in Red is the precursor to telling your manager or HR that Roger is deliberately causing harm and refuses to accept feedback on this.

USING YOUR PRIVILEGE

Historically marginalized people in the workplace shouldn't have to stick up for themselves by themselves. A good ally to people of color, LGBTQ+ folks, people with disabilities, and others will use their privilege to call out harmful behavior. It's additionally harmful to stay quiet in the moment, then later approach the only Asian person on your team and whisper, "What Chuck just said wasn't okay." If it's not okay, speak up at the time of the incident. That is how we ally, and it's only 0.1 percent as hard as *being* the microaggressed person in that room. For more on how to be an effective ally in any environment, see page 281.

My boss constantly takes credit for my ideas. I'm over it. *[This was the shortest "help me with a boundary" message I've ever received. I'm here for it.]*

GREEN: (in private) "I'm glad you thought my plan to make the event virtual was smart. I would have appreciated you giving me credit in that meeting, though. It didn't feel good."

YELLOW: Start documenting everything in writing. If you share an idea in person, follow it up with an email: "Per our earlier conversation, I presented you with my plan to move the event to virtual [share bullet points]. Let me know if you'd like me to share it with anyone else."

RED: (in the room) "Thanks for that, Chuck. Since this plan was originally my concept, can I share the budget and timelines I've already started sketching out?"

Red is basically war—but your boss is a crappy leader if they can't see that your good ideas already make them look good. Documenting everything in writing is a good interim step so they can see you mean business with this boundary. Also, ask around (gently), because chances are your co-workers have experienced this, too, and remember, there's strength in numbers.

SCRIPTS FOR SETTING BOUNDARIES AROUND PERSONAL SPACE AND ENERGY

Some parts of your job are mandatory, like submitting reports, completing projects, and attending necessary meetings. But there will always be aspects of your office culture that ask more of you than what's in your job description. Navigating socialization, various work styles, and team-building activities are an aspect of every workplace, but you have agency here, too, and there is no "one-size-fits-all" when it comes to fitting into office culture.

Establishing boundaries around your personal space and energy, such as how much physical contact you allow or how often you participate in office games, is important for maintaining a sense of comfort at work. Not everyone wants to hug their co-workers, be Facebook friends, or join the company yoga class—and establishing boundaries around what you are and aren't comfortable with will make your office (whether virtual or in-person) feel like a more welcoming, accommodating, respectful space.

My boss constantly micromanages me. It's exhausting and unnecessary, because I'm good at my job. The trouble is, I can never really prove myself with all of this "help" and supervision. How can I become more self-directed?

GREEN: "Hi, boss! I created this project management document to help you see where I am with tasks, so you can more easily stay up to date. Can we set up a weekly touch-base so I can keep you updated on my progress?"

YELLOW: "I'm clear on the direction of this project, and I'd like to work independently to hit the first deliverable. Can I touch base with you next week and show you my progress?" If they check in early or provide additional direction, try, "Would you please hold any suggestions or feedback until we meet next week? We agreed I could work independently this week, and I want to use the opportunity to show you *my* work product."

RED: "Maybe you haven't noticed, but you've been overmanaging me on this project, and to be honest, I'm a little frustrated. Can you please step back and trust me to run this? This is why you hired me, and I deserve the chance to prove myself."

That last one might feel like a lot, but your boss continuing to overstep into your role and duties benefits nobody. However, you could add an Orange (tertiary) boundary like "Are you unhappy with how this is going? You've been giving me input at every stage even though I haven't asked for help, which makes me wonder if you're unsure whether I can manage it on my own."

My manager is always touching me. It's not sexual—a hand on the shoulder when they want my attention, or a bump on the arm after a joke—but I don't like it. I know they don't mean any harm, so I'm not sure how I should approach it.

GREEN: "I believe you're just trying to be friendly, but I'd appreciate it if you wouldn't physically try to get my attention or let me know I'm doing a good job. Words work just fine."

YELLOW: (putting a hand up) "Oops, please don't do that. I don't like physical contact at work."

RED: "Stop touching me like that. It's inappropriately familiar, and I don't like it."

It's likely your manager will be uncomfortable when you bring this up. (GOOD. They should be aware of how their actions impact others.) You may also feel guilty, based on their reaction. Please don't let their response or your own discomfort push this boundary aside. We both know how necessary it is for your safety and security in the workplace. If needed, talk to their boss or HR about their ongoing conduct—which is unacceptable in any workplace setting, in case you needed validation.

Folks in my office are very friendly with one another, but I prefer to keep my private life private. How do I respond to questions like, "Are you dating anyone?"

GREEN: "You know me, I like to keep it mysterious." Change the subject.

YELLOW: "Mmm, I don't really like to talk about my dating life at work." Change the subject.

RED: "Ha—you know I'm not going to answer that!" Change the subject.

This Green response is technically what I'd call a "pre-Green" boundary. It's not the clearest statement (that's Yellow), but it gets the point across that this isn't a subject you're comfortable with. Saying something slightly coy like this, when appropriate, can be an effective "minimum dose," and changing the subject makes it even more clear that you'd rather not discuss it.

TALK ON YOUR TERMS

Much like the strategy I talked about in the "I don't want to be disturbed when I'm busy" scenario from page 75, another way to maintain a friendly vibe with co-workers is to proactively share things that *don't* cross your boundary line. Volunteer what you made for dinner, the book you just finished, the hike you did this weekend, or your dog's latest antics. Bonus: Ask people about *their* lives, too! They'll come away thinking you're friendly and a great listener, and you won't have to engage in any conversations that make you feel uncomfortable.

My boss's boss keeps calling me "kiddo." Yes, I'm one of the youngest people in the office, but I'm a grown adult in a professional environment. He says it with fondness, but I'm worried that tolerating this will impact how others see me, so I want to find a nice way to say "please don't."

GREEN: "Hey, I may be young, but I'm not a kiddo. Please call me 'Jane.' "

YELLOW: "Calling me 'kiddo' at work is inappropriate, especially in front of others. I need you to make the effort to stop, please."

RED: (interrupting) "Not 'kiddo.' It's Jane."

If they've been calling you by this nickname for a while and you've been letting it slide, it's never too late to speak up! Try, "I know you've been calling me 'kiddo' for a while, and I haven't said anything. But to be honest, it bothers me. Could you please stop?" Speak the Yellow boundary during a quiet moment when you can have their full attention—and document it for yourself, just in case.

BONUS: SELF-BOUNDARIES AT WORK

Most of these boundary conversations center around issues with co-workers and managers, but those aren't the only work relationships that boundaries can improve. We learned during COVID that working alone from home is *hard*. And yes, while many of us are back in our offices now, remote work is largely here to stay, which means we all have to figure out how to balance the pull of our laptop when the "office" is accessible 24/7.

Setting boundaries with *yourself* around your work-from-home time is critical to preserving a happy, healthy work/life flow and preventing burnout. Here are some self-boundaries I've developed over the last decade, many of which came in clutch during the pandemic, when work, school, and home life would constantly bleed into one another if I let them.

- **Work in only one dedicated space, like a small office or at a specific desk.** This helps your brain delineate "work space" from "home space" better than working at the kitchen counter (where you also prep meals, play board games, and eat breakfast). Also, when it's time to "leave" for the day, it's easier if your materials aren't scattered over the living room, dining room, and kitchen.
- **Preserve break and lunch times, as you would at a real office.** Book a midday break in your calendar if that helps—treat it like a meeting with yourself. Limit Zoom meetings you schedule to fifty minutes, so you always have a short break in between.
- **Force yourself to leave your desk during these breaks.** Eat lunch in the dining room, sit outside for a few minutes, play with the dog, or call your mom from the backyard.
- **When you're done for the day, close up "shop."** Shut down your laptop, turn off phone notifications, and close your office door. Mimic "leaving" the office as you used to do.
- **Build in a brief transition between "work" and "home," even if it's just ten minutes.** You no longer have the commute to serve as the demarcation line between working and relaxing, so find something that can do that. Try a short walk, a quick trip to the grocery store, a workout, or just heading upstairs and giving yourself twenty minutes to relax before you start the dinner/homework/meal prep rush.
- **Make a rule not to check work email or Slack before your morning routine or in the hour before bed.** You know why.

LOVING THE LIMITS THAT SET YOU FREE

In late 2010, after realizing I was letting my business take way too much of my time and energy, I set a boundary that caught everyone off guard. I was traveling to present Whole30 seminars just about every weekend, which meant I didn't usually get Saturday and Sunday off. So my entire company (all two of us) started closing on Tuesdays. Every Tuesday, no matter what was happening, became a no-work day. I didn't answer emails, respond to Facebook comments, or schedule meetings or calls. In fact, I'd often be out of cell reception altogether, off hiking in the mountains.

Nobody thought it would work. "I mean, the rest of the world works on Tuesday," my sister said. "How can you just tell them no?" The answer is, *I just did*. And sooner than I ever anticipated, everyone became used to it. My publisher, community, and brand partners all knew I wasn't online on Tuesdays; my away message made it clear I'd reply on Wednesday and everyone just worked around it. I maintained that boundary for two or three years, until we stopped doing seminars and I got my weekends back.

Granted, if you work a 9-to-5, you likely can't start taking random weekdays off . . . but that's not the point. The point is, *every boundary* feels weird and awkward in the beginning. You'll have to remind people that this is your limit. You'll have to remind yourself that healthy boundaries aren't rude, selfish, or disloyal. You'll have to resist feeling guilty for prioritizing your health and peace. You'll have to resist the urge to overexplain, justify, or cave "just this once." If boundaries are meant to make relationships better, then your healthy workplace boundaries are there to keep you performing your best, feeling your most fulfilled, and staying mentally and physically healthy—which only benefits your team, manager, and employer. Your work environment will be calmer and happier, your home time more relaxed and rejuvenating, and your work product will showcase the full scope of your energy and talents.

Boundaries at work are *magical,* and now you're completely primed to start setting those limits. Which is good news, because it's time to talk about your mother-in-law.

When the Drama Is Your Mama

Setting Boundaries with Parents and In-Laws, Grandparents, and Other Family Members

Last fall, I received an email from a man named Caleb who was asking for help setting a boundary before the holidays. Caleb's parents had been divorced for more than eight years, but they still bickered every time they interacted. Phone conversations, shared meals, and holiday celebrations were consumed by complaints and attempts to woo Caleb to their respective sides. "They're constantly gossiping about each other and making snide remarks," Caleb wrote, "like 'Can you believe your mother did that?' and 'Of course your father is too busy to help.' My wife and I are happy to celebrate the holidays separately with each of them, but we don't want to be involved in their drama, and I don't want to hear either of them speak poorly about the other. I love them both, but at this point, it's exhausting. Can you help me set the right boundary here?"

If I had a dollar for every "Help me with my parents/in-laws" boundary issue my readers have sent me, I'd be typing this from my private yacht in the Bahamas. Boundaries with family members are complicated by a number of factors, including some of the power dynamics discussed in Chapter 3. You spend your formative years letting your parents tell you what to do—for good reason. As a small human, you needed the help, and (hopefully) your parents assumed responsibility for your well-being, development, and safety. As you got older, there was probably tension between your growing desire for independence and the fact that you still needed their support and input to keep you safe, sheltered, fed, and successful. Now that you're a fully grown adult, you see how hard those patterns are to break. You no longer necessarily need or want your parents' feedback or assistance, but parents are gonna parent, and their often well-intentioned desire to "help" can sometimes feel pushy, like they're overstepping.

There's nothing that snaps me back to unhealthy communication styles, coping mechanisms, and behaviors faster than being around my parents. (Well, maybe my ex-husband, but that's in Chapter 7.) The patterns you create in childhood are stored in the body, so even if you logically realize how dysfunctional or unhealthy they were, it feels almost automatic for everyone to return to those roles when you're together now. It can also be hard for parents to see their kids as fully functioning adults with their own lived experiences, goals, and opinions, capable of making their own decisions and running their own lives. My dad still gives me advice about everything from child-rearing to home ownership to car maintenance, and sometimes he gets pretend-grumpy when I don't take it. Some of his feedback is welcomed or benign, but some (like when he oversteps with my parenting decisions) requires a boundary.

The same can apply to siblings or other relatives. If you spent time together during childhood, those patterns set when you were kids can continue to show up now, in adulthood—even if you're all in therapy. If your parents had "favorites," if one of you always got your way, if you were used to being the peacemaker, or if your family was so big you felt invisible, those childhood dynamics may still find a seat at your family dinner table, even as adults.

BETTER BOUNDARIES CREATE STRONGER FAMILIES

Setting healthy boundaries with family members isn't just about improving relations with your immediate and extended family. This practice can have a positive impact on *all* of your relationships, because the relationships you create with your family often carry forward into romantic partnerships, adult friendships, and work interactions. When Caleb was younger and his parents fought, they often put him and his sister in the middle, unfairly asking them to take sides, vying for their affection, and using them as emotional dumpsters. Caleb was used to playing the peacemaker and he grew up feeling as though it was his job to placate his parents. Now that he's an adult with his own family, he can see how that pattern extends into work discussions, disagreements with his spouse, and even dynamics with his own kids.

If you were the peacemaker of your household, as Caleb was, you might fear conflict as an adult, letting friends or co-workers run you over because it's less scary than saying no. If overly controlling parents didn't respect your needs as a child, you may not set boundaries with your romantic partner (assuming they won't be respected), only to end up resentful and angry. If arguing parents shaped your childhood, you may find yourself giving in to your child's every demand, so they don't have to experience the discomfort of an argument themselves.

This is a meaty chapter, because boundary violations with family take a wide range of forms, stem from a variety of dynamics, and prove challenging to address. I suspect that when you read the list, you might spot a few behaviors that you didn't even catch as potential boundary issues in your own life. But one person's "Oops—that's too far" is another person's "Works for me!" You may not love it when your in-laws pop over unannounced, while someone else enjoys the surprise, knowing how helpful they are with the kids when they visit. Your spouse may appreciate your parents' questions about her career path, while you would rather they support without feedback.

You also might find you need one boundary for one set of parents, and something entirely different for another. If your mom and dad are dream houseguests, fending for themselves in the morning, taking the kids to lunch, and pitching in with household tasks, you might allow them to stay with you longer than your in-laws, who expect to be waited on hand and foot during their visit.

None of these conversations or scenarios are prescriptive—you don't *have* to set a boundary in any given area just because others have decided to. Only you know the limits that work best for you, and it's okay (healthy, even) if those limits change based on the context, the people involved, or the season of life you're in.

When family members don't respect your boundaries, it can look like:

- Visiting unannounced or staying longer than is welcomed
- Inserting themselves into your plans (vacations, births, jobs)
- Gossiping, negative talk, or oversharing about other family members
- Refusing to respect names, pronouns, or gender identities
- Sharing your personal details or photos without your permission
- Saying hurtful things because they "care"
- Forcing hugs or kisses on you and/or your kids
- Taking over your space (like "reorganizing" your cabinets or gifting decorations)
- Attempting to parent your children
- Interfering with your relationship or personal life
- Setting unreasonable expectations around time together (like frequently scheduled dinners or holidays)

- Breaking your rules around food, screen time, or video games when your kids visit
- Borrowing money, cars, or other possessions in a way that feels egregious
- Assuming you'll help with babysitting, dog-sitting, or other care tasks
- Unreasonable time spent at your home eating, doing laundry, or sleeping over
- Interrupting alone time or self-care practices
- Letting themselves into your home without notice or permission
- Forcing discussions on relationships, child status, career path, or religious practices
- Pressuring attendance at family gatherings, holidays, and other events

In my own personal boundary practice and in the work I've done helping others, I've seen that the boundary issues that frequently arise with family members fall into three categories: parents and in-laws, grandparents, and other family members.

PARENTS AND IN-LAWS: Most of the boundaries we want to set with parents and in-laws involve an overstep into your life, space, time, or values as an adult. It can be hard for parents to watch their child shift their attention, devotion, and priorities to a partner or spouse, and it can bring up jealousy, a sense of competition, and regret over missed opportunities. At the same time, as in Caleb's case, parents also get stuck in old patterns, not realizing how damaging they are to their now-grown children. Setting boundaries around these behaviors is the first step in creating a healthy relationship for this stage of your life.

GRANDPARENTS: Boundaries with grandparents are designed to help you maintain a sense of security, consistency, and autonomy for your household and kids. Grandparents can be opinionated when it comes to the way you are raising your own children, and sometimes those opinions carry over into contradicting your rules, parenting style, or instructions. Whether they think you're too strict ("a little ice cream won't hurt") or too lenient ("iPads in the car—really?"), setting healthy limits with your parents on behalf of your children will make for more relaxed and enjoyable visits.

OTHER FAMILY MEMBERS: Whether you're asking Aunt Donna to stop talking politics at the table or telling your younger brother it's time to get off your couch, setting boundaries with other family members can have positive effects that reverberate through the entire clan—but may cause some shock waves in the beginning. Remember that "clear is kind," and most important, remind yourself that boundaries are not selfish, because they'll improve all of your family dynamics. Also, patience is key anytime you're looking to change generational patterns. It might not happen overnight, but with consistency, things *will* change.

IN-LAWS BEHAVING BADLY

I recently invited members of my community to share some their "best" in-law boundary oversteps. While I had dozens to choose from, my favorite read, "My in-laws just showed up at our house without notice after I gave birth. Like, the *day* after. And announced they were staying for ten days." You might be thinking, "They did *not*," but I've been giving boundary advice for so long now, nothing your in-laws do surprises me. They invite themselves on your vacations, involve themselves in your marital disputes, and fill your children with sugar and red dye 40 when you've explicitly asked them not to.

While my boundary scripts pertain to both your own parents and your partner's, in-laws add another layer of complexity to

the parental boundary equation. Any boundary-crossing, manipulative, passive-aggressive patterns you're now experiencing
firsthand are all too familiar to your spouse or partner. It's likely
your partner felt run over this same way starting in childhood.
And it's *super* likely your partner has simply learned to live with
their unreasonable demands or oversteps.

Until you showed up.

If you're the one driving the change in dynamic, be aware that
leading the charge means encountering a lot of potential land
mines. First, you run the risk of becoming the villain in this story.
Your in-laws may see you as making waves, disturbing the peace,
coming between them and their child, and taking away privileges
they've been used to for decades. To state the obvious, they're not
gonna like it. Second, you may be asking your spouse to choose
between your needs and their parents' feelings, which is a tricky
place to be—especially if your in-laws reinforce the narrative that
this is a battle where sides must be drawn.

Your partner just wants to keep the peace and is doing their
best to placate all parties. You just want your completely reasonable limits respected. And your in-laws are likely to play their kid
like a fiddle to get what they want . . . unless you two can start
working as a team. And when it comes to in-laws, I have one
overarching best practice that I affectionately refer to as "The In-
Law Rule," which states:

Present a united front, but handle your own parents.

Even if the boundary originated with you, it's most effectively
implemented if you both agree this is the healthy limit you need
to set as a couple. Then it's your partner's job to handle the conversation with their own parents on both of your behalf. This
does not include your partner telling their parents it was your
idea. Saying something like, "Well, Taylor was wondering if . . ."

is effectively throwing you under the bus and immediately weakens your collective case. Your partner needs to present this boundary to their parents in a way that shows that those preferences come from *both* of you. If you two are divided, you have no chance of holding an effective limit with an overbearing parent.

Ideally, your partner should lay it out for their parents like this: "*We* are requesting (insert limit). *We* are in agreement on this and will hold this boundary together. *We* will impose the following consequences if you do not respect *our* boundary." However, be prepared for this to feel so uncomfortable to your partner that you'll end up needing to drive the bus. If that's the case, make sure you do two things first: One, confirm with your partner that you have their full support with this boundary, even though you're the one doing the talking. Two, ask your partner how they are willing to support you during the conversation. If they can't agree to be there even in silent support (or at the very least, if their parents try to insert a wedge by asking, "Is this what *you* want?" your partner needs to be willing to say, "Yes, I'm with Taylor"), you could end up in a situation where sides *are* taken, and you feel abandoned and betrayed.

THE EXCEPTION TO THE IN-LAW RULE

Sometimes, for whatever reason, it's better if the spouse does all the talking with their in-laws. If your spouse is a man and your parents have more respect for male authority, maybe he *should* set the boundary. (Gross, but work the system here, okay?) Perhaps your in-laws respect your professional perspective (say, if you're a medical doctor or a psychologist), or are willing to do things just for the sake of the pregnant partner in the relationship. If that's the case, use whatever leverage you have to just get it done.

But what if you can't agree on the right limit? Maybe your wife likes it when her mom just drops by, even though it stresses you out. Or your husband wants his mom there right after the baby comes home, but you're praying for some quiet time to bond. The best place to start is an honest conversation with your partner. Share your feelings about how this behavior makes you feel and the ways it negatively impacts you and your family. (See my "Magic Number" trick ahead.) Boundary-crossing here may impact multiple relationships—yours with your partner, your kids' with their grandparents, or yours with your in-laws—so spell that out clearly. Then ask whether your partner can support the boundary you want to set based on that conversation.

If you still can't agree, find a compromise. And yes, there's almost *always* a compromise. Make a deal that if your mother-in-law stops by without calling, you aren't obligated to visit with her if you're already busy—your wife will be responsible for that. Set a reasonable limit on the number of days your in-laws stay with you once you have the baby, or offer to pay for a nearby hotel or Airbnb so they can be close by. Get creative, because you can do it any way you want (see YCDIAWYW on page 171), even if it's unconventional or has never been done before in your family. Until you and your partner agree on the limit that needs to be set, there is little point in having a boundary conversation with anyone else, so spend as much time as you need until you can present a boundary that works for you both as a united front.

THE MAGIC NUMBER

I've used this trick to help me through tough decisions for years. Ask yourself, "On a scale of 1 to 10, how much do I care that my mother-in-law drops by without calling? Does it bother me a 10, like *max annoyance;* or is it a 3, an eye roll but whatever?" Then ask your partner, "How important is it to *you* that your mom has the freedom to come by anytime she wants, with no notice?" Decide at the same time, without sharing your rating—you don't want your answer to be swayed by your partner. Then compare your numbers. If it bothers you a 7, but your partner only cares a 3, that helps you set the boundary—your mother-in-law has to call first, even if it's just ten minutes ahead of time. If your very pregnant wife 8/10 wants her mom here when the baby is born and you're just a 5, not really sure whether it will be helpful or annoying, give your wife what she needs to feel safe and cared for. As long as you're both committed to self-awareness, honesty, and the process of setting the limit that is best for you as a collective (and not just "winning"), this simple tool can go a long way in facilitating these boundary conversations.

While much of the nuance discussed here is specifically around your in-laws, everything applies to your parents, too. (After all, your parents are your partner's in-laws!) If your parents are the ones overstepping, reading through this section and the scripts should help you be better prepared to support your partner, and will offer guidance that can be applied to situations with your own parents.

THE GRANDPARENT WARS

As I've mentioned a few times, having children presents some big challenges when it comes to establishing boundaries with your parents. My mom often talks about how much she appreciated my grandmother's perspective. Gram was helpful and supportive to both of my parents without butting in or over-parenting. Her philosophy was, "I did my job as a parent. Now it's your turn, and I'm going to mind my business." While I'm lucky my parents also (mostly) follow this philosophy, I've had to set a few boundaries when they've overstepped into my co-parenting relationship and other decisions I've made for my child. Looking through my DMs, I can see that this is something many people experience.

- "How do I talk to my parents about not forcing my kids to hug them?"
- "What can I say when my mom tries to discipline my kids over me?"
- "My parents think my routines are overly strict—but I'm the kids' mom."
- "I hate it when my parents feed my kids sugary treats, even though I tell them not to."

It seems like grandparents get all the best parts of parenting. They can buy their grandkids all the toys, feed them all the sugar, extend all the bedtimes, and hand them right back to Mom and Dad when they're cranky, tired, and pitching a fit. I've heard plenty of grandparents say, "It's my right to spoil them rotten!" (That is, give them all the things they never let *you* have as a kid, because they knew it would wreak havoc on your routine, stability, and mood.)

It can also seem—and given the generational patterns at play, it's highly likely—that your parents do not see you in the role of "fully functioning adult capable of successfully raising this tiny human." It can seem near impossible for your parents to resist inserting their years of wisdom and experience into your own parenting, despite how much they (probably) hated it when *their* parents did that to them. In some areas, their opinions are welcomed—*Yes, Mom, please tell me how you distracted a young me from the candy at the supermarket checkout*. In other areas, though, you want to figure it out for yourself, just like they did.

Also, the way your parents raised you may be different from the way you want to raise your kid. I came from two very authoritarian parents. My mom was not about to negotiate with me in the middle of the grocery store—I either shaped up and stopped whining, or she left a cart full of groceries in Aisle 7 and dragged all of us home. (This happened once. It was legendary.) If you're into more of a gentle parenting style, firmly reject diet culture, or believe in bodily autonomy and consent, Gram saying to your child, "You'll be put in time-out / Two more bites or no dessert / Come on, give Gramma a hug" can feel extra-invasive and even harmful.

The first step is to have a general conversation with Grandma and Grandpa, probably more than once. When my son was just a few months old, I said to my mom: "I have recently realized you probably had no idea what the hell you were doing either, did you?" She laughed and replied, "Nobody does, Melissa." Establishing common ground can be helpful, as can acknowledging the ways your parents did the best they could to raise you. You might then add, as I did, "I may not do it all the same way you did, but I look forward to figuring it out. If I want advice or help, I know who to ask." (And I did, most notably calling her in tears on a Sunday afternoon, curled up in an empty bathtub in all my clothes. Parenting is like that sometimes.)

In the moment, your parents may feel like they're helping ease your burden by disciplining, correcting, or otherwise parenting your child. Ideally, address this behavior as early as possible, even as it's happening. Try, "Mom, when I'm here, please let me be the parent. It's not your job anymore, so sit back, relax, and just enjoy your time with him." They may also have very different ideas about "acceptable" behavior around bedtime, TV time, or mealtime. Explaining in front of your kid, "It's okay, Grandma, this is the way we do it at our house," can go a long way toward helping your child feel secure, while gently reminding grandparents that it's your house, your rules.

THEIR HOUSE, THEIR RULES

Things can get tricky when your kids spend time at Grandma and Grandpa's without you. I've always abided by "your house, your rules," as long as what my parents want to do isn't inherently dangerous or unhealthy for my son. For instance, in our house, I let my son get out of bed and play at 6:30 A.M., but Grandma wants him to stay in his room until 7—their house, their rules. Same for no games at the breakfast table, or no snacks in the car. But when it comes to my dad's penchant for ice cream, I set a boundary: "Please don't feed him any dairy—it triggers his eczema. Find something else to serve as a treat." This is especially important when their house "rules" tend to wind your kiddos up *just* in time for you to pick them up. Staying up way too late, eating gobs of sugar, or watching too much TV might be situations you need to set a boundary around, even if they are on Grandma and Grandpa's territory.

In the end, you may just have to remind your parents that though they disagree with your parenting style, rules, or practices, it's your life and your child, and now it's time for every grandparent's rite of passage: butting out and minding their own business. You can say it nicer than that, although you certainly don't have to.

BOUNDARIES AND FAVORS WITH RELATIVES

Here's a little bonus advice for a scenario you're likely to run into: how to set boundaries with family members who have done you a favor, like lending you money, letting you move back in, or getting you a job.

Favors can be a complicated mix of pressure and emotion. The favor-giver probably wants to help (or feels obligated to), but worries that doing this favor will change your relationship, or that they might have to give or do something they're not 100 percent comfortable with. The favor-requester is equally scared that their request will be denied—or that it will be granted, and the strings attached (invisible or otherwise) won't be worth the benefit. Favors *can* be granted in a healthy environment, where there are no demands or manipulation. But often they turn toxic, with the favor accompanied by costs, debts, and threats—and boundaries don't apply because "you owe me." Yes, you're grateful. Yes, your family member did you a solid. But does that favor mean they can insert themselves into any area of your life as they see fit? Of course not . . . but try telling *them* that.

Ideally *before* you strike the bargain, get specific on what you're both agreeing to. Think about it this way: If a family member is willing to do a big favor for you, it's most likely because they care about you and want to help. This is evidence that they want to strengthen your relationship by contributing where they can. In exchange, you can do your part to keep the relationship healthy by setting clear expectations and holding your boundaries after the favor is granted. Ask in advance, "Is there anything I can do for you in exchange for this favor?" or "If I have a different opinion about how to move forward from here, is that okay, or would you expect to be consulted?" You could also get super specific about the potential for strings, like "I appreciate your offer so much, but I will only accept it if it comes without expectations or the potential for future resentment. Are you truly comfortable granting it, without reservation? Please take time to think about this. Our relationship is more important to me than this favor."

Also, it's important here to speak *plainly*. Now is not the time to beat around the bush or make assumptions. If you'll only accept their money for the wedding if you can plan it 100 percent your way, express exactly that, or share what you are willing to negotiate. If you'd love their help with the down payment but, no, they cannot store their RV in your driveway, say so. The more you can have these conversations *before* the favor is granted, the easier it will be to decide whether the favor is worth it, meet expectations on both sides, and set a boundary if they start to feel entitled later.

If you're already in the middle of the favor situation, *yes,* you can still set boundaries, especially if the favor is taking a toll on your relationship. If you're repaying money, make it clear that the repayment is the exchange you agreed to—and doesn't come with unrestricted access to the house they helped you buy. If the strings were invisible or grew unexpectedly, have a level-setting conversation. "We appreciate your help with the wedding, but it seems the closer we get to the date, the more involved you want to be with the planning. Since we didn't get a clear picture of your expectations when you offered to help, let's talk about them now, so Chris and I can make some decisions."

PREPARE FOR PUSHBACK

When you try to initiate a conversation about boundaries with someone who has done or is doing you a favor, there's a good chance that person will try to make you feel guilty as hell. They might be seeing you as ungrateful, selfish, or a "user." Please remember, the way other people choose to respond to your clear, kind boundary is not your business. If you appreciate the favor, have truly repaid it in the way you both agreed to, and believe the favor grantor is dangling strings you never *would* have agreed to, set the boundary. Best-case scenario, they'll understand they've overstepped and it won't continue to happen. Likely scenario, they'll grumble about it, but will reluctantly acquiesce—and you might have to actively smooth things over for a while. Worst-case scenario, they're furious at your selfishness, sever the relationship (likely temporarily), and you never lean on them again for a favor. (Would you really want to anyway?) Only you can decide how much to push back for the sake of your mental health and relationship.

If the invisible demands of the favor are making it nearly impossible to set healthy boundaries, as a last resort consider what you could do to get out from under it. Could you borrow money from a bank to repay your parents? Could you pay for your own wedding, even if it's far less extravagant, to make it exactly how you want it? If the favor happened years ago, but you're still being made to feel like you owe them something, can you set a boundary around talking about it? "Yes, I remember that you paid for my last year of school so I didn't have to work. I have always been appreciative of that. But it seems like nothing I've done over the years is enough to thank you, and you holding it over my head as if I'll owe you for it forever is making it hard for our relationship to grow. Is there anything else you expect from me at this point? If not, I'm not going to let that be something I feel guilty about."

FAMILY BOUNDARIES AND PREP TIPS

Let's get back to Caleb, with the divorced-and-still-bickering parents. He needed to set a boundary with both of them, but in the past, saying things like "Mom, please stop, I don't really want to hear this" hasn't gotten him anywhere. In our conversations, I encouraged him to remember that old patterns take time to break, and that stating the boundary even more clearly, repeating it as needed, and enacting consequences if that boundary isn't respected would prove key.

You'll see the specific boundary scripts I came up with for Caleb on page 112, which involve repetition, boundary alerts, and appropriate consequences Caleb could enact if his boundary is still not respected. Caleb and his parents had the chance to test it out over Thanksgiving, and though I warned him that one stern conversation won't resolve the issue, Caleb and his wife now have scripts and guidelines to follow to ensure they are no longer the emotional dumping ground for either of his parents.

I'll be honest with you here, as I was with Caleb . . . you might find it harder to set a boundary with family than anyone else, especially if you love them. You *want* to help them, make them comfortable, and keep the peace. And if your family hasn't witnessed boundary-setting in the past, your family dynamics likely don't support someone setting healthy limits. All of this is to say, be prepared that your foray into boundaries may have the following side effects: family members ganging up on you or excluding you; guilt and anxiety around your boundaries; family tension; the desire to avoid family members or events; and being labeled "high maintenance" (or worse).

The good news is that I've got many sample conversations and best practices to help you and your family ease your way into clear, healthy limits that benefit *all* of you, even if they don't see it that way yet.

- **KNOW WHAT YOU WANT.** I'll reemphasize this here—unless you take the time to determine where your limits lie and what you actually want, you won't be able to set an effective boundary. You know that running to four different houses for the holidays makes you bananas . . . but what *are* you willing to do, and what do you actually *want* your holiday to look like? Get clear on that first (with your partner and kids where appropriate) before trying to set a boundary with others.
- **START SMALL.** You don't have to rush into the biggest, gnarliest, most family-dynamic-changing boundary first. Practice with something less intimidating, gain a small win, and let that self-confidence and those experiences carry you over into the "please don't fly across the country without telling us you're coming" conversation.
- **TIME IT RIGHT.** Have these conversations during a peaceful time, ideally outside of or before the anticipated boundary issue—so, *before* the baby is due, *before* they no-call-drop-by, *before* the holidays, and *before* you share your vacation plans.
- **BE PREPARED TO RESTATE THE BOUNDARY.** With relationships

as longstanding as those with family, it's unlikely one boundary statement will do the trick. If you're talking about changing deeply entrenched patterns of behavior, be prepared to restate your boundary again and again, consistently. Assume your family members want to be respectful, but they need time to rewire their brains to accommodate this new dynamic.

- **PRIORITIZE YOUR FEELINGS.** Without boundaries, you've essentially been telling your family members, "Your feelings are more important than my own." It's not selfish to prioritize your own health and happiness. Ask yourself, "Am I willing to betray myself just to make someone else comfortable?" If the answer is no, set the damn boundary.

- **REFUSE GUILT, JUDGMENT, OR BLAMING.** Allow your family members space to process the request and the opportunity to talk about it (but not to try to change your mind), but don't let them sucker you into believing *you're* the one who ruined Christmas. If your boundary is clear, kind, and designed to make the relationship better, other people's temper tantrums in response are not your business. Think about yourself as a trailblazer, changing dysfunctional family dynamics for future generations to come! It might not be easy, but it'll be worth it.

- **IT GETS EASIER FAST.** In most cases, the first few instances of holding your boundary will feel awkward or uncomfortable. But sooner than you might imagine, it just becomes what you all do. If you can make it through the discomfort in the beginning, you may find it's smooth sailing from then on out.

Setting boundaries with family will have an incredible impact on your energy, mental health, time, and physical space. Plus, if your boundary-setting precedent spills over onto other family members, just think about how much more relaxed, happy, and comforting your time together will be. You can do it! I'll help you find the right words.

SCRIPTS FOR SETTING BOUNDARIES WITH PARENTS AND IN-LAWS

As I've mentioned, setting boundaries with either set of parents (yours or your partner's) comes with its own complexities, including getting your partner's buy-in up front, a commitment to presenting a united front, and ongoing partnership in holding them. Still, the hard work is worth it. Chances are, your parents or in-laws have been driving a wedge (big or small) between you and your spouse since the beginning. Your spouse says, "That's just how they are, they can't change." (Meanwhile you're thinking, "That's how they've trained you to do what they want.") Setting these boundaries can make a world of difference in your relationship, allowing you all to coexist in peace, with no one needing to choose sides, and making space for visits that are free of anxiety, pressure, and resentment.

> **My parents are long divorced but continue to gossip and talk poorly about each other when I'm around. They even drag me into it, trying to get me to choose sides. I love them both, and I don't want to be brought into their drama. How can I set a boundary around this?**
>
> **GREEN:** "Mom, please don't talk about Dad in front of me. I love you both and I don't want to hear it." Change the subject.
>
> **YELLOW:** "Oops. Mom, I've asked you not to talk about Dad in front of me. Please stop." Repeat as needed.
>
> **RED:** "Stop—Mom, I'm not going to listen to this. I'll be back." Go for a walk, or to another room.
>
> *These are some sample scripts I shared with Caleb during our boundary conversations. Remember, you can't make your parents feel or do anything. I say this in case some of your earlier*

pleas were centered on getting them to change their behaviors, like "Mom, get over it already," or "Dad, you can't still be angry." Your boundary has to be centered on your limit—in this case, your unwillingness to be a party to these conversations. Said with love from a woman with divorced parents.

My in-laws show up at our house unannounced all the time. I've asked them to call first, but they keep "popping in" because they were "in the neighborhood." It can be disruptive, especially on a busy weekend, but I don't know how to make it clear that we really need them to call first.

GREEN: (for your spouse to say to their own parents) "Sarah and I have talked, and we both really need you to call before you come over. It's too disruptive for you to just show up, and it's causing us both some stress. Pick up the phone first and make sure we're free."

YELLOW: (when they're at the door) "Oh, you didn't call first, and now isn't a great time. The kids are doing homework, and Sarah is working. We'll call you later."

RED: Don't answer the door.

You might have to spell out the Green even further, like "Call first to make sure we're free—and not when you're on our front steps." You also may need to enforce the consequence once or twice before they get the point. Not answering the door might sound mean, but if you're watching a family movie, doing work/ homework, or getting ready to head out for the day, their discourteous demands are not more important than your family plans. Picking up the phone isn't hard, fam.

My parents attend church faithfully. I stopped going when I was a teenager, and my husband isn't religious at all. When we

visit, they're always pressuring us to go with them. How can I respectfully say no?

GREEN: (before the next visit) "We can't wait to visit, but we won't be attending church with you. I'd rather get that out of the way now, so you don't have to ask again next weekend. We'll stay home and make breakfast for when you and Mom return."

YELLOW: "We've already discussed this—we don't want to go to church, and please don't pressure us. Church isn't for us, and we need you to respect that."

RED: "If you won't respect our decision not to attend church, we'll start heading home now."

I've personally witnessed this discussion become a tipping point for families, where visits are avoided because parents won't respect your boundary. You can automate this boundary by visiting during the week (when church isn't in session), booking your flight home on Saturday, or make other plans for Sunday morning, leaving early and avoiding the issue altogether.

AUTOMATE YOUR BOUNDARIES

It's not tricky or manipulative to navigate boundaries by simply eliminating the stressful scenario—for some, it may be the most helpful solution! If your parents know you're leaving on Saturday, they may feel relieved that they don't have to witness you staying home from church *again*. And you can enjoy your time with them, knowing that particular pressure isn't in the works. This could offer you yet another strategic but still kind way of establishing your limits.

My parents just informed me they plan on staying with us as soon as the baby is born, to "help out." We'd love for them to visit, but not until we've had a few days alone at home to settle in. How should I handle this?

GREEN: "Mom and Dad, we're excited for you to meet the baby, but we want at least a week at home alone to settle in before anyone comes to visit. Let's talk about it after the baby arrives."

YELLOW: "We're not accepting visitors right away—not even her grandparents. We need that time alone as a family and are asking you to respect that."

RED: "If you insist on flying out before we invite you, it's going to hurt our relationship—and you still won't see the baby. Don't do that to us."

I'm using "at least a week" in the Green response because if you decide you need more time at home alone, you've already set that expectation, but if you change your mind, you can always surprise them with a "Mom, I was wrong, we could really use your help." And if they still fly out before you're ready . . . I hope they enjoy their hotel and sightseeing.

My in-laws are always inviting themselves on our family vacation. Two years ago, we let them come on a cruise with us, and it added a layer of complexity that made it not fun for any of us. We're planning our next trip, and I'd like to head this off at the pass. How can I nicely say, "You're not invited?"

GREEN: "Oh, we've just decided to book our next trip! We'll be flying to Mexico for a week sometime in January. This one is just for us and the kids, and they're really excited about it."

YELLOW: "No, you can't join us for this one. We're looking forward to having quality time with the kids, and we've promised them that this time, it's just the four of us."

RED: "We're not including you in this one. It's not up for discussion."

A few of you have told me your in-laws or parents just showed up at the cabin/beach house/hotel as a "surprise," and that is WILD. If this is a possibility, keep your plans vague on purpose. You can always say, "We'll let you know more details soon," or "We want the trip to be a surprise for the kids, so we're not telling anyone." If they don't know where you're going, they can't just show up. (That's a Fuchsia-level boundary right there.)

Both my spouse's parents and my parents are divorced, and all four families expect us to be present on the holiday itself. It's a lot of running around, with no time to ourselves. It's too much, but we don't want to disappoint anyone.

GREEN: "We'll be by to see each of you on Christmas Day, but we'll only stay for an hour or so. We want to spend our evening at home relaxing as a family."

YELLOW: "This year, we'd love to stop by on Christmas Eve (or the weekend after Christmas) instead and extend the celebration. We've decided to keep our Christmas Day unscheduled and relaxing."

RED: "We've decided to stay home on Christmas this year. We'll FaceTime you after we've opened presents."

Remember, the first part of the discussion is, "Hey, family—what do we want to do on Christmas Day?" Once that's clear, you can spell out your limits to extended family. There is no right answer here—but remember now that you are adults, you should feel empowered to have the holiday you want.

THE HOLIDAY GUILT TRIP

Sometimes the boundary you want to set isn't about the travel or the specific holiday at all—it's how you're treated during the visit. If you want to spend time with multiple households but get guilt-tripped when you leave one family for the other, that's the boundary you need. You can say something like, "Hey, Mom, we love spending time with you and with John's family on Christmas, but it's not cool how you guilt-trip us when it's time to leave. It's not fair to us, or his parents. Please don't do that this year." This is another reason why discussing what you want ahead of time is so important. Your family might have a vague idea that visiting everyone on Christmas Day is stressful, but when you really get into it, it's not the drive or the moving around, but the dinner talk, guilt-tripping, or food-pushing that stresses you all out. *Now* you know where to set a boundary!

My dad lent me and my wife money to buy our house. We're on track to pay him back, but until then, he seems to think this entitles him to stop by without asking. We gave him a key for emergencies, so he lets himself in and stays for hours and hours, often inviting himself for dinner. I feel guilty, but this wasn't the agreement—can I say something?

GREEN: (between visits) "Dad, I appreciate that you did us this favor, but we have to set some boundaries around your visits. If you want to stop by, you have to call first. If we're working or have plans, you have to be respectful of our time. And if you'd like to stay for dinner, you have to ask first—if we can prepare, you are welcome to stay, but some nights that won't work, and I need you to respect that, too."

YELLOW: "Dad, we need our key back, please. We've asked you to call before you come over, and you're not respecting that."

RED: Let him know you've changed the locks to preserve your privacy, and remind him yet again that if he doesn't call before stopping by, you reserve the right not to answer the door.

Lending you money doesn't give your dad the right to enter your home and do as he pleases. And if you are able, pay him back even faster than the agreement. It's a shame when someone does you a favor that turns out to have major strings, but when someone shows you who they are, believe them—and create as many fences as you need to reestablish trust.

SCRIPTS FOR SETTING BOUNDARIES WITH GRANDPARENTS

It's important to set boundaries with grandparents around the way you choose to parent your own children. You probably have feelings and opinions about how you want your parents to engage with your kids (especially when you're not around) and that's totally okay. Over-parenting you, contradicting your family rules, imparting values that aren't aligned with your own, and allowing (or reprimanding) different behaviors than you would can be confusing for your kids and can create an environment where the stress and tension are palpable for all.

Healthy boundaries with grandparents aren't controlling or restrictive—they're a gift! Through these limits, you're allowing your parents to live out the very best parts of being a grandparent. They get to visit without the responsibility of raising or disciplining your kids and will have the opportunity to see your kids at their best—happy, relaxed, and appreciating their special time with Grandma and Grandpa. Your kids will enjoy a tension-free visit, knowing that there will still be consistency in their routines and rules. And you'll be happier and more relaxed, knowing your kids are being cared for in the way that is aligned with your parenting and values. Imagine how weightless you could feel, knowing you could ship your kids to Grandma and Grandpa's for the night with zero anticipation of conflict. Boundaries could get you there.

My parents try to set the rules in my house, even when I'm there. They'll tell my kids they have to clean their plates after I've already excused them, or ask them to get off their iPad during their allowed time. How do I request that they don't override me?

GREEN: (away from the kids) "If the kids are with you and I'm not around, they obviously follow your rules. But when I'm here, please allow me to make the parenting decisions for them. It's confusing when you contradict me."

YELLOW: "Mom, I told the kids they could have an hour of iPad time. Please don't override my decisions."

RED: "Oops, Grandma, no, I already said he could be excused. Casey, you can be done, honey."

You may need to repeat some version of the Red boundary a few times until they break the over-parenting habit. You can also take your kids aside and say, "I know it's hard when I tell you one thing and Grandma tells you something else. I've reminded her that if I'm here, I'm in charge, so if you get confused about something she's said, come ask me."

My son has eczema triggered by dairy and gluten. I've told my parents multiple times not to feed him these foods, but invariably I'll pick him up and he'll tell me Grandpa gave him ice cream or cookies as a treat. How can I explain that I'm serious about this request?

GREEN: "When I leave Hunter with you, I need to know that I can trust you to respect my wishes. Please don't feed him anything with dairy or gluten—not even as a treat. I'll be happy to send him over with snacks that he can eat, or recipes you can make together."

YELLOW: "Dad, I've asked you many times not to feed Hunter ice cream. If you can't respect that, I won't be able to leave him with you again."

RED: "I won't send Hunter for an overnight, but you're welcome to come to the house to visit."

You don't need a medical reason to make a request like this. If you prefer your child follow a low-sugar diet, not drink soda, or not eat fast food, anyone in a caretaking position needs to respect that. In this case, the Red boundary is the consequence, where your child can no longer visit your parents unsupervised.

THE BAD GUY

What if the recipient of your boundary tries to turn it around and make *you* look like the bad guy in front of your kids? Statements like "Grandpa wanted to get you an ice cream, but Mom said no" are an immature and manipulative way of responding to a boundary—but it happens. In this case, respond quickly in front of the kids: "Grandpa, stop teasing, that's not nice. We know that ice cream makes Hunter's skin itchy, that's not his fault." Then, away from the kids, set *another* boundary on the spot with Grandpa: "It's not okay that you are manipulating Hunter like this. If you can't respect my boundary without resorting to childish tactics, I'm going to send you home / we'll be heading out right now."

My four-year-old daughter isn't a big hugger, but her grandmother insists on a hug and kiss every time she visits, often forc-

ing her to comply. I'm teaching my kids about consent, and I want people to respect when my daughter says no. Any tips?

GREEN: (before the visit) "Fran, I know it's hard to leave without a hug and kiss, but we're teaching Jenna about consent, and if she doesn't want to hug, I'm asking that you don't force her."

YELLOW: (in the moment) "Oh, remember, we don't make Jenna hug if she doesn't want to. Jenna, would you like to give Grandma a high-five or just wave goodbye?"

RED: "Fran, Jenna doesn't want a hug today. [Scoop up your daughter if she wants to be held, or just stand right next to her.] Jenna, let's wave goodbye to Grandma. Bye!"

Some folks will insist that you have to hug or kiss to be polite. Uh, NO. A friendly wave or "Goodbye, Grandma" is perfectly polite—but you may have to be the one to spell that out. I have empathy for a grandparent who just wants to love on their grandbaby—but that doesn't override my child's right to bodily autonomy. I offer my son options ahead of time, like "When Auntie Kelly leaves, you can kiss, hug, elbow-bump, fist-bump, high-five, make a funny face, or just wave."

My teenage son just came out as trans. He's told the family and most people have been supportive, but my parents still use his old pronouns and name, and when I correct them, they tell me it's going to take them time to "get used to this." How can I best advocate for my boy?

GREEN: "Your grandson has asked you to call him Travis, and he deserves that respect from you. I have faith that this is a change you can quickly grasp and immediately implement, for his sake."

YELLOW: "No, Mom, *HE* got an A on *HIS* math test. I understand that you might slip up, but I expect you to correct yourself on the spot, because otherwise you're being disrespectful. I need you to make more of an effort, because this is hurting our relationship."

RED: "I won't allow your behavior to cause Travis further harm. If you won't use his correct name and pronouns, I'm going to limit your communications with him until you can."

If it becomes necessary to protect your child from other family members, please do that, no matter who they are. Limit communication to emails filtered through you, or don't allow any contact until they commit to demonstrating respect for your child's identity.

IT'S JONATHAN, NOT JON

I had a friend growing up whose name was Jonathan—and if you called him Jon, his mother would immediately and sternly intervene. If your child has a preferred name or nickname, it's perfectly acceptable for you to request that family members honor your child's preference. Correct people in the moment if they don't get it right. It's the same for a nickname your kid *doesn't* like. My dad got into the habit of calling my son "Pumpkinhead," and after about a year, my kid decided that wasn't funny anymore. He asked Grandpa to stop, but at five years old, this request wasn't taken seriously. It wasn't until I said, "Hey, that nickname upsets him now— I don't know why, but let's retire it" that my dad made the effort. (Aside: My son now loves that nickname again, and often signs cards to his grandparents "Love, Pumpkinhead." As I've said, boundaries should be flexible.)

My doctor is recommending anyone who spends time with our newborn have up-to-date Tdap, flu, and COVID vaccinations. My parents aren't vaccinated, and they are angry that we're not letting them visit right away. How can I hold this boundary nicely but firmly?

GREEN: "Our doctor told us that newborns are at the highest risk for viruses, so unless you're vaccinated, you'll have to wait six weeks to visit, until her immune system is stronger. When you do visit, you'll need to wear a mask and not kiss the baby. We can FaceTime until then."

YELLOW: "I know you love this baby, too. We all have to do our best to protect her from viruses and infections. If you want to visit in person, these are our rules."

RED: "You can't come visit her yet. We'll let you know when we feel comfortable, and under what conditions."

Remember, boundaries can be flexible. If your parents are willing to meet outside, wear a mask, and abide by your other requests, you can flex here as much as you are comfortable. You can also hold this boundary as firmly as you choose. Ultimately, you are responsible for your baby's health and safety, even if that means keeping Grandma and Grandpa at a distance.

RESPONDING TO ACCUSATIONS IN THE FACE OF A BOUNDARY

Even though this limit is designed to keep your baby healthy, expect to get pushback from your parents here: "You've been pressuring us to get vaccinated, and now you're using the baby to force us to do so." It may feel like that to them, but remind your parents that this limit is about your baby's health, and you're not forcing them to do anything—they still have choices. They can choose to get vaccinated and snuggle the baby, or they can choose not to and find other ways to visit, like FaceTime or a socially distant gathering outside. Assure your parents that you will respect their decision, just as they need to respect the decisions you're making as a new parent.

My spouse and I have decided to keep all photos of our new baby off the Internet. We've asked family members to do the same, but my mom still shares pictures on her Facebook page, saying, "I barely have any followers, and I have to show off my new grandbaby." What can we do here?

GREEN: "Mom, when you share things I've asked you not to, it's a major violation of trust. I need you to understand how serious this is, and how much this compromises my sense of safety. You have two choices—either make your page private and limited to immediate family and friends, where we'd be comfortable with you sharing photos, or stop posting photos altogether and exchange them with friends via text or email."

YELLOW: "You continue to share photos after we've asked you not to, and that's not okay. If you can't respect this simple request, we won't share photos with you anymore, and will remove you from our social media pages." (Remind her of her Green boundary options, in other words.)

RED: "I won't be sharing photos of the baby with you any longer. And you're welcome to visit, but please do not take photos while you're here. We are responsible for our child's safety and privacy, and this is an unfortunate step that you've demonstrated we have to take." You may even go so far as to limit visits—it's a pretty egregious violation at this point.

This is a limit we set with our son when he was born, and happily our families and friends immediately respected it. I can't imagine this would go beyond a Yellow boundary, but grandparents never cease to surprise me. Offering to help your mom with technology, like creating a private Facebook page, setting up a group chat via text, or installing a digital photo frame at her house might help ease the Green boundary.

SCRIPTS FOR SETTING BOUNDARIES WITH OTHER FAMILY MEMBERS

If your family didn't have healthy boundaries modeled for them, you might be the first to rock the boundary boat. The bad news: That can get you plenty of negative attention—you might be labeled "the demanding one," "the prima donna," and most certainly the s-word ("selfish"). The good news is that you may start a boundary conga line, where others who were once too nervous, anxious, or guilty to speak up may follow your lead, rally, and have your back! (Surely *nobody* likes your sister's Yorkie begging at the dinner table.) Normalizing healthy boundaries throughout the family helps to smooth communications, reestablish trust, and eliminate resentment, and that benefits everyone.

A lack of boundaries, much like trauma, is often passed down from generation to generation. Someone has to be the first to break the cycle, and you're now better prepared than anyone to start communicating your limits in clear, kind words. Expect some pushback, sure, but you may also find some unexpected allies in your boundary conversations, too. And if no one steps up, invite them into the conversation. There's power in numbers, and if *everyone* tells your sister to leave her dog at home, you're far more likely to be successful.

> **Some of my family members and I don't agree on political or social justice issues. When we spend time with them, they're not shy about expressing their perspectives. They're entitled to their opinions, I suppose, but this kind of commentary is unacceptable to me. Can I even set a boundary here?**
>
> **GREEN:** (before the visit) "I know we don't see eye to eye on political or social justice issues, so let's please agree to not bring up, discuss, or provide viewpoints on those topics during our

visit. It's the only way we'll enjoy our time together, and I really want to."

YELLOW: (in the moment) "Stop, Jeff. We all agreed to not bring up immigration, so please change the subject." Change the subject.

RED: "If you won't stop talking about your views on immigration [or sexuality, gender identity, reproductive rights, etc.], we're going to leave."

Yes, *you can set a boundary here. If it's important to you to maintain the relationship and/or it's inevitable that you'll see these family members at gatherings and you'd rather not have it turn into an episode of* The Jerry Springer Show, *setting and holding a healthy boundary is the only way you'll accomplish that.*

My sister insists on bringing her dog everywhere, including to our house every Sunday for family dinner. My son is mildly allergic and we don't want dog hair all over the house, but she insists the dog can't be left home alone. I need to draw the line.

GREEN: (before the visit) "Andie, the dog can't come with you tonight. You can leave her either at home or in the fenced-in area out back, but we can't have her in the house, just so that's clear."

YELLOW: "Wow, I reminded you not to bring the dog. Do you want to run her home, or leave her in the backyard?"

RED: "If you won't leave the dog outside, then we'll reschedule dinner. I'll call you tomorrow."

It's actually pretty easy to hold a boundary like this, because if she's got the dog, you just don't let her in the house. It should only take one boundary-push here before she realizes you mean business and finds other accommodations.

CHANGING THE RULES

It's common at this point for someone to point out, "But you used to be okay with this!" You used to let the dog in the house, you used to let them rearrange the furniture, you used to let them stop by without calling . . . they're attempting to paint you as volatile or overreactive for reversing your position without notice. But guess what? You *can* change your mind! You can decide to speak up instead of feeling resentful! You can start putting your own needs first! A good way to respond to this is, "Yes, I used to allow that, but I was also resentful and upset about it. I'm speaking up now because I don't like feeling that way about you, and I'm sure you don't want me harboring those negative feelings, either. This will only make our relationship better, and I have faith that we'll adjust quickly."

My sister-in-law has a longstanding habit of criticizing me when no one else is around, whispering, "You look tired" or "Are you eating enough?" When I call her on it, she tells me there's no reason to get so defensive—she's just "worried." I feel like I can't win.

GREEN: "I appreciate you caring about me, but your comments aren't helpful. Maybe you don't realize how mean they sound, or maybe you do. Either way, please don't do it again."

YELLOW: "To be clear, I'd rather not hear about how you think I look." Change the subject.

RED: (just as quietly) "For the last time, your feedback on my appearance is not welcome." Hold direct eye contact, then walk away.

This is where keeping a cool, calm, collected demeanor goes a long way. State your boundary (bonus if you do it in front of someone else), and don't allow your sister-in-law to gaslight you. If she protests or tries to play the victim, a brief "Amanda, I don't need to hear any more—do better" would do the trick. You can also discuss this behavior with your spouse and have them back you up. Chances are, they're not surprised by this behavior from their sister.

My younger brother constantly asks to borrow money—$20 or $50 here and there. Sometimes he pays me back, but often he doesn't. I hate to see him struggle, but I'm not an ATM ... how can I set limits without looking like a jerk?

GREEN: "I can swing $50 today, but that's it, and I won't be able to help again this month."

YELLOW: "I can't give you any more money right now, Rob. Is there some other way I could help?"

RED: "I can't lend you money, Rob. I'm starting to feel used and resentful, and that's not healthy."

You could create a "no lending money to friends or family" policy (automation) ahead of time to avoid this tension in the first place. But if you're already in, remember that your financial status has no bearing on your boundary. You can be in a position comfortable enough to give them $20, and you still don't have to. It's up to you to decide your limit.

MONEY TALK

Money is one of the most uncomfortable boundaries to set—for both parties, usually. Here's how I think about it. First, I assume the person will not pay me back, even if they say they will. I evaluate whether or not I want to *gift* this person this money, no strings attached. I also don't ask what it's for, because that's not my business. So the question becomes, "Do I want to give this person this gift and walk away? And can I do so without resentment?" If I can't say yes to either question, I won't give them the money. If the answer to both is yes, I give the money and we never speak of it again. I don't expect a gratuitous thank-you, an update on how it was spent, or a follow-up about how it helped. That's the only way I've been able to help people financially without any resulting resentment, regret, or anger.

I'm a stay-at-home mom of a four-year-old. My sister has a son a year younger, and assumes I'll babysit anytime she needs me to. She'll just show up with him, asking, "Do you mind?" and it's hard to say no in the moment . . . but just because I'm home doesn't mean I'm free! Help.

GREEN: (between visits) "I'm happy to watch Ben sometimes, but you can't show up unannounced, and you can't just assume I'm free—you have to ask me ahead of time. Here are three local sitters that I've used and really like, for the next time you need someone and I can't."

YELLOW: "I can't watch him all day, but if an hour would help, you can drop him off at noon. We're heading out at 1 P.M., though, so please be back by then."

RED: "Oh, I can't watch him today—we have a full schedule already."

One way to mitigate this is to set up a regular playdate or babysit swap. If you agree to watch Ben every Thursday for a half day, and your sister can watch your kiddo on Saturday morning so you can go to the gym and run errands, that could be a win-win, and make the boundary easier to swallow.

I have a small apartment in a desirable part of the city, walkable to many tourist attractions. Any time family members visit, they expect to stay with me. I don't really have the space, as I just converted my only spare bedroom to my work-from-home office. How can I say no politely?

GREEN: (before the visit) "You're going to have a great visit. Here are some hotels and Airbnbs in awesome areas of the city, and I'd love to meet you for lunch or dinner one day—let me know what works for you."

YELLOW: "My apartment is quite small, and I don't have space for guests. Do you want help finding a hotel or Airbnb?"

RED: "Staying here isn't an option. Let me know if you want help with finding a suitable place."

One thing not to do here is cite their comfort as the reason for your boundary. Saying, "Oh, I barely have room for an air mattress, you won't be comfortable" opens you up to "I'd be perfectly happy on a couch, I'd just love a free place to stay." Your boundary is your limit, not about them or their comfort. Make it clear that even if they'd be willing to sleep in a closet, your home is simply not an option.

BONUS: SETTING BOUNDARIES WITH KIDS

Let's address the elephant in the room: Yes, you can set boundaries with your own kids. Even if they're young. *Especially* if they're young! Normalize healthy boundary-setting and teach them to respect others' boundaries earlier, and they won't grow up with the same challenges you and I had. Healthy boundaries with kids establish a sense of safety and security, teach patience and consequences, and provide them with a framework for autonomy—within age-appropriate limits.

This is one area where I'd invite you to work with a play therapist, pediatric psychologist, or childhood educator, because you'll need different strategies, approaches, and language for different age groups. (You can't rationalize with your toddler the way you do with your mother-in-law—although they sure do sound the same sometimes.) Here are some general tips for working through boundaries with all ages.

TODDLERS (2–4 YEARS): Set reasonable boundaries around when they can have your attention, be picked up, or ask you for things. For example, when I was on the phone and my son wanted me, I'd say, "I see you, but I'm talking to Nana. Please wait until I'm done." I'd then find a natural pause in the conversation quickly and praise him for waiting, asking him to wait for longer periods of time as he learned patience and got older. You can do this around picking them up ("I have these groceries in my hands, I have to put this down first") or giving them a toy ("I'm going to put these dishes away, then we'll get your toy"). You can also model boundaries on their behalf, like not forcing them to hug or kiss if they don't want to, or not allowing their sibling to snatch a toy from their hands.

PRESCHOOL (3–5 YEARS): As my son got better at entertaining himself, I started setting boundaries around when I'd drop everything to play with him, when he could wake me up, and what went into his bedtime routine. I'd tell him, "I need to work until the clock says 4:15, then I can play with you." He knew he could get out of bed and play when his frog clock glowed green, but he couldn't come into my room until 6:23. (He negotiated me down from 6:30.) And thanks to boundaries, I got his bedtime routine to go from twenty-seven hugs, fourteen sips of water, and a hundred and two I-love-yous to a reasonable one hug, one water, and one I-love-you, with a bonus hug at the end. *Kid, I love you, but go the hell to sleep.*

SCHOOL-AGE (6–12 YEARS): My son is in fourth grade now, and boundaries for him include not watching TV in the morning before school (because it makes getting ready for school stressful for all of us); not entering our offices unless he has permission (because that is disrespectful of our privacy); not using my phone without asking (same); and if I ask for fifteen minutes of alone time to recharge before we play, he respects that. On the flip side, he's become so comfortable with boundaries that it's not unusual for *him* to set them with *us*. We're not allowed to read his private journal, he's comfortable saying, "I don't want a hug" if he's not feeling it, he will ask for half an hour to FaceTime with friends before we tackle his school projects, and he doesn't want me telling him what to wear anymore. My counter—as long as it's clean and fits the school's dress code, he can wear whatever he wants. (Some of his choices are, shall we say, *creative*.)

ADOLESCENTS (12–18 YEARS): Boundaries can be challenging as kids get older and you want to afford them more privacy, autonomy, and the opportunity to make mistakes while still keeping them safe. Younger adolescents might be allowed to stay home alone but not have friends over; have their own social media accounts but only if they're private; and go on vacation with friends if you know their parents well. Older teens may be able to borrow the car as long as they leave it clean and with a half tank of gas; buy a new iPhone if they earn enough money to pay for half of it; and make their own decisions about attending events with extended family.

Boundaries will vary widely based on your parenting style, relationship, and context, but the most important thing is that they're established and communicated clearly and kindly, and that parents recognize that boundaries with their kids are a two-way street.

LOVING THE LIMITS THAT SET YOU FREE

If you've made it this far (hooray!), here's your reward: Let me paint a picture of how your family dynamics *could* look, with the implementation of healthy boundaries. Visits would be more predictable, knowing house rules were clearly understood. Interactions would be more pleasant, knowing certain conversation topics wouldn't be brought up. Resentment, anxiety, and exhaustion would be a thing of the past, knowing you all understood the same set of expectations, needs, and consequences. Channels of communication would be far more open, so no one had to guess about how you feel, what you need, or how you can best support each other. Your kids would be more relaxed, your guests would feel more at home, and you could enjoy your time together with an estimated 82 percent less stress, worry, or frustration.

Doesn't that sound just *lovely*?

It won't happen all at once. It may take patience, persistence, and a thick skin. And the hard truth is that some relationships may have to change in order to achieve this happier, more peaceful coexistence. But all of this is possible through the practice of clear, kind boundaries in a way that it wasn't before you read this book.

Remember when things feel scary or challenging that boundaries are designed to make your relationships better, and someone has to go first to create a new generational pattern for your family. I'm proud of you for being that person.

CHAPTER 5

Relationships We (Mostly) Choose

Setting Boundaries with Friends and Neighbors

I first heard from Lucy in the winter. She was at her wit's end with her friend Olivia, and she wrote me a series of DMs asking for advice. When Lucy and Olivia first became friends, Olivia was going through a hard time with her on-again, off-again boyfriend. Lucy was a good listener and often spent hours on the phone with Olivia, offering advice, a shoulder to cry on, and the occasional "Just dump him, girl. You can do *so* much better." Eventually, however, Lucy started to notice a few things. One, Olivia never took her advice. Ever. So their conversations would repeat themselves like Groundhog Day, even though Lucy offered lots of (solicited) feedback for how to take action. Two, their entire "friendship" seemed based on Lucy's willingness to listen while Olivia complained. Work, her relationship, her family—it never ended, and none of Olivia's problems were ever her fault.

At first, Lucy assumed Olivia was upset and distracted, and that's why she never asked Lucy about *her* day or *her* life. Lucy even tried inserting herself into the conversation more, saying things like "Let's talk about some good things now," or "Guess what—I just booked a vacation with my parents!" But Olivia never picked up the thread and would occasionally accuse Lucy of being insensitive by bringing up something good or happy when it was clear Olivia was struggling.

When I read this part of the story, I sent Lucy a single emoji: the vampire. I explained, "You have an emotional vampire on your hands, and if you have any chance of saving this friendship—if you even want to—you need some boundaries. STAT."

In this chapter, I'll cover boundary scenarios that fall into two categories: friends and neighbors. I've grouped these together because there can be overlap between categories. There is an element of mutual choice in the relationships you have with friends and neighbors, as you have some control over how they appear in your life. And these relationships can blur if you move in with your bestie or make friends with your new neighbors.

However, these boundaries can also have some sticky spots. Relationships frequently change over time, often necessitating the adjustment of existing boundaries or the establishment of new ones. And it's not always easy to enforce consequences on someone you've signed a lease with, or a neighbor behaving badly from their side of the property line. You'll find scripts in this chapter that will help you build the figurative fences you need to keep each of these relationships thriving.

FRIENDS: We'll be talking specifically about friends who take advantage of your time, energy, effort, and money. They take without giving back, make their friendship conditional, use you when they need you, or are simply incapable of being thoughtful, empathetic, or giving. This can be one of your biggest sources of energy drain, and learning how to set boundaries here *will* be life-changing.

NEIGHBORS: The last thing you want is to be stuck in disagreement or drama with the people who live right next door . . . and might be there for the next ten years. There's a reason people fence their properties, and building your own healthy fences in the form of boundaries can create the structure and distance necessary to make your relationship healthy and happy.

Rather than giving you tips for navigating these boundaries as a whole, I'll include tips unique to those relationships in each section. Let's start with friends, as I'm betting everybody can relate to Lucy's predicament.

FRIENDS OR FRENEMIES?

We've all had that one friend who complains about the same thing over and over, but never seems to do anything about it. This isn't *venting*—a healthy exchange in which someone sticks to one subject, takes responsibility for their feelings and actions, is open to feedback about how to move forward, and expresses gratitude for your listening and support. This is *emotional dumping*, when your conversation partner repeatedly dumps all of their emotional baggage in your lap, portrays themselves as the victim, takes no advice or follow-up action, and expects you to hold their problems without any expression of gratitude or reciprocity. In my research, the *number-one reason* people are desperate to set a boundary with a friend is to halt this kind of emotional dumping.

Emotional dumping is overwhelming, exhausting, and frustrating, because your conversation partner isn't taking accountability for their circumstances. They might play the victim in every situation, refusing to see how they are contributing to their own issues. They may appear to thrive on drama, even as they're complaining about it. And they certainly don't seem to be *doing* anything about their problems, even though they've asked you for advice and could take steps to make changes.

Problematic friends can take on many shapes and forms, but "emotional vampires" like Olivia deserve their own category. These are people who consciously or unconsciously steal your time, energy, and attention with their toxic behaviors, as if drawing the life force out of you will somehow fill them up. (It never does.) These people leave you feeling depleted, depressed, overwhelmed, frustrated, or insecure with every interaction, as if you've been put through an emotional wringer. Here are a few of the most common types of Emotional Vampires:

- **THE NARCISSIST:** Needs to feel superior, doesn't care about your feelings, and will keep you around as long as they can continue to emotionally manipulate you
- **THE SOAP OPERA STAR:** Turns everything into a production, loves to gossip and create drama, and wants everyone else to get caught up in their performance
- **THE CONTROLLER:** Always needs to get their way, offers unsolicited advice (and gets mad when you don't take it), and is constantly criticizing you in an effort to be "helpful"
- **THE VICTIM:** Dumps all of their emotions and problems on you, refuses to take any accountability, won't implement your advice or try to change their own circumstances

If you're running through a mental Rolodex of your own friend group, here's how to identify an Emotional Vampire in your life:

- You avoid their texts or calls.
- You dread social meet-ups that include them.
- You never know where you stand with them.
- You change your behavior specifically for them.
- You make excuses or apologies for them often.
- You don't feel good during or after your encounters with them.
- Other people point out that your friendship is unhealthy.

If you've discovered you've got one of these Emotional Vampires (especially a Victim) in your Rolodex, you must accept that no matter how much you give them, it will never be enough. These friends will drain *all* of your energy, time, and attention if you let them. Don't panic, though; you'll soon see how *boundaries* are the vampire-repelling garlic you've been searching for.

SET THE BOUNDARY, SAVE THE FRIENDSHIP (IDEALLY)

To state the obvious, maintaining a friendship with someone who constantly dumps their emotions and problems on you is unsustainable. If you have your own Olivia, think back to the beginning of your friendship. I bet the first time this friend came to you with an issue, you poured yourself into the conversation. You were an active listener, validating your friend's feelings, empathizing, and offering thoughtful advice about exactly how they could make changes or improvements. You left feeling certain you were able to help your friend through this challenging situation. But after days, weeks, or months of the same scenario replaying over and over again, you're *fully* tapped out. There's nothing new to be said here; the advice your friend asked you for isn't being applied, and it feels like they've somehow absolved themselves of all accountability, relying on you to sort through their issues, absorb their negative emotions, and come up with a solution.

Lucy's friendship with Olivia had blown way past the line of "mutually supportive" into "all take and no give" territory. As a result, Lucy began avoiding Olivia's calls and texts, putting off plans to spend time together, and feeling emotionally drained at just the thought of interacting. If this sounds all too familiar, I'll tell you what I told Lucy: You need to set some healthy boundaries to get the relationship back on the right track—for *both* of your sakes.

Despite the emotional and physical toll this is taking on you, you want your friend to receive the support they need, and if you continue to allow them to dump on you, there is little impetus for them to seek more effective help elsewhere. Remind yourself (because you'll probably feel guilty) that your ongoing participation in this toxic pattern is standing in the way of not only your friendship, but your friend's growth. If you continue to allow them to dump their emotional baggage on you, they'll never learn how to process it in a healthy way. Setting firm boundaries here is necessary for both of you, whether they see it that way or not.

WHEN TO OUTSOURCE

If your friend's situation isn't threatening their health or safety, it's appropriate to set the boundaries we're about to discuss. However, if you have reason to believe your friend is being physically or emotionally abused or harassed, or if their problems are leading to or are exacerbated by serious mental health issues, please encourage them to seek professional help, or offer to help them find a therapist that can support them in ways that you cannot. Equally important: Seek therapy yourself if your friendship is taking a toll on *your* mental health, or if you need guidance on setting appropriate boundaries in your specific situation.

If you're in the same boat as Lucy, I advise you to begin by setting the tone at your very next interaction. Start with, "It seems like you continue to have this same issue, even though we've talked about it a dozen times. Before we get into it again, tell me what you've done since our last call to change things on your end." This places the responsibility firmly in your friend's lap, where it belongs. If they haven't done anything, you can end this part of the conversation right there. Say something like, "Last time we talked, we agreed you could try doing these three things.

Until that happens, it's unlikely things will change. Let's talk about this again once you've taken some action."

If they start playing the victim here, as if nothing they do could effect any change, then it's time for some tough love: "I don't believe you have no power here—we've talked about this extensively, and you haven't tried anything we've discussed. At this point, you have two choices: You can either take responsibility for doing your part to change the dynamic, or accept things the way they are and decide to live with it. You came to me because I'm action-oriented, but I can't do it for you. So what do you think the right solution is?" Again, you're placing the ball in your friend's court, asking them to assume responsibility for next steps.

If they continue to push back, get angry or defensive, or otherwise refuse to respect the boundaries you're trying to set, it's time to get honest. Say something like, "I've tried so hard to help you, but at this point, I can't do anything else, and continuing to talk about the same things over and over is taking a toll on my mental health, and on our friendship. Maybe it's time to talk to a therapist about this, someone who has experience with these kinds of situations and can offer a new perspective. Whatever you decide to do, I need to take a break from this topic of conversation. And if you can't or won't do that, I'm going to take a break from the friendship itself."

Then hold your boundary. That might mean continuing to talk about other things but saying, "No, I'm not talking about your office dynamic anymore," if they try to drag you back into it. I'd be shocked if you didn't feel immediately lighter after setting this kind of boundary with this person. (I bet just the *idea* of setting a boundary here makes you giddy.) And if you're wondering whether or not this friendship stands any chance of survival . . . how they ultimately respond to your boundary will tell you everything you need to know. (For more on how to deal with other people's reactions to your boundaries, see Chapter 11.)

During their next phone call, Lucy interrupted Olivia with her first boundary. "Olivia, we talked about this last week. Did you talk to your co-worker directly, or show your boss your project-management spreadsheet?" When Olivia said no, Lucy held firm and told her that until she took action, she wasn't going to rehash the issues. She then changed the subject to her job. Lucy told me, "The conversation was really awkward from there. I could tell Olivia was annoyed, and we hung up pretty fast after that, but to be honest, I wasn't mad about it. I got an hour of my life back!" (This last statement jumped out at me—it's what movies call "foreshadowing.")

While emotional dumping is the most common reason you might want to set a boundary with a friend, there are certainly others:

- Friends who ghost, popping in only when they need something from you
- Friends who gossip or create drama amongst your friend group
- Friends who try to shove their beliefs or values onto you
- Friends with unreasonable expectations around how you show up for them
- Friends who don't respect your time (showing up late, bailing last minute)
- Friends who don't support your goals
- Friends who don't act like friends (making fun of you, sharing private information, or behaving competitively)

We'll address all of these scenarios (and then some) in the scripts section.

BREAKING UP IS ~~HARD TO DO~~ DOABLE

Should you continue to set healthy boundaries, and your friend continues to disrespect those boundaries or prove incapable of honoring them—it is probably time to invoke a consequence. Yeah, I'm talking about a friendship breakup. If the idea makes you squirm, pull a face, or feel like hiding under the covers, there's a reason: Friendship breakups can be even more awkward and uncomfortable than dating breakups.

For one, nobody expects you and your friend to spend every day together till death do you part, which means the differences that can split up a couple are generally expected to be better tolerated with friends. That can make ending a friendship feel unfair, unreasonable, or overly dramatic, even if the problem has been going on for years. Also, unlike monogamy, you're not limited to just *one* friend at a time, so one person's not-so-positive traits are often endured because you've got other friends to fill the gaps. Sure, Lucy felt like Olivia talked about herself a lot, but Lucy had lots of other friends who asked about her life, and she should be able to handle being the strong, capable go-to for one person who needed the support . . . right? Finally, each friendship is unique, emotionally tangled with shared (and often life-altering) past experiences. Letting go of the friendship can feel like you're letting go of a piece of your own history—and many friendships last far longer than they should for that very reason.

There's a psychological fallacy that likely plays in here: the Sunk Cost Fallacy. It describes our tendency to stick with a task, job, or relationship because we have already invested time, effort, or money in it, regardless of how well (or not well) it's working for us now. It's a big part of why we continue to hold on to long-standing friendships, even if the other person is no longer a good friend. "We have history. We've been through a lot together! I can't just throw that all away!"

Can't you, though?

Yes, you've invested all kinds of resources in this person. But the reality is that even though you *keep* spending, you're getting little to nothing in return. Taking an honest inventory of how the friendship feels today can be helpful here. Setting aside history and how the relationship used to feel, isolate how it's going *now*. Do you dread spending time with this person? Do you leave exhausted instead of recharged? Are you frustrated with their behavior more often than not? Have they ignored the boundaries you've set in an attempt to get the relationship back on track? It's not a fun exercise, but if you take history out of the equation, it may be time to give up friendship CPR and call it.

You'll never recoup what you've already spent . . . but you *can* keep yourself from going even further into friend-debt by ending things clearly and kindly now. If it's helpful, remember that people come into your life during specific seasons. Holding on to something because of what used to be isn't living in the present or rationally acknowledging what this relationship is stealing from you *now*.

Losing a friend is hard—especially if the friend is reacting poorly to your boundaries or trying to make it appear as if you're the unreasonable, insensitive, or demanding one. So how do you know when enough is enough?

When you establish limits to make the relationship a healthy space for you, and someone repeatedly refuses to respect those limits, it's time to end the relationship.

I can't tell you how much grace to give a friend or how many chances they deserve, but if the relationship continues to feel one-sided, disrespectful, or full of resentment, anxiety, or dread long after you've tried to set healthy boundaries, what are you hanging on to here? I know you'll say, "I don't want to hurt their feelings," but let's start prioritizing *your* feelings, please. Your friend hasn't been too concerned with them, and it's about time that someone is. (You. That's you.)

There are two ways to break up with a friend: the slow drift and the cutoff. In the slow drift, you let the friendship go over time. You stop replying to texts so quickly, with as much information, or at all. You decline invitations or stop extending them. When you do see this friend at events or in groups, you're polite and kind, but you keep things on a more superficial level. In this version, you each drift off peacefully into your own alternate friend groups without tension, conflict, or confrontation.

This might be appropriate for a casual acquaintance, a new friend, or someone you see or speak with infrequently anyway. If your friendship is one-sided, where you're always the one reaching out, or things have been so dramatic or heated that a pause or break is necessary and understandable, taking some time away and letting the friendship slowly drift off might be the smoothest way to let things go.

However, the slow drift isn't always the right move—even if it feels like it would be the easiest. If you've been friends for a long time, see each other regularly, or have a more intimate friendship, avoiding your friend until they get the hint isn't clear *or* kind. It's also far more likely in this scenario that they'll wonder what they did wrong, not take the hint, and keep calling or texting—or that they'll stay angry, wondering why you're ignoring them. This only complicates the issue, drawing out the process, allowing them to blame-shift to you, and leading them to demand even more of your time, effort, and energy.

With some friendships, the right thing to do is explicitly cut it off. Scary, I know, but it doesn't have to be messy, mean, or drawn out. Think of it as Marie Kondo–ing, but with friendships instead of sweaters: Hold it in your hand, thank it for the joy it has brought you in the past, and say goodbye.

FRIEND BOUNDARIES, AND PREP TIPS FOR BREAKING UP

If you do find you need to end a friendship, here are some best practices to help you communicate clearly, minimizing the potential for drama and giving each of you the opportunity to go with grace.

- **DO BE CONSIDERATE WITH YOUR TIMING.** Choose a quiet time for a brief interaction, ideally when you can speak in private. (If you can't meet in person or it's a long-distance friendship, it's okay to write a letter, email, or thoughtful text.)
- **DON'T APPROACH IT FROM A PLACE OF ANGER OR FRUSTRATION.** If you suspect you're going to verbally vomit all of the ways this person was a terrible friend to you, wait until you're calm and grounded. (You can vent to your therapist in the meantime.)
- **DON'T ATTEMPT TO DICTATE THEIR EXPERIENCE.** Saying, "I don't think this friendship is healthy for either of us" almost makes it sound like you're doing this for *their* sake. Stick to how *you* are experiencing the friendship, and why it's no longer working for you.
- **DO EXPRESS THE CUTOFF DIRECTLY.** Once you have shared your feelings, be clear about what this means: "It's best for me if we don't continue to try to make the friendship work" or "At this point, I'm going to move on from the friendship."
- **DO EXTEND GRACE, IF THAT FEELS AUTHENTIC.** Add, "I wish you nothing but good things," or "I'll look back over the years we've spent together with gratitude."
- **DON'T ALLOW THEM TO DUMP HOW TERRIBLE THEY FEEL AND**

HOW SORRY THEY ARE ALL OVER YOUR LAP. This forces you to once again comfort them, and at this point, you're done spending your energy here. Cut it off with a short "I appreciate that, but let's not dig that up again. I'm ready to move on."

- **DON'T LINGER, ESPECIALLY IF THEY'RE ANGRY.** Allow them the courtesy of processing their feelings in privacy, and excuse yourself from the conversation.

- **DO ALLOW SPACE FOR GRIEF.** You can feel immense relief and deep grief in the same moment, so allow for both. The end of a friendship is a loss, and of course you would grieve for the days that were good, the lost potential, and the hole that friendship once filled in your life.

DID I DO THE RIGHT THING?

After you end things with a friend, you may feel deeply sad. Often, people take that grief or sadness as an indicator that they made the wrong decision. Here's a trick to reassure yourself you did the right thing, and that you're just grieving the loss of what was or could have been: Imagine I told you, "Hey, that breakup conversation never happened. Your friend is about to call you, and you two will pick up exactly where you left off." If you feel anxiety, dread, or any other negative emotion, *that's your sign*. If you don't want the friendship back exactly the way it was the day before you ended things, then you made the right decision—you're just understandably sad about it.

Eventually and unsurprisingly, Lucy had to end her friendship with Olivia. I encouraged her to talk about how she felt during the friendship and after spending time together, and to make it clear this friendship was no longer serving her. She sent me the script she used to keep herself grounded and calm during their discussion: "This friendship isn't feeling reciprocal, and it's no longer healthy for me. I don't like how I feel after we spend time together, and that's a big sign that our friendship has run its course for me. I wish you nothing but good things, but it's time for me to move on." Lucy said it immediately felt like a weight had lifted, which is how she knew she made the right decision. She hasn't spoken to Olivia since.

Sometimes, with time, space, and maturity, friendships come back around; sometimes you were just meant to be there for each other in that particular season of life. Either way, you'll never regret learning how to set healthy boundaries in your friendships, because the ones that work will lead to fulfilling, happy relationships—and the ones that don't will make themselves crystal-clear real fast.

HOWDY, NEIGHBORS! (NOW PLEASE STAY OFF MY LAWN.)

There's a reason they say, "Good fences make good neighbors." Literally and figuratively, a boundary can mean the difference between a peaceful, easy, healthy relationship with your neighbors—or anger, resentment, and anxiety every time their garage door opens and the leaf blower comes out. Neighbors might be friends, which often makes these situations easier, but they could also be strangers you just have to live with in a copacetic fashion, often for many years.

I used to have a neighbor who would walk her dog past my house every morning. She had one of those retractable leashes and she would often let her dog wander way into my yard while she stared at her phone. The dog usually tore up my lawn or trampled over my flowers before its owner even noticed. I could never get outside fast enough to talk to her about it, and I wasn't sure where she lived. One day I finally caught the dog plowing through the bushes in the *back* of my yard, and I ran out to say, "Can you please not let your dog run around my yard like that?" It didn't happen again, but this neighbor did not take the request well; she wouldn't look at or speak to me when we passed each other on the street from that day on.

Boundary situations with neighbors are challenging, because there are things neighbors might do in their own yard or house that negatively affect you. They might play loud music late at night, leave their barking beagle outside all day long, install security lights that laser-beam straight into your window, or decide that 7 A.M. is prime leaf-blowing time. Unfortunately, you can't always set effective boundaries here, because your limit might interfere with how they want to live on their own property. You'll find examples of actual boundaries you can set in this chapter, but even if you can't set and hold a boundary, you might still need to have a tough conversation.

NEIGHBOR BOUNDARIES AND PREP TIPS

A big part of healthy boundaries with neighbors starts *well* before you experience conflict. When I was growing up, my parents knew all our neighbors well. I'd been inside all of their houses, we often had block parties and socialized together, and I was sent next door to Cindy's house to borrow an egg or cup of milk on more than one occasion. Today, it feels like we're all in our insulated bubbles, and unless we go out of our way to introduce ourselves to the neighbors, it's likely we'll never speak to them . . . until there's an issue. That's never a great way to establish a relationship, so here are some tips straight from the 1980s to help you pave the way for easy fences, low fences, or no fences at all, because your whole neighborhood has achieved Sesame Street–level cooperation.

- **GO OUT OF YOUR WAY TO BE NEIGHBORLY.** Make friends with the people who live nearby—even if it's just a "Good morning, how's the landscaping coming?" kind of relationship. (Bonus if you bank some goodwill by shoveling their sidewalk or lending them your ladder.) If you're "that nice neighbor" instead of a stranger, they'll be far more receptive to a boundary conversation if one has to arise.

- **HAVE POSITIVE ASSUMPTIONS.** Go into any boundary conversation assuming your neighbor wants to be a good member of the community, and just doesn't realize how their behaviors are impacting others. Assuming the best can go a long way toward ensuring the type of polite, friendly conversation that actually gets you somewhere.

- **BE REASONABLE.** Approach your neighbor for a conversation during a calm period, explain the issue, and pose your reasonable request. You can't ask them to *never* turn their music up, but you can mention you just had a baby, and ask them to keep it down or wear headphones after 10 P.M.

- **PICK YOUR BATTLES.** If their dog poops on your lawn once and they don't notice, is it worth knocking on their door if they're an otherwise great neighbor? If the pattern continues, that's a different story, but know when to let it go, so you can set boundaries where they really count.

- **DIY.** Even if you do set a boundary, do your part to look for solutions on your end, too. Sleep with earplugs or a white noise machine, buy blackout curtains for late-night lights, buy poop bags just in case, or put up a literal fence to keep the neighbor's kids out of your flowers.

You may find yourself in a situation where you've been nice, asked politely, and still aren't getting cooperation. If you need to step up your efforts to make sure your neighbor is holding up their end of the (unwritten) rules of the block, start documenting what you notice. Write down the time period their dog was barking while they were at work, snap a photo of the flowers their kids stomped through while cutting across your lawn, or shoot a video of their security light shining straight into your living room. Having this evidence will help if you have to escalate things, but you could also share it with your neighbors to demonstrate that you're not exaggerating the issue.

If you still can't get resolution, it may be time to contact your landlord or HOA, or explore your local ordinances. For example, Salt Lake City has a "Good Neighbor Guide," which offers a variety of resources and contacts to deal with noise issues, property in disrepair, graffiti, lighting issues, and more. You could also invite everyone to a neighborhood meeting to discuss the issue, look into community mediation, or file a "nuisance suit" in small claims court.

One last thing *not* to do is stoop to your problematic neighbor's level. Blaring *your* music at 5 A.M., throwing their dog's poop back into their yard, or buying your own super-bright light to shine into their windows is a recipe for trouble, perhaps in the form of a lawsuit or criminal complaint. This kind of behavior is neither clear nor kind, so take the high road here, even if it would feel so satisfying to crank up "Baby Shark" on repeat. The boundary scripts in this chapter will help.

SCRIPTS FOR SETTING BOUNDARIES WITH FRIENDS

Setting boundaries with friends helps to keep your relationship healthy and reciprocal; ensures that your mental health is protected; and identifies when you might need to create distance or adjust the terms of the friendship before it becomes problematic. It's never too late to establish a healthier dynamic! Plus, you'll learn real fast what kind of friendship you *really* have based on how your friends respond to the clear, kind boundaries you set with them.

> **I made a new friend at the gym, and they seem great—but I've started to realize they talk a lot about themselves and don't ask me much about my life. If I'm going to invest in a new friendship, it has to be a two-way street. How can I say, "Stop talking about yourself so much!"**
>
> **GREEN:** "I know so much about your job by now—can I tell you about mine? I have a few exciting things happening and I'd love to share them."
>
> **YELLOW:** "I feel like our conversations are very one-sided. It doesn't feel great that you never ask about me or my life."
>
> **RED:** "I feel like our connection is missing something, so I'll pass on hanging out again. See you at the gym."
>
> *You can use the Green boundary to see if they check themselves and realize they haven't been a good conversation partner. If the conversation continues to stay one-sided, as awkward as it feels, you're totally justified in not pursuing it. Friendships take work, and this person doesn't seem as invested as you are.*

> **I have this one friend who keeps ghosting me for months at a time, then popping back in when she needs something. It doesn't feel very good. How can I express that to her?**
>
> **GREEN:** "It's been a while, and it seems like you only reach out when you need something. That doesn't feel good to me, and I'd like to talk about that first."
>
> **YELLOW:** "It's not okay that you drop out for months at a time, then pop back in when you need something. I can't help you

right now, but if you'd like to talk more tomorrow, give me a call."

RED: "I hear that you need help, but you completely disappeared on me, and I'm upset about that. I'll reach out again if and when I'm ready to talk."

It's up to you whether or not you help, or even if you want to continue in this friendship. Context matters: Is your friend struggling with mental health or a chronic illness? Do they only call when they're not dating someone? Those two scenarios likely deserve different limits. Think about what might explain why your friend is ghosting you and take that into account when you set your boundary with them. If they need more support than you can provide, encourage them to find it.

A casual friend keeps sending me political articles and memes that I don't appreciate or agree with. I've asked them to stop forwarding these things, and they reply, "I just want you to be informed." Help me find nice words here, because what I want to say is not nice.

GREEN: "Please stop sending these kinds of emails to me. You know I don't share your views, and I don't want you forcing them on me."

YELLOW: "I haven't opened your last two emails because you continue to send content that I've specifically asked you not to. If you won't respect this, our friendship won't continue."

RED: Block and be blessed.

I went on an unfriending, unfollowing, and blocking spree in 2020—between the election, social justice uprisings, and COVID, it was a necessary step to preserve my mental health and keep my social media feeds a healthy, safe space. If you need permission to unfollow someone, here it is: Click the damn button. Nobody—not your family, friends, and certainly not the girl you haven't seen since high school—is entitled to that kind of access to you.

THE BEAUTY OF THE BLOCK

Blocking or unfriending a real friend on social media should never be your first step, as that behavior is neither clear nor kind. However, if you've set several boundaries already and find your friend is simply not able or willing to respect them, removing the connection and their unlimited access to you is the natural consequence of that disrespect. (Remember, a boundary is *your* limit, so if they're not respecting that limit, you'll have to enforce it yourself.) At that point, muting, blocking, or unfriending them is a last-ditch effort to preserve your emotional and mental health—and I can tell you firsthand, it works. By blocking them, you're also blocking the anxiety, irritation, resentment, and anger you experienced every time that friend's name showed up on your feed or in your in-box, and the time you spend on social media will be far more pleasant and joyful.

I have a friend who gets mad when she texts me and I don't reply back right away. She'll even stalk my social media and say, "So, you can post on Instagram but you can't text me back?" I need to (nicely) explain that I'm not at her beck and call.

GREEN: "You're right, I won't always text back right away, and I'd love it if you could be a little more understanding about that. Sometimes things come up, or I get distracted, or I just can't do the back-and-forth in the moment. I'd love to give each of us some grace here."

YELLOW: "Jess, I can't always reply right away, and it doesn't feel good that you're checking up on me like that. Is there a bigger conversation we need to have about our friendship?"

RED: "Our dynamic isn't working for me right now. I'm going to take a break from the friendship. I'll reach back out if I'm ready to start talking again."

This situation can escalate quickly: You delay in responding because you just don't want to deal with how demanding your friend can be, and they get even more angry around your delay in response. The Yellow boundary of "Is there a bigger conversation we need to have here?" can help you feel out whether your friend's expectations are simply too high for you to meet given your energetic capacity, and whether you want to maintain the relationship going forward.

I have a friend who bails on me constantly. I understand that things happen, but more often than not, we make plans and then my friend will cancel last minute, always with a weak excuse. What should I do?

GREEN: (on Friday) "Hey! Confirming the movie on Saturday at 7 P.M. still works for you? It's been hard to get together lately so before I buy the tickets, I wanted to check in."

YELLOW: (if they cancel) "This is the third time in a row that you've canceled last minute. I don't want to keep making plans if you're not able to stick to them."

RED: (if they reach back out to reschedule) "You've canceled so often, I'd rather not make plans like this again. If you want to stop by one night this week to talk, I'll be home."

The Red boundary puts the ball in their court—if they show up, great. If they don't, you're not put out one bit, and you can probably call this friendship over.

REACH OUT

If you have a friend who used to be reliable but now seems to bail regularly, consider reaching out to them. Mention that they've canceled a number of times now, and you're wondering if they're going through any specific challenges that are making it hard to socialize—and if so, would they like to talk, or can you help? Yes, sometimes people are careless and inconsiderate. But sometimes they're suffering from depression, anxiety, or financial stress, which makes it really hard to do normal social things. Or maybe their ADHD is worse, which makes keeping a calendar, schedule, or time commitments challenging. Or maybe they have a chronic illness that's flaring, leaving them with little energy for anything besides basic care tasks. As a caring friend, it's worth checking in before you assume the other person is just being a jerk. If a friend is in a busy season (new baby, new job) or is experiencing personal challenges, instead of trying to force meet-ups, offer alternate ways to stay connected, like text message touch-bases, a quick Sunday night phone call, or trading funny TikToks. (That's my current friendship Love Language.)

I have one friend who is always gossiping about others—sometimes people I know, often people I don't. I've asked my friend to stop, because I don't like the drama and it doesn't feel kind, especially when she's talking about mutual friends. How can I make it clear?

GREEN: "Ooh, wait. Talking about Mia like that isn't nice, and I'm not comfortable with it." Change the subject.

YELLOW: "I don't want to talk about other people behind their backs, and this makes me wonder how much you talk about me when I'm not around. I don't like it."

RED: "I don't want a friendship that includes talking about other people behind their backs. I wish you well."

If your friend is talking to you about others, I guarantee they're talking to others about you. And a friend you can't trust isn't someone you want in your circle.

One of my friends likes to put me down in front of other people, especially men. She'll say something like, "Yeah, she's pretty, but don't ask her anything about current events." I think it's because my friend is insecure, but this isn't nice, and she needs to hear it. What should I say to her?

GREEN: (after the fact) "That was quite the backhanded compliment, and it felt pretty sucky. I would never do that to you, so what was that?"

YELLOW: (in the moment) "Ouch. I thought we talked about catty jokes like that? It's not cute. Please excuse me." Leave the conversation.

RED: "I don't let my friends say things like that about me. I think I'm done here."

If that's what your friend is saying to your face, I can't imagine what she says behind your back. If setting a boundary and having an honest conversation about what's behind those comments don't change her behavior, the friendship may not be worth saving.

BACKHANDED COMPLIMENTS

"You look so tired; I don't know how you do it all." We've all been the recipient of a backhanded compliment, and they often leave us flummoxed. Do you say thank you, tell whoever offered it to get bent, or both? Responding to comments like this doesn't *necessarily* involve setting a boundary (although you might want to do that if this person is a backhanded repeat offender), but here are three ways to address a compliment like, "Your presentation was surprisingly good!"

- **Make them explain it:** "Huh, that's a strange way to put it. What do you mean by 'surprisingly'?"
- **Ignore the slight:** "Yes! I *was* fantastic, wasn't I? I'm thrilled it was so well received."
- **Call it out:** "If that's the way you compliment people, I can't imagine what your insults sound like. Next time just say, 'Good job.'"

If this person has a habit of couching their "compliments" in backhanded nastiness, it might be time to point it out to them and to set a boundary. "'Surprisingly good' . . . you know, I've noticed all of your compliments also include some kind of insult. Next time you feel the urge, please skip the feedback. Whatever is happening here, it's not about me, and I'd just rather not."

One of my friends is such a one-upper. If I tell a funny family story, they'll interrupt with a funnier one. If I was out sick last week, they'll talk about a time they were even sicker. It's exhausting and makes me feel like they don't really hear me, they just listen to interject their own stories. How can I interrupt this process?

GREEN: "Oh, I wasn't done telling my story, actually. I'd love to be able to finish."

YELLOW: "It feels like you don't really listen when I tell you things. You never comment or reflect back on what I just said, you just rush in to tell your own story. It doesn't feel great, to be honest."

RED: "You're not giving me the space I need in this relationship. Every time I try to talk to you, you immediately make it about you. I don't know how to continue the friendship this way."

Whether your friend's one-upmanship stems from jealousy, insecurity, or self-centeredness, it doesn't demonstrate that they're concerned with your feelings, personal growth, or experience. That doesn't sound like a very caring or reciprocal relationship.

SCRIPTS FOR SETTING BOUNDARIES WITH NEIGHBORS

You don't have to be friends with your neighbors, but it makes life a lot nicer (and more convenient and safe) if you all look out for one another. At the very least, you don't want to have to run inside and hide every time Jerry's garage door opens across the street. Creating relationships with your neighbors is the first step in establishing healthy boundaries; you don't want the first conversation you have with a neighbor to be, "Your poodle just took a dump on my lawn." Start laying the foundation for your fences before you need them, and you'll find the construction process goes much smoother.

My neighbor is always letting their dog poop on my lawn, and they often don't pick it up. I've pointed this out to them politely, but nothing has changed. How do I address this?

GREEN: "I understand dogs poop where they poop, but as a good neighbor, please pick it up if it's in my yard."

YELLOW: "Your dog pooped in my yard just now—can you please come back and pick it up?"

RED: (in the moment) "Here's a poop bag for your cleanup."

You can't make your neighbor pick up their dog's poop, you can only set your own limit, which is, "I won't let dog poop sit in my yard." That might mean you have to pick it up yourself, unless you can catch your neighbor while their dog is in the act. However, you could also attempt to automate the boundary by erecting a "Please pick up after your dog" sign, installing a prominently placed camera as a deterrent, placing a "Take a poop bag" basket by your mailbox, setting up motion-detector sprinklers to keep dogs (and their owners) off your lawn, or building a fence.

We have the only in-ground pool in the neighborhood, and people are always asking if they can "stop by with the kids for a quick dip." This is fine sometimes, but other times we just want to enjoy the pool by ourselves. How can I say no without looking like a jerk?

GREEN: "We're not ready for guests today, but Saturday we'll be poolside from noon until 4 P.M. and you're welcome to come by then."

YELLOW: "We're having a family day, so it's not a good time."

RED: "We've run into some problems letting so many people drop by, so we're closing the pool to guests for now."

Could you automate this boundary? I read a story about a family purchasing a large orange flag for their backyard. If the flag was up, the pool was open! You could also have structured times (like Saturday afternoon) when guests are encouraged to drop by, but otherwise the pool is for family and invited guests only.

My neighbor always comes over when he sees us outside, and he stays forever. He'll talk our ear off if we let him, and we can't

really escape unless we go back inside. We're starting to avoid our own yard because of this! How can I talk to him without being rude?

GREEN: "Walter, we're going to let you go so we can get back to our day now. See you later!"

YELLOW: (without stopping what you're doing) "Hey, Walter, we can't chat now but we'll wave you over the next time we're outside and have a moment."

RED: "Now isn't a good time, Walter." Wave goodbye and continue about your business.

You should feel safe and comfortable in your own house and yard, and you shouldn't let your neighbor, no matter how well-meaning he may be, hover. If you speak to him about needing space and he continues not to respect it, you may have to be more straightforward: "Walter, I hope you understand that sometimes we just want our privacy. If we're outside, please don't treat it as an automatic invitation to socialize. In order to be good neighbors, we need to respect one another's boundaries."

The people next door have a different schedule than we do, and they often play loud music late into the night. We have a new baby and would love to agree on "quiet hours" with them, but we don't have a landlord or HOA. How can we approach this?

GREEN: "Here are some cookies I just baked. I also wanted to introduce you to Emma [point to baby in sling]—she's a month old today. I'm wondering if you could please turn your music down after 10 P.M.? It would make our life as new parents so much better."

YELLOW: "Your music level is still loud on weekends, and lots of the neighbors here have young kids. Can we ask again that you work with us and turn it down after 10 P.M., please?"

RED: "Our local ordinances for noise regulation prohibit loud music at night between the hours of 10 P.M. and 7 A.M.—here's a copy. A few of our neighbors have signed this letter, asking for you to please abide by these regulations. I don't want to have to take this further, so please work with us here."

Killing a neighbor with kindness is never a bad approach, especially in the beginning. And just in case it takes a while before their behavior changes, make sure you're doing everything you can to protect your family from their noise, from investing in white noise machines to wearing earplugs to bed to moving the baby's crib as far away from their house as possible.

My neighbor is always sending her kids over to my house. While our kids play well together, I don't always want to be responsible for watching her kids, too, even if they are just outside. Plus she never invites my kids to her house. How can I talk to her about this?

GREEN: "Hi, Jessica, the kids always seem to end up at our house. I don't mind if they're outside and playing well, but can you call me before you send them over to make sure it's okay?"

YELLOW: (walking the kids home) "Sorry, Jessica, I can't have them over today. Next time please call."

RED: "Sorry, kids, we can't play today." Send them home.

First, ask yourself whether you're objecting because of the perceived "unfairness" of the situation, or whether having her kids at your house really is too much effort for you. If they're good kids capable of entertaining themselves without much supervi-sion and your children enjoy the company, do you really need a boundary here? If you do (no judgment), consider proposing standard playdates (like Tuesdays at your house and Thursdays at Jessica's), or make a rule with the other parents that their kids can come over to play if they see your kids outside, but they may not knock on the door unannounced.

I lent my neighbor a tool once, and when he walked into my garage and saw my workshop, his eyes lit up. Since then, he's been stopping by to borrow equipment and ask my advice on projects. I don't mind lending a hand, but I'm not my neigh-bor's personal Home Depot. What should I say?

GREEN: "I can let you borrow it one last time, but you really need one of your own at this point. Let me know if you want help picking one out."

YELLOW: "I can't help today, Glenn—why don't you run down to Home Depot? They're all super knowledgeable and friendly."

RED: "I'm not lending tools out anymore, I've had some bad experiences."

If your neighbor is responsible with your stuff (tools, books, shovels, whatever) and brings it back on time, consider being a good neighbor and continuing to help him out, as long as it's not cramping your style. But if your neighbor is forgetful about returning your things, brings them back damaged, or expects your help at the drop of the hat, you can feel comfortable shar-ing the Red boundary—because those are the bad experiences.

I live in a row of four townhouses. Lately, my neighbor has been taking my packages inside his house if they're delivered when I'm not home, or knocking on my door repeatedly if there's a

package outside and I am home. All of this makes me uncomfortable. I'm sure he's trying to be helpful, but how can I ask him to stop?

GREEN: "I appreciate you looking out for me, but I'd prefer my packages are left where they are, even if I'm not home."

YELLOW: "Please don't concern yourself with my packages, just leave them where they are."

RED: "Stop taking my deliveries or I'll report this to the HOA."

You might want to ask if there's a reason he's bringing your packages inside—maybe your neighborhood has had a rash of "porch pirates" that you're unaware of, which could change your opinion. You could also ask carriers to deliver packages to a more discreet location, away from your neighbor's prying eyes.

LOVING THE LIMITS THAT SET YOU FREE

I have a group of girlfriends here in Salt Lake (there are five of us) who truly embody what it means to be a good friend in a caring, compassionate, boundary-respecting environment. Here are the unspoken-but-clearly-understood rules of our friend group:

- We keep inviting one another to do things but we understand that everyone's capacity is different—even if someone says no five times in a row, the invitations keep coming. Nobody takes a "no, I can't right now" personally.
- We respect that we all have rich, full lives with families, other friends, work, and challenges. If someone isn't responding to group texts, we don't take that personally, either.
- If someone has ducked out for a while, we'll check in gently. "You doing okay? Mental health hanging in? Need a coffee or some Botox?" (We have a plastic surgeon in the group.)

- If we see someone skiing with her other friend group after she said no to brunch, no one gets upset. In fact, everyone will comment on her Instagram post, "So happy you had a fun day!" and mean every word.
- If someone sets a personal boundary, like "I'm not drinking right now," everyone else is immediately and unquestionably supportive in honoring that boundary.
- When something is really important, we show up, regardless of what else we have going on. (And if we honestly just can't, it's understood that we would have if we could.)
- We look for small, thoughtful ways to let one another know we're thinking about them—sharing memes or tagging each other on Instagram is a respected form of connection.

These friendships have been going strong for nearly a decade, and the group represents the most mature, caring, respectful friendships I've ever had. The good news is that if your friendships don't sound like this, it's *never* too late to introduce boundaries. In fact, that goes for everyone who appeared in this chapter, whether it's your neighbor you've been tolerating (and grumbling about) for years or a friend you're considering moving in with. You'll be surprised and delighted by how much happier, healthier, and stronger your relationships with friends and neighbors can become when you take the initiative to establish and share some well-placed limits.

CHAPTER 6

Love, Marriage, Sex, and Dishes

Setting Boundaries in Romantic Relationships

When my husband, Brandon, and I bought a house together in late 2019, we quickly discovered that I needed way more alone time than he did. When we were dating, he'd spend a night or two at my townhouse, then head back to his apartment for a night or two so we could juggle work, my schedule with my son, and our household responsibilities. I assumed he enjoyed and appreciated his alone time as much as I did.

I was wrong.

After we decided to move in together and bought a house, I asked for a head start moving in, so my son could get adjusted before Brandon joined us. But as Brandon's move-in date approached, I realized I was feeling claustrophobic . . . and I was the only one. (This was also prime pandemic, which certainly factored in.) I tried to ride it out, because I didn't want to keep kicking him out of what would soon be his own house. But not saying anything made me resentful, snippy, and generally awful to be around—which he clearly picked up on. After a day of moving boxes in while tiptoeing around me, Brandon went back to his old apartment in frustration, and I felt equal parts relieved and guilty.

He knew spending time alone was how I recharged—we'd

talked about it a ton. But neither of us had a plan for how that would work once we lived together, and clearly "sucking it up" wasn't a viable strategy. We needed clear communication, a shared set of expectations, and of course . . . boundaries.

Brandon and I have been together off and on since 2017. We dated for five months before he broke up with me, a tidbit that I enjoy pulling out at parties now that we're married. He was insecure and in a period of transition in his life, and I still carried baggage from my last relationship. It turns out that time apart (and therapy) was exactly what we needed. When we bumped into each other again eight months later, we were vastly different people, so we decided to give the relationship another try.

This time, it worked from day one, and the biggest difference (aside from the therapy) was the boundaries we were both willing to set and respect. My communication around sex, how we handled conflict, the way I needed us to continue to show up for ourselves and the relationship, and the pace at which we moved had never been more clear and direct. Brandon matched that energy with thoughtful periods of introspection, offering equally vulnerable and clear statements around what he needed from me, and the ways he planned to contribute to our family and our household. Our greatest boundary hits included:

- I'm not into that in the bedroom, but I'm down with this, this, and this (both of us).
- When I tell you I need to take a break during an argument, please give that to me (me).
- Please don't post photos of the kid on social media (me).
- I don't want to share a bank account (both of us).
- Being married but living in separate houses doesn't work for me (him).

Yes, that last one was an actual conversation. After one of my claustrophobic episodes, I cautiously suggested: "Why don't we get married but, like, not live together?" Brandon promptly shut that down—no hiding his feelings, no mumbling "maybe" and shuffling off disappointed or confused, no blowing up in anger over the idea. Just a firm "That would not work for me," which it turns out was the kindest thing he could have said. (After all, we're married *and* we live together now.)

This conversation was also grounded in one of the most important agreements we made in the second half of our relationship— what I call our Relationship Golden Rule.

THE RELATIONSHIP GOLDEN RULE

Well before we talked about moving in together, we had what was perhaps the most important conversation of our relationship. What we agreed on that day has become my Relationship Golden Rule—the one law we live by that supports all other aspects of our relationship. It goes like this:

> *Say what you mean and trust your
> partner to do the same.*

During the course of an otherwise unremarkable conversation, Brandon asked if something he had done was bothering me. I thought for a minute, then said, "Nope." He proceeded to dig a little more. "Are you sure? I felt bad, and . . ." I interrupted him. "This is one thing you can count on—if I'm upset, I will tell you. If it had bothered me, I would have said so. But if I tell you it doesn't, you can trust that I'm telling you the truth and you don't have to keep asking."

It took him a while to trust that, understandably. Not many people actually say what they mean. I still sometimes have to reassure him, "Hey, I said we'd be fine if you go on that trip this weekend—I promise I meant it." But I firmly believe this is the number one gift you can give everyone in your life, especially your romantic partner. Because the alternative is crappy, and I suspect we've all been on one side or the other.

> **SPOUSE:** "Is it okay if I go out with friends tonight?"
>
> **YOU:** (seething—don't they see how much that would put you out?) "Sure, babe."
>
> **SPOUSE:** (crossing fingers that you mean it) "Okay, thanks!"
>
> **YOU:** (three hours later, still seething)
>
> **SPOUSE:** (creeping in, bracing for a fight) "Hi, I'm back!"
>
> **YOU:** (sarcastically) "*GREAT.* I hope you had an AWESOME time while I stayed HOME and DID EVERYTHING ALL BY MYSELF."

If you are a woman and you read that assuming "spouse" was a man, there's a reason for that. It's an established gendered trope that women never say what we mean because we're coy/people-pleasing/indecisive/manipulative, and it's the man's job to drag our true feelings out of us, attempt to mind-read, or tell us how we really feel. (Fun digression: Google "Why don't women say what they mean," then prepare to fume.) But no matter the gender, it can be ruinous to a relationship when people don't say what they mean or take responsibility for their feelings.

This Golden Rule isn't unique to my romantic partnership; I operate like this in all areas of my life. My friends and colleagues know I don't say things just to be nice. (I'm not that nice.) I don't say yes if it's not really a yes. I don't swallow my feelings just to spare others'. And I am comfortable saying no, clearly and kindly. Here's how it works:

SAY WHAT YOU MEAN. This requires introspection, a moment (or more) of pause to check in with how you really feel, and a commitment to clear, kind communication. In the instance above, if your spouse going out for the evening would leave you feeling abandoned or overburdened, then say that. Instead of, "Sure, babe," try, "That idea stresses me out because we have a party planned for tomorrow and there's a lot of prep work we still need to do. If you leave, I'll have to do it all by myself."

In the moment, this provides a much clearer path to resolution. Your spouse can now process the information you've provided and say, "Okay, I'll skip it, then. Show me the list." Or maybe, "Okay, but it's Sam's birthday today. How about I go for an hour, then come back and help?" Or "I remember! I'll wrap all the presents, hang all the decorations, and clean the patio furniture first thing tomorrow morning. Would that make you feel less stressed about me heading out for a few hours?"

Now it's your turn to reflect and tell the truth. Options include, "Yep, that's a good compromise, tell Sam I said happy birthday," or "No, I'm feeling a 7 out of 10 that I really need your help tonight," or, "Actually, that works, as long as you have it all done by 10 A.M. Deal?" Continue to communicate clearly and kindly. Say what you mean.

TRUST YOUR PARTNER TO DO THE SAME. If your partner says, "I want to go 9 out of 10 tonight—my mental health is struggling and I really need this time with my friends," accept this as truth, and consider if you can willingly give up your preference in service of your partner, and in service of your relationship. If your partner says, "Okay, I understand, I'll skip it tonight," believe they are making the right choice for themselves, not giving in resentfully, angrily, or bitterly. Hold them to the same standard of clear, kind communication that you've committed to, and suddenly your night looks and feels so much better, whether or not they go out.

REPEAT OFFENDERS

This approach requires a basic level of trust. If you communicate clearly and kindly that you really need your partner at home tonight and they go out anyway, determine if this is a one-off situation in which you underestimated how important a night out was to them, or if this is a pattern of behavior in which your partner continually fails to respect your needs, demonstrate reciprocity, or communicate as honestly as you do. If it's the latter, a therapist could help you work through these fundamental issues.

With the Golden Rule approach, you and your partner have agreed on a path together, and you can both go about your lives knowing each person will be communicating honestly and taking responsibility for their own feelings. The Golden Rule is huge for preventing unnecessary conflict. When you are willing to say no instead of agreeing resentfully and fuming silently, your yes will carry more meaning. Your partner will know if you say, "Yes, your parents can stay with us," "Yes, go ahead and spend the money," "Yes, it's cool if you go out tonight," then you *really mean it*. They don't have to brace themselves for backlash, simmering anger, and an argument down the line, and that builds a deeper level of trust in your relationship.

This behavior is also a path toward establishing clear, kind boundaries, even if you've never had them in your relationship before. Your willingness to say no in alignment with your integrity also gives your partner permission to say no to *you*. You're now modeling a clear, kind communication pattern and encouraging your partner to explore their own healthy boundaries for the good of the relationship. This means your *partner* will not begrudgingly or angrily say yes either, and now you're both free to enjoy your life without worrying there's a sneak attack coming.

The Relationship Golden Rule Brandon and I established early on laid the foundation for the clear, kind boundary conversations that were to come, and made them ten times easier. But there's one more principle I want to share before we get into how we boundaried our way out of the alone-time puzzle. It's a term I invented called YCDIAWYW, and I still can't figure out how to turn it into a pronounceable acronym.

YCDIAWYW (YOU CAN DO IT ANY WAY YOU WANT)

Ironically, this theory (YCDI for short) started with a conversation I had with a friend about being in a committed relationship while maintaining individual residences. Over breakfast one day, my friend was telling me about life with her longtime partner. "He still has his place, and I still have mine. Some nights, I want to put on a face mask and sleep alone. Some nights, he wants more solitude than my kids can offer. We've been together for six years, and this just works for us."

My mind was blown. At the time, Brandon and I had just started dating again. We were navigating our relationship history, what we both wanted now, and when and how to introduce him to my son—it was a lot. When my friend explained how she and her partner structured their lives, I realized for the first time that two consenting adults really could run their relationship *any way they wanted*. It didn't have to be conventional, it didn't have to fit societal norms, and it didn't have to make sense to anyone but us. This is another game-changing relationship hack that can be applied to every area of your life and can help you set the healthy boundaries that work best for your partnership. Here are some of the areas you and partner can navigate together, committing to doing it *any way you want*:

FINANCES: You can merge finances, or maintain entirely separate bank accounts. You can split expenses, or have one person pay for everything, or do anything in between. You can agree on making big purchases together; have a "don't ask, don't tell" policy around what things cost; or decide if it's in your bank account, it's your money. You can do it any way you want.

INTIMACY: You can agree on monogamy, have an open relationship, or practice polyamory. You can sleep in the same bed, have separate bedrooms, or a combination of both. You can get married without living together, live together without getting married, or get married and live together for just half of the year. You can do it any way you want.

GENDER ROLES: Any partner can be the breadwinner, child caretaker, or household manager. Any partner can cook, clean, change the oil, or whack the weeds. Any partner can pay the bills, hire the contractor, landscape the backyard, or design the new bathroom. You can do it any way you want. (I'm looking at you, straight couples.)

SOCIALIZATION: You can arrive at and leave parties together or separately, or send one of you home early in an Uber. You can always invite your partner, never invite your partner, or sometimes invite your partner. You can have shared friends, friends that are just yours, or few friends because you prefer your solitude. You can go out regularly, go out never, or entertain only in your own home. You can do it any way you want.

Though the idea of getting married and living apart wasn't in the cards for us, the YCDI concept helped us explore and successfully navigate other aspects of our relationship—whether we wanted another kid, Brandon's career path, how we handled money, and how we maintained a sense of privacy when I already had a pretty public life. Because we never felt pressure to do it any one way, we were free to explore any solution we could imagine, no matter how unconventional. Ultimately, YCDI allows us to create a life that works for *us,* having talked through all of the aspects that are important to us both and meeting in the middle, often in unconventional ways.

Which is why I went back to therapy before Brandon moved in. Having separate households wasn't going to work for him. Living together the way we'd been trying to definitely wasn't working for either of us. The idea of not getting married made me sad. So, I resumed therapy with the specific goal of figuring out how Brandon and I could successfully cohabitate.

I spent a few sessions with my therapist identifying and discussing how to plug a number of energy leaks in my own life. Most of those leaks stemmed from my phone. They were sapping the available energy I had to connect with Brandon, so I enacted some self-boundaries around how I engaged with social media, Slack, and email. Then, my therapist and I moved on to communication strategies and brainstorming the boundaries I could set to ensure I got the alone time I needed without Brandon feeling slighted or "wrong" for simply existing in our space.

In the spirit of healthy communication, I shared high-level details of my therapy sessions with Brandon, so he could see I was taking responsibility for my own feelings. We talked about the strategies I was employing with social media and work to reclaim some of my energy. We also explored ways that I could get the space I needed to recharge without him having to sleep in the car—this included my taking long solo hikes on the weekend and going to bed extra-early (and alone) to read for an hour.

At the same time, I encouraged him to share what *he* needed from me in this situation. He does not require as much alone time as I do, but he still wanted to maintain his independence, taking nature trips with friends and traveling for jiu jitsu tournaments. We discussed how we could both get what we wanted if we were more communicative. He also expressed that he missed the ways we used to connect before he moved in. He asked if I'd make more of an effort to pause and physically connect during busy days, even if it was just a long hug or a quick kiss, and he asked me to stay up later with him on weekends for Netflix-and-cuddle sessions on the couch.

We both recommitted to the Relationship Golden Rule, understanding that if we were clear and kind in expressing what we needed, we could trust each other to take responsibility for our own feelings about it. That meant no more holding it in to preserve his feelings—if I was feeling itchy for some space, I had to say so; if he was feeling disconnected, he had to say so, too. These three things—communicating more, exploring solutions together, and committing to speak our truths—solved the vast majority of my "alone time" issues; the ones that were left simply required a boundary. In the moment, those boundaries sound like:

- "I would love to watch a movie, but I don't want to snuggle right now, okay?"
- "I want to hike alone tomorrow. Can we do something together on Sunday?"
- "I'm heading to bed right after I put the kiddo down—I need some quiet time."

Brandon and I have been living together for almost two years now, and it's remarkable how much I've expanded my capacity for sharing space. In fact, we've used the Golden Rule and the YCDI concept to create healthy boundaries in every area of our relationship, from the division of household labor to how we handle conflict to S-E-X. But before we get into all of that, I want to warn you this chapter isn't as cut-and-dried as the others. Though boundaries are magical, they can't solve everything, and that holds especially true for the most common challenges I've witnessed between romantic partners.

DO YOU NEED MORE THAN A BOUNDARY?

In this chapter more than any other, you're going to hear me say, "That's not really a boundary issue." Yes, there are plenty of scenarios in which setting a boundary is appropriate and helpful. If your partner buys something expensive without talking to you first, proposes something in the bedroom that makes you uncomfortable, or involves their mom too often in your relationship, yes, you need a boundary, and we'll cover those in the scripts. But many of the most common issues that come up in romantic partnerships need to start with *communication* and *expectation-setting*, not boundaries.

- Division of household labor
- Finances and spending
- How you handle conflict
- Socialization preferences
- Privacy and personal space
- Physical intimacy
- Trust and fidelity

Can you set a boundary that says, "I do not have the emotional or energetic capacity to do the dishes again this week?" You sure can. But what are you going to do if the dishes still don't get done, and you find yourself ready to eat a meal without a clean plate, fork, or knife in the house? (If you said, "Be petty and buy myself a secret stash of paper plates," I'd silently love that, but out loud I'd point out that is not a long-term solution.) And a boundary like, "My limit is not to go more than five days without sexual intimacy" isn't often viable, because holding that depends on someone else—and their boundary may conflict with yours. (Like, "I won't consent to sexual intimacy under pressure.")

In exchanges with my community, I've heard just about every relationship issue there is, and having been married, divorced, and remarried, I've experienced a lot of them myself. I wish there were simple boundary scripts that could adequately address the really hard stuff, but these situations can't be solved by one party setting a limit—they require clear communication from everyone involved, and the establishment of shared expectations, perhaps facilitated by a therapist.

There are a few ways I'll tackle these issues in this chapter. First, if there is a clear, kind boundary that can be set, I'll outline that in the scripts. Second, if the issue can't be solved by setting one healthy limit, I'll share my best strategies for initiating the right kind of conversations or offer tips that will help you move closer to the goal. Finally, for more weighty subjects (specifically, fair division of household labor, establishing "rules of engagement" around conflict, and sexual intimacy), I'll point you to entire books that have been written on those topics, so you can do a deeper dive with your partner to improve the specific aspect of your relationship that's causing you stress or draining your energy.

I've broken these conversations, resources, and boundary scripts into the issues that most frequently arise in five different categories: household management; interpersonal conflict; styles of socializing; privacy and trust; and sex and physical connection.

HOUSEHOLD MANAGEMENT: These are boundaries around how you and your spouse navigate the division of labor, childcare, finances, and other aspects of your home. Running a household is as complex and challenging as running a business, and we all want to be recognized and appreciated for the very real (and often invisible) labor involved. As discussed, holding a healthy limit around your labor may not be easy, as respecting that boundary often requires your partner's cooperation. Still, there are limits you can set within each area of household responsibility that will encourage your partner to acknowledge the labor you're regularly performing and invite them to co-create strategies that work for both of you.

INTERPERSONAL CONFLICT: These are healthy boundaries you set when you and your partner disagree, argue, or engage in challenging conversations. Establishing healthy "rules of engagement" is key to ensuring your arguments remain respectful and safe. Setting boundaries around how you will allow yourself to be spoken to or treated by the one you love is one limit you *can* enforce. I'll share resources here that will help.

STYLES OF SOCIALIZING: It's common for couples to have different preferences around the way they socialize with friends and family, spend quality time together, and get adequate time alone. Recognizing there is no one "right" way to socialize as a couple is a necessary first step; all that matters is that you find strategies that work for both of you. If one partner is feeling either stifled or energetically drained by your social encounters, I'll share some healthy boundary conversations you could initiate.

PRIVACY AND TRUST: Maintaining a sense of autonomy, personal space, and trust within your relationship is a must, and each of you has to determine what you are and are not comfortable with. Behaviors around the sharing of private relationship details; the security of your phones or email accounts; personal space (either individually or as a couple); and the agreements you make about your partnership are mission-critical to discuss, agree upon, and respect.

SEX AND PHYSICAL CONNECTION: I've saved this for last, because this could be its own chapter (and this issue is right up there with household management as a major area of conflict in relationships). When one partner wants or needs more physical connection than the other, it can lead to a negative feedback loop of nagging, feeling pressured, withdrawing, and feeling lonely or abandoned. This can't be solved with a boundary conversation—it requires a deeper level of communication and problem-solving, often with the help of a therapist. In the case of a partner initiating contact that feels uncomfortable, setting healthy boundaries around what kind of intimacy or touch feels good for you can be empowering and productive. We'll cover both boundary conversations and resources related to this topic.

ROMANTIC PARTNERSHIP BOUNDARIES AND PREP TIPS

Before we get into the scripts and resources, I want to stress how valuable a therapist or counselor can be for these conversations. The first thing I did when I realized Brandon and I were at an impasse with our plans to move in together was return to therapy. A therapist can be your relationship lifeline, acting as a neutral party, a safe space to vent, an experienced source of advice, and the most likely person to see things in your situation that you never would have seen on your own. Here are some tips for (and benefits of) seeking therapy to support your communication and boundary efforts with your partner.

- **GO FOR YOU.** While couple's therapy is an amazing tool to help partners communicate more effectively, you don't have to wait for your partner to agree to seek help. There are tremendous benefits to going by yourself, even if your intention is to improve your relationship.
- **BE THE CHANGE.** One person *can* change a dynamic. Going to therapy can help you notice patterns in how you respond to issues in your relationship. It is possible to change a partner-

ship by changing your own behavior. By working on yourself, you will show up differently for your partner, and that means things will shift.

- **TAKE RESPONSIBILITY.** Seeking therapy shows your partner that you take responsibility for your own feelings. This can model the kind of behavior you hope to see from your partner. It can also help to reassure them that you're doing your part; at the very least, it will help you regain your power in a situation in which you've likely felt powerless.

- **GET EXPERT ADVICE.** Some situations feel so big or heavy, it's hard to know what to do, or even what you can do. A therapist has probably seen the issues you're confronting before and can offer the most effective strategies for navigating challenging situations.

- **RECEIVE SUPPORT.** If things still don't change for the better, your therapist can support you in whatever decisions need to be made, offer advice for next steps, and share alternative resources.

While being able to attend therapy is a privilege, there are resources to help you find support within your budget, and apps or websites that allow you to meet with a therapist virtually. I always recommend that people start therapy *before* something stressful or painful happens, so when you do hit a speed bump, you'll already have an established relationship, history, and trust with a mental healthcare provider. And should your individual efforts later transition to couple's counseling, maintaining your individual sessions will help you process your own feelings and get the support you need to see you through during difficult times.

SCRIPTS FOR SETTING BOUNDARIES
AROUND HOUSEHOLD MANAGEMENT

For all the women reading right now, show of hands, how many of you wish you had more time for yourself? Oh look, it's literally ALL OF YOU, including the moms reading this on the toilet because that's the only place you can truly be alone in your own home. (And even that isn't a guarantee.) The women I talk to every day are *constantly* tired, and if my direct messages are any indication, their biggest source of fatigue is how much they're expected to do and how little their time is valued—most notably, by their own husbands. Let's talk about how unbalanced our division of household labor still is, at least in heterosexual couples.

Thanks to the patriarchy, sexism, and stereotypical assumptions about gender roles, women are overwhelmingly responsible for laundry, cleaning, cooking, caring for children, shopping for groceries, and washing dishes. In fact, a 2020 report by Oxfam and the Institute for Women's Policy Research estimates that women in the United States spend two hours more than men *every single day* doing this unpaid work—and that was *before* the pandemic. That figure doesn't disappear when women work full time, either—working women still spend an extra 1.1 hours a day, every day, on household labor.

That's between 401 and 730 hours of *extra* unpaid labor we do every year. Is it any wonder the subject of household labor comes up so often in straight relationships? (Of note: Research demonstrates that same-sex couples manage this division much more effectively and fairly. It's almost like removing traditional gender roles from the equation allows each partner to work toward a solution that benefits the family as a whole, delegating chores based on interest or proficiency rather than sexist stereotypes. *Interesting*.)

Every time I talk about setting boundaries with romantic partners, I receive an onslaught of messages from women, all asking the same thing: "How can my husband and I divide chores evenly?" "How can I get my husband to help more with the kids?" "I need him to do more around the house—is that even a boundary?" The number-one complaint I hear from wives in straight relationships is around the unfair division of household labor. And the truth is, that's not really a boundary issue; it's a communication and expectation-setting issue.

(Another interesting note: It appears the men in heterosexual relationships also want more time for themselves, and the thing they say would help the most is if their wives nagged them less often. Of course, that nagging usually comes in the form of . . . their wives asking for more help with household tasks. This section is gonna be *lit*.)

RESOURCE: *FAIR PLAY* BY EVE RODSKY

Entire books have been written on this subject, and my favorite by far is *Fair Play* by Eve Rodsky. It's a guide to aligning your expectations around household management; identifying the tasks that need managing; and having one person own all three components of every task: conception, planning, and execution. Here's an example of how I've applied Rodsky's philosophy to one household task in my own life: "trash day":

- **Conception:** Noticing that the trash needs to be taken to the curb every Monday night. If you don't know that, "trash day" can't be completed.
- **Planning:** Observing that it's Monday, several garbage cans throughout the house need to be emptied, and there are cardboard boxes from deliveries that need to be broken down for recycling.
- **Execution:** Breaking down the boxes and taking them out to the recycling bin; taking out the kitchen, bathroom, and office trash (and re-

placing the trash bags); and rolling both bins to the curb for garbage pickup.

In heterosexual relationships, men often handle some of the execution piece when their wives say, "Remember, tomorrow is trash day," but all too often that means just rolling the bins to the curb. That leaves the burden of conception, planning, *and* the bulk of the execution on the women in those relationships—and that's just one task out of hundreds that go into successfully running a household and family.

In Rodsky's *Fair Play* system, each household task is fully owned by one person all the way through, from conception to planning to execution. This encourages partners to evenly manage the invisible labor that goes into so many household tasks. Rodsky also recommends establishing a "minimum standard of care" for each task, where each partner agrees on what it means to say a task is "completed"—so when you say "it's garbage day," everyone understands that means dispensing of all of the garbage in the house *and* the cardboard boxes.

This model is borrowed from corporate organizational management and helps you treat your household like the complex and dynamic business that it is. Rodsky says her *Fair Play* system accomplishes two things: It alleviates the mental load for the partner managing the household tasks (typically women), and it eliminates nagging, which is the number-one complaint men have about home life. Win-win.

The scripts you'll find in this chapter can help you preserve your own time, energy, and capacity as you establish an equitable system for household management—although you'll still find that holding your own boundary may not be in the best interest of your family. That's where the *Fair Play* system comes in. Between Rodsky's system and the conversations and boundary scripts I'll outline in this section, you'll be well on your way to identifying, acknowledging, and redistributing the incredible amount of labor that goes into running a household, and setting limits where needed to ensure your time and input are valued and respected.

> **My spouse says they'll help with tasks, like doing the dishes or folding the laundry, but then they only do half the actual task— they'll wash the dishes but not put them away, or fold the laundry but leave it in the living room. This doesn't meet my expectations. How can I communicate this?**
>
> **GREEN:** "Hey, babe, when someone does the dishes, we agreed that also means putting them away."
>
> **YELLOW:** "Billy, we need the dishes—the kids are about to set the table, and my job is dinner, not dishes."
>
> **RED:** (away from the task, in a calm moment) "We've discussed my need for a fair division of household labor, and I'm still regularly completing tasks that we agreed are yours. This is bigger than just the dishes, and the resentment I'm feeling isn't healthy for our relationship. I'm going to talk with a therapist about next steps, because this is not working for me."
>
> *Establishing an agreed-upon minimum standard of care (as recommended in* Fair Play*) for household tasks is the first step here, but ultimately, your boundary is, "I'm not swooping in to do the things you've committed to doing." There are no easy answers here, because you can't force your partner to do their fair share or value your efforts, but your Yellow and Red boundaries demonstrate that you are taking responsibility for your own needs, and that you'll do what needs to be done to ensure they are met.*

> **We have an infant and I'm going back to work. I need my partner to start waking up earlier to share in the responsibilities of**

everything that needs to get done in the morning. How can we tackle this?

GREEN: "Can we talk about what the morning routine looks like once I return to work, and who's going to do what?"

YELLOW: "You can be on baby duty from 6 to 6:30 A.M. so I can shower and get ready, or you can get ready first, and take her from 6:30 to 7 A.M. What's better for you?"

RED: "Next week, I need you on baby duty from 6 to 6:30 A.M. so I can get ready for work."

Start with Green, and outline everything that needs to happen in the morning for you and your partner to be able to walk out the door—from showering and making breakfast to packing bottles to dropping the baby off with your caregiver. Involve your partner in the process of figuring out who does what and when, so they feel the true partnership in this big occasion and so they can see all of the invisible labor that goes into caring for a new baby when both parents work.

PUT IT ON A SCHEDULE

I remember complaining to my therapist that I was struggling to stick to my morning routine and get my kid to school on time, but I felt bad asking Brandon to take him. My new husband frequently asked, "How can I help?" but I was so used to doing everything myself and wasn't yet over the hump that my son was now *our* child, and therefore *our* shared responsibility. "Why don't you put it on a schedule?" my therapist asked me, and the clouds parted and the angels sang. Now on Tuesdays and Thursdays, my husband is on kid duty, from wake-up to breakfast to getting dressed and going to school. Even if I'm home, *it's not my day,* which leaves me free to work out, start work early, take the dog for a long walk—whatever I want. It was the single best piece of advice I've received around sharing household responsibilities, and now I ask everyone, "Can you put it on a schedule?"

My partner doesn't consult me when making big financial purchases. He bought a second "fun" (and expensive) car without even talking to me! But he's the wage earner in our family (I stay home with the kids) and he says it's his money. What can I say in this situation?

GREEN: "This marriage is a partnership in all areas. I'd like to make decisions involving our finances together, just like the decisions we make about the kids or the house."

YELLOW: "I expect to be consulted before we make a large purchase. When you don't do that, I feel disrespected and disregarded, and that's not a healthy place for a relationship to be."

RED: "This relationship isn't going to work if you don't value my contributions or input."

When a spouse says something like "It's my money," that demonstrates a lack of value or respect for everything you do to manage your household. Fun experiment: Tally up everything you do around the house—all of the cleaning, meal prep and cooking, nannying, chauffeuring, pet care, errands, and personal-assistant work—and figure out how much it would cost to outsource all of that work. Perhaps being presented with a bill at the end of the week would change your husband's perspective. An alternative (if you don't want to go that hard) is to request a monthly finance meeting where you and your spouse meet to go over bank balances, spending, and budgets together. You could also establish an "up to" limit where each of you can spend without asking below the limit, but anything above that limit requires a consultation. Establishing shared expectations and why they matter, then approaching the issue as a team and holding each other accountable is key.

My partner and I recently moved in together, and slowly all of my "things" started to disappear. My art isn't to their taste, my furniture isn't as comfortable, and now everything we have in our shared space is theirs. Decorating a home together was something I looked forward to, but now, where I live doesn't feel like me. What can I do?

GREEN: "I'd like to design our new space together, so we both feel comfortable and at home. Let's talk about which pieces are important to each of us, and where they might fit."

YELLOW: "These three pieces are really special to me, so let's find a place for them."

RED: "My favorite rocking chair is staying, as is this piece of art."

If your velvet "dogs playing poker" is a real clash with the space's mid-century modern design, what else could you do? Can you decorate your office however you want? Sell most of the furniture and buy new things together? Take a purely objective approach (like "Whose coffee table is in better shape?") or find a less prominent spot for things that are meaningful or sentimental to you?

SCRIPTS FOR SETTING BOUNDARIES AROUND INTERPERSONAL CONFLICT

Every relationship experiences conflict, and how you handle it can make or break your sense of trust, safety, and connection. One of the first things relationship experts recommend is to create "rules of engagement" around arguments *before* they happen. This helps set the stage for how you'll behave when tempers flare and emotions run hot. Some general rules include no name-calling, no threats, and no yelling, but here are some additional guidelines that my husband and I have found helpful:

DO NOT USE THE OTHER PERSON'S DEEPEST FEARS AGAINST THEM. Brandon and I know each other well—we know what the mean voices inside our heads tell us when we're feeling insecure or stressed, and we know the one button we could push that would inflict the most damage. Using that knowledge against the other person in the midst of an argument (or at any point, really) is strictly off-limits.

CREATE A "CODE PHRASE" TO INTERRUPT THE PATTERN. We use one that immediately puts the conversation into perspective if one of us is feeling overwhelmed: "Remember we're a team." It's a reminder that we're not actually adversaries, no matter how it might feel in the moment. Our shared goal is to figure things out *together*. Invoking our code phrase is almost always effective at shifting the energy and our moods.

STICK TO ONE SUBJECT DURING ARGUMENTS. This helps us come to actual resolution and not deviate down the path to Everything That's Ever Been Wrong Ever–land. Bringing up fights from two years ago or "well, what about when you do this" is never helpful or productive, so we made a deal that we stick to one topic at a time, and stay with it until it feels appropriately resolved.

HONOR REQUESTS FOR A TIME-OUT. At any point, either one of us may ask to remove ourselves from the situation to gain perspective or cool off, and giving each other that time always helps our shared cause. However, the person who requested the time-out must come back to the conversation within a reasonable amount of time. Yes, sometimes we do go to bed angry, but we agree to talk about it the next morning after a good night's sleep, and that works for us.

RESOURCE: *NONVIOLENT COMMUNICATION* BY MARSHALL B. ROSENBERG, PHD

Don't let the title of this book scare you—you don't have to be engaged in shouting matches or throwing dishes to recognize that the way you and your partner argue often harms each other. *Nonviolent Communication* (NVC) will help you learn to express yourself clearly and honestly while actively listening to your partner's needs. NVC is an active practice of compassionate communication that invites collaborative problem-solving instead of the typical ways you're used to framing discussions (with a lot of "you did this" and "you shouldn't do that"). The objective of NVC is to help you and your partner understand your feelings, express clear requests to have them met, listen empathetically and compassionately to each other, and arrive at a solution together.

There are four steps to the NVC communication model: observations, feelings, needs, and requests. Using a situation I often hear from my community—when one partner goes out more than the other expects—here is how the NVC process would look for the *speaker*:

- **Observations:** Share whatever you noticed without judgment, using neutral descriptors. So "You'd rather go out with friends than be with your family," turns into "I noticed you came home at 8:00 today instead of 6:00." Shifts like this can help prevent defensiveness in your partner.
- **Feelings:** Take accountability for how you feel. (If it helps, refer to a "feelings inventory" resource to help you pinpoint what you're experiencing.)

- **Needs:** Connect those feelings with the need left unmet. In this model, instead of "You're so inconsiderate," you might say, "I feel frustrated and hurt [feelings] because I end up eating dinner alone [my need for connection and inclusion was not met]."

- **Request:** Directly ask your partner to help you address those feelings and needs. That turns "Stop going out for drinks after work" to "Would you be willing to come home three nights a week after work so we could have dinner together?"

For the *listener*, NVC prioritizes listening instead of gearing up for our response, seeking understanding rather than "winning" an argument, and compassion for the partner you love so dearly. A word of warning—it does sound like therapy-speak, which might turn some people off at first. But the structure is just a starting point to give you a new framework for communication, and with practice and commitment, it'll feel natural to use statements like "I feel" and "Would you be willing . . . ?" This framework can be radically transformative for so many relationships, and it might be just the tool you and your partner need to shift the way you listen, understand, and communicate.

I apply some of the NVC framework in these boundary scripts, as well as some common rules of engagement. Once you have basic communication styles and a set of shared expectations around conflict, setting and holding boundaries around your mental health, sense of safety, and relationship will be much easier.

When my spouse and I argue, I am pretty good about staying calm and speaking cordially. They struggle with this, and often use an aggressive tone or say mean things. I'd like to make a rule that we don't let arguments turn personal or nasty. How can I do this?

GREEN: "You just called me a name, and now I'm feeling anxious. I need to feel respected and safe when we communicate. Are you willing to do a quick reset with me?"

YELLOW: "I will not stay in this discussion if you continue to speak to me like that. I'd like us to go back to our NVC model. Are you willing to do that?"

RED: "The way you're speaking to me is not okay. I'm going to step out; let me know when you're ready to have a respectful conversation."

During cooler moments, explain that when things get heated or one of you breaks your "rules of engagement," you're more likely to say things you don't mean, or behave in a way that would be harmful. Taking a break allows you to calm down and show up again as your best self so that you can reach a resolution together. Explaining this can reassure your partner that you're not abandoning them or punishing them by leaving.

My partner comes home from work and immediately starts to vent about the hardest parts of their day. Their job is stressful, I know, but I also just got home, and it makes me even more stressed when I should be trying to unwind. Help?

GREEN: "Hey, babe. I for sure want to hear about your day, but could I get twenty minutes to decompress before we get into it?"

YELLOW: "Ooh—can we pause? I just got home, too, and I'm going to take a quick shower first to reset from my day."

RED: "I'm over capacity and can't handle a vent session. Can we take the night off from work talk?"

Even better, can you automate this boundary? Sit down during a relaxing weekend and talk about what you'd like your first thirty minutes at home together to look like. "I hate starting our nights together by venting about work the second we walk in the door. Can we make a rule of no work talk until after dinner, so we can both relax and decompress?" Maybe your partner

will find a half hour of reading, a quick workout, or cooking
dinner so relaxing, they won't need to vent so hard.

My spouse often agrees to things, then gets mad at me after the
fact. Last weekend, they agreed we should skip brunch with
friends so we could finish the yardwork, but an hour into it,
they blew up at me for "making" them miss the fun. How can I
nicely say, "I'm not a mind reader, and this is passive-aggressive?"

GREEN: "Honey, I'm feeling frustrated. You agreed we needed to
finish the yardwork, and I trusted that you were okay with that
decision. You can be upset about missing brunch, but please
don't take that out on me."

YELLOW: "I can't help if you won't tell me the truth about how
you really feel."

RED: "We aren't communicating effectively here, and I'd like to
bring in an expert to help us."

Remind your partner that you're not a mind reader, and that it's
an unhealthy communication pattern for them to expect you to
guess how they really feel or try to tease it out of them. Model
the Golden Rule for them by sharing your truth clearly. And if
they do get mad after the fact, show empathy ("Yeah, brunch would
have been way more fun"), rather than taking it personally.

My partner constantly criticizes my appearance, like what I'm
wearing or the way I've applied my makeup. Sometimes I'm not
dressed up enough, other times I'm overdoing it. I'm not very
confident in my style anyway, and this just serves to make me
even more insecure. How can I explain this?

GREEN: "Babe, unless my pants have a hole in them or I have
lipstick on my teeth, please don't offer unsolicited advice about

my appearance. Regardless of your intention, it doesn't feel supportive."

YELLOW: "Hey—please don't. You're either trying to hit my self-confidence or control how I dress, and neither is okay."

RED: "I'm not asking for your opinion."

This speaks to a bigger issue, which is you getting confident in your own style and preferences, and your partner's not-so-subtle attempts to control your body and appearance. (Might I suggest talking to a therapist?) I also had a partner who used to do this—once I bought a pair of leather pants and was so excited to wear them out to dinner, until he said, "You're not wearing those out with me." I looked him straight in the eye and said, "I am, unless you're gonna stay home." We did not have that conversation again.

During arguments, my partner is constantly projecting my feelings, using "always" and "never" statements, and telling me what I want. This is not a healthy way to disagree, but I don't know how to change the dynamic. Is this even a boundary?

GREEN: "I notice you're making assumptions about how I feel. What I'm actually feeling is sad because I hoped this discussion would be more collaborative. It would help if I knew how you felt—are you willing to share?"

YELLOW: "You're still trying to assign me feelings, and now I am frustrated, because I don't think we're communicating effectively. To continue, we each need to take responsibility for our own feelings."

RED: "I'm feeling really unheard right now. I'm going to take a break. I'll come back in an hour and we can try again."

A reader sent in the phrase "Please don't assign me feelings," and I loved it so much I'm using it here. You can't make your partner use certain phrases, but you can model "I" statements for them. Therapy is super helpful here, too. Remember you're only responsible for your half of this relationship, but one person can influence change: Even if only one of you is using NVC, that's a 50 percent improvement already.

THE "ALWAYS" AND "NEVER" TRAP

It can be tempting to follow an "always" or "never" statement with examples of when you didn't or did, but that's only going to take you further off track. Yes, you *do* help around the house, but bringing up the last three instances in great detail isn't addressing a deeper issue. Instead of chasing after the "always" or "never," think about the feelings and needs behind those words. "You never help with the kids" means "I'm totally overwhelmed and need your help." "You always take her side" means "I'm not feeling like a team here, and that scares me." Read between the lines, ignore the hyperbole, and address what you're hearing. Remember, the goal isn't to win; it's to approach the discussion with compassion and arrive at an agreeable solution together.

SCRIPTS FOR SETTING BOUNDARIES AROUND SOCIALIZING

If you and your partner struggle with how much you each like to socialize, how you socialize, and how much of it you do together, I'd apply the YCDI framework here immediately. I know couples who spend *all* their time together, socializing with other people very little and preferring each other's company. (The idea gives me hives, but you do you.) I also know couples where one person goes out with friends or colleagues most nights of the week, and often leaves their more introverted spouse at home—and that works for them both.

Get over the idea that a healthy relationship "should" look a certain way. Recognizing that each person has different needs around socializing and friend groups, and structuring your lives in a way that suits both people, is the big win, even if nobody else "gets it." I'll share boundary scripts here that run the gamut, helping you find the words to set the healthy limits that could bring you and your partner even more freedom within your relationship.

> **I love social activities because they boost my energy. My partner is the opposite; they don't love socializing and would rather spend time at home. So I often make plans without them, but then they get upset and resentful. How can I balance our needs?**
>
> This isn't really a boundary issue, unless your limit is "I can only stay home with you four nights in a row before I'll lose my mind." (Which *might* be necessary to say out loud.) Instead of Green/Yellow/Red, let's talk about options for partners who have different social drives and preferences.

- **Invite feedback.** Is there something specific about your social activities that your partner would like to talk about? Maybe they get worried when you stay out late drinking, or they get frustrated because you're always picking up the bill— something you could address (or not, but at least hear your partner out).
- **Seek to understand.** Does your partner worry your socializing means you like your friends better than you like them? Or that you're getting tired of them? Having an open conversation

about your partner's deeper feelings, especially their insecurities, might help.

- **Find ways to improve the dynamic.** Ask if there's anything else you could do to make your partner enjoy socializing with you more. Maybe they don't like being left in the dust the second you get to the party and see your friends, or they would love to join you for dinner, but not at a nightclub. Or perhaps they'd enjoy socializing from the comfort of home, and inviting people over makes everyone happy.
- **Be flexible.** Invite your partner to join you for part of the night. Maybe they'd like to be more social with you, but don't enjoy staying as long or as late as you. (This is why God invented ride-sharing.)
- **Be conscientious.** Ask if there are nights your partner would really like you to be home during the week, or offer to split the weekend with them, so you're always home either Friday or Saturday for quality time.
- **Agree to a compromise.** Suggest you'll only ask your partner to attend events that are really important to you, and if they ever tell you they really want you to stay home, you will. (This works as long as neither of you abuses it.)

If your partner would truly rather stay home and you need the social engagement for your mental health, set a boundary. That could look like: "I'm not asking you to socialize when you don't want to, because I know you wouldn't enjoy that. Please don't ask me to stay home when you know that being around friends is good for my mental health." If your partner just can't get past the resentment or frustration, talk to a therapist about next steps.

I need regular alone time to recharge and I don't know how to ask for it in my new relationship without sounding selfish or

cold. What can I say when my partner asks for an overnight I just don't want?

GREEN: "I could use a night to myself, so I'll call you tomorrow. Have a great night."

YELLOW: "No thanks, I can sense I'm ready for some quiet time to recharge."

RED: "Alone time has always been important for my mental health. If we're going to continue dating, we need to find a way to work this into our routine."

I'm sharing boundary scripts here because the specific wording might be helpful, but even before setting a boundary, it's important to have a conversation with your partner about what alone time means to you, and specifically how it benefits you as a couple. When I take an hour, a night, or a weekend by myself, I come home happier and more enthusiastic about reconnecting deeply and intimately, and the time apart helps me preserve my sense of independence and autonomy—which my husband finds attractive.

I'm a working mother of three boys, and by Sunday afternoon, the constant interruptions, lack of personal space, and noise levels have me spinning. Can I ask my whole house—including my wife—for a moment of silence? I'm only half kidding.

GREEN: "Please take your Nerf guns outside / people playing video games need to be wearing headphones / the TV volume can't go above 15."

YELLOW: (agreed upon with your wife) "I'm taking a quiet hour in my room. You can keep playing, but if you need something, please ask Mama."

RED: "This house is taking a quiet hour today from 2 to 3 P.M. You can read, take a nap, or watch something on your tablet with headphones."

We do "quiet hours" on many weekends, and it's magical—my son doesn't have to sleep, but he has to stay quietly in his room and read or play on his own, and I get the silence I'm craving. Also, may I suggest investing in a pair of noise-canceling headphones? Automate that boundary.

My boyfriend enjoys fast-paced hobbies, like downhill skiing, motorcycle riding, and CrossFit. At his encouragement, I've tried them all, and they're just not for me—I have a low risk tolerance and prefer hiking or reading books. I love that he has his own things, but he gets mad at me when I won't participate with him.

GREEN: "I don't enjoy all the same things you do, and I need you to respect that. It's good that we have our own interests, and I'll never force you to go hiking with me."

YELLOW: "You know I don't like to ski, so please don't pressure me. Go have fun."

RED: "The way you behave when I say no is a problem for me."

Use this as an opportunity to start a conversation about why it bothers him that you don't enjoy the same hobbies. Maybe he's never had a healthy relationship where each partner encourages the other's independence, or maybe he thinks this disparity will lead to too much time apart. Talk about what's behind his anger so you can determine your next steps.

SCRIPTS FOR SETTING BOUNDARIES
AROUND PRIVACY AND TRUST

Here's where clear communication and expectation-setting really come into play. Yes, it's relatively easy to hold a boundary around not sharing your email password, spilling your friend's secret, or opening up about past romantic partners, but having a conversation up front about issues of privacy and trust can go a long way in not needing a boundary at all, or feeling more empowered to set one should someone cross a line.

From the questions people have written me about privacy and trust issues in romantic relationships—and from my own experience—these are the topics that come up with the most frequency:

- Sharing personal details or photos of your partner with friends, family, or on social media
- Sharing personal details with your partner, such as your sexual history or specific details around trauma
- Sharing passwords for phones, computers, or online accounts
- Looking through each other's texts, photos, emails, or credit card statements
- Respecting personal space at home or in public

If you haven't already, consider discussing each of these topics with your partner and ask each other how you feel about things like posting photos of them on social media without their permission; whether you're okay with them going through your phone; or how much privacy you expect at home. Can you agree on a policy of knocking before entering, asking permission before sharing photos or details of your vacation on Instagram, or respecting each person's right to privacy when out with friends?

Remember the YCDI principle—just because other couples

share every password doesn't mean you and your partner have to. Having the conversation, setting expectations, then reinforcing them with clear, kind boundaries will ensure you'll preserve the sense of respect and trust that every relationship deserves.

> **I've caught my partner going through my texts and photos a few times now when my phone was left unlocked. This is a violation of trust and not how I want us to treat each other in our relationship. How can I talk about this with them without making it seem like I'm hiding something—because I'm not!**
>
> **GREEN:** "Please don't go through my phone without my permission. That's a violation of my trust and that isn't how I want us to behave toward each other."
>
> **YELLOW:** "Snooping on each other is not healthy for our relationship. Please don't do it again."
>
> **RED:** "I can't stay in a relationship that isn't trusting or respectful. I've made an appointment with a relationship counselor—you can join me, or I'll go alone."
>
> *How you choose to handle privacy in your relationship is up to you, as long as you agree on what is and is not acceptable. If you have agreed to reasonable expectations of privacy, your partner needs to respect that, and address any issues of insecurity, jealousy, anxiety, or control in a healthier and more straightforward manner.*

> **My spouse overshares details of our private life (especially arguments) with his parents, and it impacts our relationship. I feel that my in-laws are judgmental and already overinvolved in their son's life, and hearing details about our relationship has affected how they treat me. How should I handle this?**

Is your boundary that you don't want your spouse to discuss certain things with his parents, or that you don't want his parents to bring those things up with you? Get clear on your request before having a conversation with your spouse. I'll assume it's the former, as the latter boundary would need to be set with your in-laws directly.

GREEN: "To be clear, this argument/discussion/situation is not something I want you sharing with your parents. What you tell them impacts how they treat me, and long after we've resolved an issue, they continue to hold it against me. That isn't helpful for my relationship with them or you."

YELLOW: "I will only have this conversation if you agree not to share it with your parents. It's not their business and their input is harmful."

RED: "I'm talking to my therapist about how I should respond to your lack of respect for my privacy and our marriage."

If your spouse (understandably) wants someone to talk to about these issues, think about who you are okay with them confiding in or seeking advice from. Agree on people you know will maintain perspective and not insert themselves into your relationship inappropriately. For me, it's my sister. For my husband, it's one of his best friends, or his therapist.

I'm dating someone new, although neither of us is looking for a serious relationship right now. If the person I'm seeing starts dating someone else, though, I'd like to know. Is that fair to ask?

GREEN: "You said you're not dating anyone else right now. If that changes or you decide to get active on Tinder again, would you please let me know? I'll do the same; I'd like us both to be transparent here."

YELLOW: "I have one rule: Please let me know if you start seeing anyone else. If you can't agree to that, I can't keep seeing you."

RED: "I asked for one thing, and you weren't honest with me. This is over."

This is an example of a boundary you can't hold; you have to trust that your partner hears your limit and will respect that. Unfortunately, the Red boundary means it's too little, too late, and all you can do is enforce the consequences of their disrespect.

My spouse has no concept of personal space—she'll pee with the door wide open, walk into the bathroom when I'm showering without knocking, and will stand outside the door to the toilet to ask me a question. She doesn't think twice, but I need some boundaries here.

GREEN: "Hey, babe, I'd like a little more mystery in our relationship. Can you knock first if I'm in the shower or wait until I'm done, and close the door when you use the bathroom?"

YELLOW: "Jeez, honey, I've asked you to please knock before barging in. Please let me finish."

RED: "Hey, I'm jumping in the shower now." Automate the boundary by locking the bathroom door.

Continuing the conversation by discussing differences in how you were raised, self-consciousness you might have around your body or bodily functions, or the private rituals you'd rather your spouse not bear witness to (ahem, shaving down there) can deepen your connection and reduce hurt feelings.

My new boyfriend keeps asking me for details of my past relationships—how many sexual partners I've had, whether we've done this or that in bed, have I ever had a one-night

stand. I don't think sharing that at this stage would be helpful, but do I owe him a conversation about my past?

GREEN: "I don't want to talk about our past relationships, especially sexual details like that. Is there a reason you're bringing it up?"

YELLOW: "I can't see why that's important at this stage, and I'd rather not talk about it."

RED: "If we can't move past these kinds of questions, I don't think this is the right relationship for me."

Your Green boundary invites follow-up conversation around why they might be asking. Maybe they're worried because they're inexperienced in the bedroom, or they have an STI (sexually transmitted infection) and they're using this line of questioning as a roundabout route to talking about it. If those kinds of conversations don't evolve and your partner keeps asking questions you're not comfortable with, this could be a relationship red flag.

SCRIPTS FOR SETTING BOUNDARIES AROUND SEX AND PHYSICAL CONNECTION

Setting boundaries in other categories of your life may be uncomfortable, but for many people (especially those with a history of trauma), setting boundaries around sex and physical touch can feel extra-intimidating. The patriarchy, stereotypical gender roles, religious and political influences, and the media have imprinted onto women that our role is to serve/please/give. People who have suffered sexual or physical abuse or trauma are often left feeling like their value resides in their bodies and what they're willing to do with them, or that they don't have or deserve full bodily autonomy. I struggled for many years to set any boundaries with romantic partners, and I often found myself saying yes to things I didn't want to do out of a sense of obligation, pressure, or fear around what would happen if I said no.

The most important piece of advice I've been given when it comes to setting and upholding boundaries around my body in romantic relationships is to take responsibility for my own sexual pleasure—a sentiment echoed by many marriage and sex therapists. When you are focused on your partner's pleasure ("does this feel good for them, am I turning them on, am I going to satisfy them?"), the only successful outcome is the result *they* achieve. And if your partner doesn't indicate that you've performed a 10/10 for them, then you worry that says something about you—cue the insecurity, self-esteem issues, and anxiety around sex, your body, and your worth.

Even if your partner does give you a sex gold medal, who was looking after *your* pleasure while you were together? Surely, you'd hope, your partner . . . but what if they don't? (Something women in heterosexual relationships say happens far too often.) And how much responsibility can another person even take for what's going on inside *your* head, heart, and body—especially if you aren't communicating that in the moment?

The bigger picture here—to bring it back around to boundaries—is that focusing only on your partner's pleasure makes it hard to see whether or not your own boundaries are being respected, or even where those boundaries are. If your partner's erection is the signal that sex is imminent and their climax is the signal that it's over, where does that leave your desires, mood, readiness, or agency? (Again, we're mostly talking about straight couples here—it appears, once again, that same-sex partnerships tend to fare better in terms of sexual desire and, notably, orgasm achievement, particularly in lesbian couples.)

Taking responsibility for your own sexual pleasure doesn't mean gratifying yourself at the expense of your partner. It simply serves to reconnect you with your own body, desires, and feelings in the moment. When you take responsibility for your own pleasure, you're constantly checking in with yourself, asking, "Does this feel good? Do I want more or less? Do I want something else? Do I want this to continue?" If you develop a practice of holding yourself accountable for your own pleasure, you're more likely to communicate your needs to your partner, ask for what you want, and use clear, kind language to get there. (It's like we're wrapping up the Golden Rule, YCDI, and the clear, kind tone of healthy boundaries in one beautiful package.) In addition, the kind of self-disclosure, open sharing, and vulnerability that comes with this level of communication can be wickedly sexy, and very connecting.

Shifting the focus back to your own sexual pleasure doesn't guarantee an earth-shattering orgasm every time you couple—but it does put you back in the driver's seat as to what you do with your own body, and that makes it easier to know what you want *and* helps you to communicate that in the form of boundaries, if you need to.

RESOURCE: *COME AS YOU ARE: THE SURPRISING NEW SCIENCE THAT WILL TRANSFORM YOUR SEX LIFE,* BY EMILY NAGOSKI

Considered one of the most important books on sexual desire, *Come As You Are* is a scientific exploration of how women's sexuality works, and the most important factors for women to create a fulfilling sex life. If the idea of owning your sexual pleasure feels intimidating or you don't know where to start, Nagoski wrote *the* book on it. And though it focuses on people with vaginas, when relationship legend John Gottman says it's a "necessary guide for all couples," people with penises should also pay attention.

Nagoski's book goes beyond "what happens" in sexual response—desire, arousal, orgasm—and delves into the *why* and *how* processes that underlie those behaviors. The mechanism is based on two functions that occur in every human being: the sexual accelerator, known as "turn-ons," and the sexual brakes, or "turn-offs." How those two functions show up varies greatly from person to person, and understanding and embracing how *your* accelerator and brakes work is the key to long-term sexual fulfillment. Ultimately, the true gift of *Come As You Are* is to help you answer the question "Am I normal?" (spoiler: YES), and provide you with a path to change and heal your sexual functioning, no matter where you're starting from.

Communicating your boundaries in the bedroom (and in other intimate spaces) can be a powerful step toward reconnecting with your needs, taking responsibility for your own pleasure, and reminding yourself of your worth and value. Let's practice how you could do that in the moment with this scripts section.

I do a lot of things in the bedroom I don't want to do because my partner gets hurt feelings so fast when it comes to sex. How can I communicate what I do and don't want in the moment?

GREEN: "Ooh, I'm not into that / I'm not ready for that yet / I don't like that / that's not something I want to try right now. Can you/we [offer alternative] instead?"

YELLOW: (stop the action) "No, I don't want to do that. Are we clear? Don't do that again."

RED: "No." Physically remove yourself, as this is now assault.

Repeat after me: I am not responsible for my partner's feelings. You can certainly initiate a conversation around your sexual preferences, what a no means (I'm uncomfortable, it hurts too much, I don't enjoy the sensation, it doesn't feel safe for me), and reassure your partner that you're declining the action, not them personally. If they are so easily hurt by a clearly communicated no in the bedroom, they have work to do, and you cannot "fix" it by giving in when you don't want to. (P.S. By refusing to take responsibility for their feelings, you'll find out real fast if their "hurt feelings" were actually a manipulation tactic.)

LET'S TALK ABOUT SEX

Communicating clear boundaries leads to a safe and pleasurable experience for both of you. In the moment, your partner needs to respect your no and *immediately* shift into something you both consent to. Things that are *not* an excuse for pressuring you or disrespecting your boundaries:

- You've really turned them on.
- They're "so close" to finishing.
- You've done it before with other people.
- You've done it before with them.
- You did say yes, and have changed your mind.
- You're married.

It may feel uncomfortable to open up a conversation with, "So, how do you feel about anal?" but the alternative is the awkwardness of discovering your partner *really* isn't into something in the heat of the moment. My husband and I have had our best conversations about sex during relaxed moments on vacation, where we're not feeling pressured or stressed and we can approach the subject with curiosity and playfulness.

I want new sexual partners to wear a condom, but you wouldn't believe the excuses I hear and pressure I receive when I bring it up. I've given in more than once. How can I stand my ground?

GREEN: "Did you bring a condom? If not, I have one for you."

YELLOW: "If you won't wear it, none of this is happening."

RED: "Bye."

Tee this up early, well before your clothes come off. "We can do that, if you wear a condom, and that condom stays on. Is that an issue?" If they give you any back talk, interrupt: "It's non-negotiable, buddy." Any pushback after a Yellow boundary is a permanent deal-breaker—if your partner won't respect your boundaries here, they're not worthy, and sharing your boundaries early and seeing how they respond is a great litmus test for the relationship.

My partner wakes up earlier than I do and loves to reach over and snuggle me. I appreciate the loving act, but I'm usually still in my sleep cycle and I don't like to be disturbed. How can we compromise here?

GREEN: (the night before) "If you wake up early tomorrow and I'm still sleeping, please don't snuggle me. We'll get some time in tonight while we watch a movie."

YELLOW: "I don't want to snuggle in the morning before I'm awake."

RED: "If you keep touching me in the morning after I've asked you not to, I'm going to sleep in the guest room."

Yes, you can set a boundary in the moment, but it's kind of too late at that point, as you're already awake! Start the night before by talking about your differences in sleep preferences and looking for compromises. Maybe you want to sleep until your alarm goes off during the week to make sure you're rested, but weekend mornings can be for snuggling. Or maybe your partner would be happy with an extra-long hug once you do wake up. The best way to avoid snuggling when you don't want to (and then being resentful all morning) is to communicate clearly before you even get in bed.

There is one area of my body that I just don't like to be touched—my stomach. How can I let any prospective partners know that area is off-limits?

GREEN: "Ooh, anywhere but my stomach. I don't enjoy that."

YELLOW: "I don't like having my stomach touched. Please don't."

RED: Remove yourself from the situation.

You may need to remind someone new a few times and forgive accidental or unintentional contact (like if they reach over you for something). Feel free to explain that it's a sensitive area for you, it's related to trauma, or it just feels too ticklish to be enjoyable. Or don't. Consent must be respected even without an explanation.

My partner makes sexual advances during the most inopportune times, like when I'm fresh out of the shower and getting dressed for work. It looks sexy in the movies, but in real life, no, I cannot be late. How can I get my partner to read the room?

GREEN: (during a quiet moment) "It's not you—I just can't get into the mood right before work when I'm already pressed for time and thinking about my day. How about Saturday, I put on a suit for you . . ."

YELLOW: (with a kiss) "I love you, and sadly this isn't happening for me right now. Save this energy for after work."

RED: "No." Leave the bedroom.

Some other thoughts: If the idea of "making you late" is a turn-on for both of you, find other (less pressing) events to be late for. Maybe your partner is just more eager in the morning—could you get up a little earlier once in a while, or make it a point to spend longer in bed on Saturdays? Or maybe your partner just wants a moment of connection before they start their day, and an extra-long hug with a butt-grab would do the trick without making you late.

LOVING THE LIMITS THAT SET YOU FREE

Some of the most important boundaries you set in your romantic relationships might just be with yourself. With my history of sexual trauma and addiction, and having experienced infidelity in the past, I didn't always operate as my highest self in relationships. When Brandon and I started getting serious, I knew I had to set some boundaries with myself so I could be the best version of me, and not bring any of my own baggage into our connection. I silently committed to myself that when it came to my new relationship:

- I would not snoop through any of Brandon's private things—phone, email, or packages.
- I would not grill him for details about who he was with or what he did when he went out.
- I would not search for his female friends on social media.
- I would not agree to anything I wasn't comfortable with physically.
- I would never fake my own pleasure during sex.
- I would not run away if I was feeling vulnerable.

And I committed to doing the following:

- I would tell him if my recovery was feeling shaky.
- I would tell him if I was feeling jealous or insecure, and why.
- I would take active responsibility for my own mental health.

Many of these boundaries became irrelevant pretty quickly. Once Brandon and I established a baseline level of trust and I unpacked some of what happened in my last relationship, I found that the anxiety I had around things like fidelity simply disappeared. Other boundaries, I hold to this day, like not faking my own pleasure (a remnant of my sexual trauma, and something I did regularly pre-Brandon) and taking responsibility for my own mental health.

Boundaries are a two-way street: You can expect others to respect yours, and you need to make it a priority to respect others' for the good of your relationship. But don't overlook the power of *self-boundaries* in all of your relationships, too. For me, creating strict guidelines around what *I* would or would not do in my relationship contributes to its success just as much as the boundaries my partner and I set with each other.

CHAPTER 7

When You Can't Just Walk Away

Setting Boundaries with Co-Parents

Emily wrote to me after hearing my podcast episode about divorce. She was recently divorced herself and was struggling to establish a new relationship with her ex-wife, Shannon. They had two young kids who went back and forth between Emily's and Shannon's homes, and though the divorce was settled relatively amicably, there were still hurt feelings and big emotions just under the surface. "Sometimes I fall back into talking to her like she's my best friend. Sometimes we're fighting like mortal enemies. We're trying to keep the kids in mind through all of this, but I'm not always proud of how I'm acting."

I've been co-parenting with my ex-husband for over eight years now—since my son was just a year old—and reading Emily's email brought it all back for me. In the past, when I'd ended a long-term relationship, the person I was splitting up with and I almost always went our separate ways. I certainly didn't *have* to talk to them again if I didn't want to, and it was often less painful to just move on. When I divorced, that wasn't an option. I had to keep my ex in my life for the sake of our child, and we had to find a way to work together in the healthiest way possible.

Despite having good boundaries in other areas of my life, I had very few when it came to my ex—at least not at first. In the midst of our divorce, I was so emotionally distraught and under so much stress that I'd flip-flop between chatting with him like we were still a couple and insisting he could only speak to my attorney. Neither communication style was helpful, but I didn't know how to set the limits I needed to successfully divorce, keep our child safe, and preserve my mental health.

BOUNDARIES WITH AN EX

When it comes to co-parenting, most of the questions I get from people cannot realistically be solved with a clear, kind boundary. Here's just some of what readers have asked me:

- "My ex says terrible things about me to our kids—how do I get him to stop?"
- "My ex feeds my kids all kinds of junk food that she knows I don't allow. How can I set a boundary around their diets?"
- "My co-parent shows up late all the time when it's their day with the kids. What can I do?"
- "My son plays lots of video games at his dad's house, but we seriously limit screen time here. Can I make his dad get on board?"
- "My ex goes out a lot, leaving the kids with his mom. I wish he'd spend more time with them during his week, or let me keep them if he's going out."

Unfortunately, situations like these cannot be effectively remedied by setting a boundary.

Remember back to Chapter 1: A boundary isn't about controlling someone else or telling them what to do. Boundaries are a limit around what *you* will or will not do in order to keep yourself safe and healthy. And the cold, hard truth is that when it comes to co-parenting, boundaries aren't always a viable solution.

In many of these instances, a "boundary" would be attempting to dictate what the other parent does at their own house with their own child—something you can't realistically influence without a court order or a binding legal agreement. You can't make your ex provide only the kinds of food you consider healthy, or set a limit on your son's screen time when he's at his father's house. You can't make your ex speak kindly about you, send you pictures from the birthday party, or show up on time when your kids are waiting patiently by the door. These are not boundary issues, because a boundary cannot control someone else's behavior.

Second, even if you could set a boundary here, enforcing it would likely harm your child. Imagine saying to your ex, "If you show up more than fifteen minutes late, the kids will not be available for your visit." That boundary may make *your* life easier, as you'll no longer have to put your own plans aside to wait for your co-parent or make excuses for their tardiness to your kids. But holding that boundary hurts your children, who really want to (and should) spend that time with their other parent. (Plus, that "boundary" would likely violate your legal agreement—something you want to avoid at all costs.)

In an ideal world, you and your co-parent would agree on every major parenting decision, from bedtime to screen time, approved caretakers to "healthy" diets, haircuts to playdates. But in reality, unless it's something you've memorialized in legal paperwork, it's impossible for you to enforce *your* standards of care, health, communication, or socialization on a co-parent.

HEALTH AND SAFETY

If you have reason to believe that your child's health or safety is in jeopardy, you should take immediate action through the appropriate legal channels. But no lawyer is going to encourage you to take a co-parent to court over screen time, junk food, or the number of nights your daughter spends with her gram instead of her dad, unless those behaviors are negatively impacting her school attendance, health reports, or other metrics of safety and wellness. I guess *Judge Judy* (now *Judy Justice*) is always an option, but why don't you finish the chapter before sending in your application, okay?

I *have* heard of unusual clauses in parenting plans (a legally binding document), like the number of evenings a child can spend with a babysitter or whether or not the parents can share photos of their child on public social media. If you can think of those situations ahead of time and talk them through with your attorney, you're well ahead of the game. However, if you're beyond that point (as Emily was when she wrote to me), you'll need other strategies to help you co-parent effectively.

SHIFT THE FOCUS

One area where you *can* set boundaries here is the communication between you and your co-parent. Outside of their behavior with your children, which you largely can't control, what kinds of limits could you set so that your communications with your ex are healthy, kind, and effective? I explained to Emily that shifting the focus to the *way* she's communicating with Shannon (and allowing Shannon to communicate with her) would prove huge in smoothing out this new phase of their relationship. I pulled from my own experience to outline some suggestions to get her started, and I'll share those here with you as well.

LIMIT COMMUNICATION METHODS. I recognized early on that phone calls or in-person meetings were far more likely to turn into fights. My ex and I knew how to push each other's buttons, and it was too easy to claim, "I never said that!" I set a boundary that all communications needed to happen in writing, so we each had a record of what was agreed to. If the topic demanded a face-to-face meeting, we met in public, where it was easier for me to keep my cool, and I followed up with a summary of the conversation via text.

LIMIT COMMUNICATION TOPICS. One of the best decisions I made early on was to limit communications with my ex to topics directly involving my son. I set a boundary around sharing anything about my personal life—how work was going, whether I was dating, how my family was—and I made it a point not to ask or know anything about his. In fact, when mutual friends tried to tell me something about his work or his travels, I'd interrupt them and say, "Oops, I'd rather not know anything about his life right now. We're respecting each other's privacy." The *only* thing he and I talked about was our child, which made it so much easier for me to move on and heal.

SPEAK CLEARLY ABOUT EXPECTATIONS. Though I couldn't set a boundary around whether he introduced our son to his new romantic partners, I did request clearly (and in writing) that if someone was going to be a regular part of my son's life, I wanted to meet them. I defined what "regular" was (someone he was serious about and who had ongoing and meaningful contact with our son), explained that I trusted him to loop me in when the time was right, and volunteered to do the same. I could not control whether or not that was honored, but I laid the groundwork for what it would look like to cooperate in good faith, and was a good role model by acting in kind.

REESTABLISH "RULES OF ENGAGEMENT." My ex and I were better behaved in our divorce than we were at the end of our marriage when it came to handling conflict—in part because each of our attorneys gave us the advice not to say or do anything that a judge wouldn't look kindly on. Agreeing to boundaries around yelling, name-calling, threatening, using our child as a pawn, and generally being mean did help our discussions go more smoothly, and enforcing those boundaries by stepping away from discussions that weren't productive proved even more helpful.

SELF-BOUNDARIES FOR CO-PARENTING

In sharing these tips with Emily, I also realized that I had set quite a few boundaries with *myself* as a means of keeping my co-parenting relationship healthy. These were limits I decided were the healthiest for me around our relationship, my communication style, and the way I wanted to show up for the good of my son. Setting these boundaries with myself helped me stay in my business, kept me out of my ex's, and helped me show up at my best during some seriously stressful situations. Here are some of the self-boundaries I set around co-parenting:

DON'T RUN OVER MY OWN LIMITS. It was *so* tempting to check my ex's Instagram feed, and when I hung out with mutual friends, they would have answered if I'd asked about him. But putting distance between us and respecting that limit was necessary for my own mental health and healing, so I held that boundary for myself. (I didn't concern myself with whether or not my ex was checking up on me—I could only control my own behavior.) Note that I didn't choose to block him on social media—I trusted myself not to look at his public feeds, and I didn't have a need to hide my public content from him. But blocking might be a reasonable and helpful step for you; if it is, take it.

LEAVE THE KID OUT OF IT. There were times when my son would tell me about his weekend with his dad and he'd share details of my ex's life in the process—the "friend" his dad had visiting, or the trip he was planning. I let my son tell his story, but I set the limit that I would not press for any extra information. Asking questions like, "Who is this friend, and how often do they visit?" or "When is your dad's trip?" was an invasion of my ex's privacy, and a sneaky way of overrunning my own healthy limit. I vowed never to put our son in the middle of our communications like that.

BE GENEROUS WITHIN THOSE LIMITS. My boundaries with my ex included speaking to him only about my son—but within that boundary, I decided to be generous when it came to communicating. During the weeks when my son was with me, I would regularly send photos, funny stories of the things he said and did, and updates on important milestones, new foods he liked, or games he was enjoying. My co-parent picked up on this and responded in the same way, which meant we each maintained a strong connection to our son during the times when he wasn't with us.

SPEAK KINDLY. It would have been so easy to trash my ex to family, our friends, even the public, as I had a large social media following and our relationship had been quite visible . . . and I decided from the outset that I was not going to do that. I had a few people I trusted—my sister, my therapist, and one good friend—and I let myself speak freely with each of them, even to vent. Outside of those folks (who didn't have a relationship with my ex anyway), I committed to saying *nothing* unkind about him, especially around the reasons we divorced. Also, I knew falling into a pattern of speaking negatively about him would hurt my child once he was old enough to notice. For that reason alone, I decided I would never speak unkindly about my ex.

LIMIT MY RESPONSIVENESS. Part of the reason I struggled to keep communications kind and cordial was that I was lightning-fast to respond to every text or email. My ex would send a button-pushing text about the house, custody, or some other aspect of our proceedings, and I'd immediately fire back. This would trigger a volley of frantic text exchanges that became increasingly impolite, threatening, or downright mean, until I was so angry, I'd throw my phone and go off to fume. Then one day, I realized I didn't *have* to respond right away. I started pausing before replying, waiting until I was calm and could see the situation more clearly. This helped me reply more kindly, which made our conversations more productive.

NOT EVERYTHING REQUIRES A RESPONSE

My ex and I both sent some unkind texts in the early phase of our divorce, but there were times when I suspected he was saying something *just* to get a rise out of me. When it came to his most provocative texts, I responded by . . . simply not replying at all. I'd force myself to put the phone down, giving myself time to sit in how the text made me feel, noticing what was coming up for me, and committing not to text back until I could reply in a way that would make me (and my lawyer) proud. You know what started happening? My ex began *apologizing* before I even said a word. "Hey, that was lousy of me. Sorry about that. Can we try that discussion again?" Before long, our unkind texts became few and far between, likely because we were now asking ourselves *before* we pressed "send," "Is this the way I want to show up?" Sometimes the best response is no response, so consider whether staying in your power and your business and declining to feed that energy at all might be the most effective course of action.

GO HIGH. This was the most important boundary I set with myself here. During the divorce process (which took over a year), my ex and I had some pretty hostile exchanges. I remember I was bingeing the show *Suits* during this time period, and I felt like my energy matched the energy of the show—there was lots of backstabbing, manipulation, and trying to win at the expense of someone else. I wanted to fight fire with fire, match threat with threat, and triumph in whatever battle we were waging that day . . . until I realized that trying to get back at him and "win" our exchanges was making me feel terrible. I was stressed and anxious, and felt like I was still carrying him everywhere I went. This was not the energy I wanted to bring into a new phase of my life. I did some work with my therapist and made the decision that no matter how my ex behaved, for my own mental health, I had to stay in my integrity and be kind. (And if I couldn't do that, I would use my lawyers to communicate for me.) Michelle Obama's now-famous quote sums it up beautifully: *When they go low, we go high.*

Setting these boundaries with myself was the most important thing I did to preserve my mental health during this incredibly stressful period—and I found that when I changed my own behavior, our entire dynamic improved. I'm not sure whether my example altered the way my ex behaved, or if my self-reflection and commitment to integrity changed the way I viewed his actions and communication, but either way, it turns out it really does take just one person to improve a relationship.

SEEK SUPPORT AS NEEDED

Emily acknowledged that she was lucky that her co-parent was cooperative and committed to behaving in the way that was best for their kids. She agreed to implement many of the boundaries that we talked about, and a few months later she reported back to me that a combination of time and the boundaries she had established with herself and with Shannon had smoothed out their communications tremendously.

If you aren't as fortunate and you are still struggling to maintain a healthy relationship with your ex, there are resources that could help. A co-parenting class can give you valuable strategies for establishing a healthy relationship, and will connect you with a group of people going through the same challenges. (Bonus if you attend together, but it's still 100 percent worth attending on your own.)

If a co-parenting situation (one in which you're both committed to working together for the good of the child) is proving challenging, consider looking into *parallel parenting,* which is like enacting the Red version of the self-boundaries I set earlier. Parallel parenting strictly limits the nature of interactions between parents, and maintains businesslike documentation of schedules, requests, and agreements. It gives you tools to effectively work together during a high-conflict divorce, helps to shield your children from any conflict you and your ex may still be experiencing, and can provide a bridge between where you are today and a more cooperative parenting style you may come to in the future.

There are also co-parenting apps, like Our Family Wizard, Co-parently, and 2Houses, to help each parent communicate, share schedules, and document expenses. Apps like this minimize the need for direct or face-to-face contact, and can help provide more of a buffer as you and your ex work on your dynamic. You can also involve a therapist or family mediator to assist in difficult conversations.

Finally, work with your attorney to see if mediation or parenting coordination may be an option to help you establish new co-parenting or parallel parenting terms, or at least agree on general "rules of engagement."

YCDI

The principle of "You Can Do It Any Way You Want" from page 171 applies here in a *big* way. There is no one right way to co-parent, and releasing expectations about how it "should" look and not comparing yourselves to other relationships can go a long way in helping you establish the kind of co-parenting system that works for your family. In addition, it's likely your co-parenting relationship will change as you both evolve. We used to celebrate birthdays separately (so our son had two parties), but a few years ago, we began inviting each other (and our partners) to celebrations, and once we saw how much our son enjoyed having all of us in one place, that became our standard practice. Allow for grace, flexibility, and growth; remember you can chart your own path as long as you both agree; and keep the best interest of your child as your North Star.

SCRIPTS FOR SETTING BOUNDARIES WITH YOUR CO-PARENT

Though you may not be able to set all of the "boundaries" you were hoping to set when you arrived at this chapter, here are a few sample scripts you can use with your co- or parallel parent to maintain healthy limits around your communications, privacy, and mental health, and some consequences you can enforce should those boundaries be disrespected.

> **My ex-spouse still pokes around for personal details about my work or weekend plans when we're talking about the kids. I don't want to share details like that, and it feels invasive for them to be asking. How can I nicely say, "Please don't?"**
>
> **GREEN:** "I'd rather not talk about that, but I'm so glad the kids had fun at the movie. Thanks for sending me those photos."

YELLOW: "I'm uncomfortable sharing my personal plans, and I'd rather you didn't ask."

RED: "I'm only discussing the kids right now."

If the questions come in via text or email and you've already expressed a Green boundary, feel free to simply not respond to the personal questions and answer only what is relevant for the children. Make sure you do set a boundary first, however, as simply avoiding their question with no explanation is neither clear nor kind.

My co-parent invited me to coffee to "talk about the kids," but when I got there, he sprung a conversation on me about how he thinks I owe him money. I need to set a boundary around this, but I'm not sure where to start.

I'm going to give you two boundary scripts here: One for in the moment, if you find a conversation in-person or on the phone isn't headed to a place you're comfortable with; the second set of scripts is for you to set a boundary around how you communicate after the fact, to prevent this from happening again.

GREEN: (in the moment) "Stop—that's not what we're here to discuss. Have we covered everything you wanted to around our son? If so, I'll be heading out."

YELLOW: "I'm not talking about this with you here. Please work through your attorney."

RED: Leave the coffee shop.

GREEN: (after the fact, in writing) "From now on, please share communications around our son using email or text. I'd like to make sure we both have a record of what we speak about and agree to."

YELLOW: "I won't meet you in person—please send me an email, text, or voice message."

RED: "When you send me your thoughts in writing, I'll be happy to respond."

In this case, you're still being fully cooperative—you're just ensuring you aren't surprised in an unpleasant way, and that your conversations are easy to refer back to should either of you need to. This is super helpful even if your co-parenting relationship isn't contentious, I've found.

My ex-spouse calls me late at night to talk about non-urgent issues. I think it's her way of checking up on what I'm doing. I've tried not answering the phone, but she'll just call back multiple times, or leave an angry voicemail. I need some help.

GREEN: "Unless it's an emergency, please don't call me after 8 P.M. If you just thought of something and don't want to forget, send a text or email and I'll reply in the morning."

YELLOW: (answering the phone) "This doesn't sound like an emergency. I'll call you tomorrow, bye."

RED: (in writing) "I'm no longer accepting calls or listening to voicemails from you after 7 P.M. If you have an emergency, please text me, and if I don't respond, call my sister or my mother."

This is where communication apps can come in handy. You can both share information, schedules, and requests via the app at any time of day or night, and save phone calls for true emergencies. Setting a boundary that all communications are done through the app maintains a record of communications, helps you stay organized, and ensures your privacy is respected.

My ex demands to know details of my personal life now that I'm in a new relationship, like whether the kids have met my new partner or if we plan to take the relationship further. How do I walk the line of wanting to cooperate for the good of the kids, but not oversharing?

GREEN: "If my new relationship becomes important enough to involve the kids, I'll let you know, and I'll introduce you to my partner if you'd like. Until then, I don't need to share the details of my personal life."

YELLOW: "I told you, when I need to loop you in because of the kids, I will. We're not at that place."

RED: "Stop asking about my dating life. When I have something to share, I'll let you know."

Treat this situation as you'd want to be treated. If your partner had a new romantic interest, when would you want to be in the know? My rule of thumb was, "If this person is going to be in my son's life regularly, I'd like to meet them." I then left it up to my ex-husband to determine that tipping point.

My ex uses our pickup and drop-off times to communicate about changes they'd like to make about our parenting plan, like with scheduling or time around holidays. Though my daughter is young, she picks up on our tone, and I don't like discussing her care when she's around. How can I say, "Now is not the time?"

GREEN: (in writing before the visit) "Let's make a rule not to talk about custody or co-parenting issues at pickup or drop-off. Katie has big ears, and I don't want to stress her out with these conversations. You can call me after her bedtime tonight if you have anything you want to talk about."

YELLOW: (in the moment) "Okay, but let's talk about that later—text me either tonight or this weekend. Katie, come say goodbye!"

RED: "Now is not the time. Say goodbye to Katie and we'll talk later."

If needed, meet for pickup and drop-off at a neutral location, or meet on the front steps so it's easier to set this limit should your ex insist on starting an inappropriate conversation. Make yourself available to have these discussions (within your limits) in a timely fashion, to reassure your ex that you're committed to cooperating.

My ex-husband will still walk into my house without knocking, or he goes upstairs to the kids' rooms without asking. I've asked him to remember this isn't his house anymore, but the behavior persists. Help me say no without getting into a fight?

GREEN: (in writing, before a visit) "Please wait to be let in when you arrive, and please don't go elsewhere in the house, even if the kids invite you, without asking me first. It's important that I maintain some boundaries around my space."

YELLOW: Keep the door locked so your ex is forced to knock, and remain with him in the house if you choose to let him visit the kids' rooms.

RED: Meet him outside with the kids all ready to go.

If you'd rather your ex not be in your home (other than the entryway), communicate this in writing, and ask that they simply tell the kids, "No, honey, this is your mom's house now, so I'm going to stay down here" if they're asked to go upstairs. If you don't mind your ex seeing the kids' toys or art, keep the other doors in the house closed for your privacy, and set a limit on

*how long they can stay by saying, "Just a minute, kids, then it's
time to go."*

LOVING THE LIMITS THAT SET YOU FREE

I remember early in my separation, I had a real lightbulb moment
through the grief and stress. I was sitting in my living room one
night, my son asleep upstairs, and I thought about what life
would look like beyond the lawyers and the courts, the divvying
of possessions and custody issues. It came to me all at once:
"Once this is over, you can have whatever you want."

I realized that though the next year was going to be hard, I was
moving into an exciting new phase of my life. I didn't have to
settle for an unhealthy, unfulfilling relationship ever again. I
could do whatever I wanted with my time, socialize as often or as
little as I liked, resume old hobbies, and sleep like a starfish every
damn night if I wanted. Even more empowering was that I knew
I could take the practice of healthy boundaries with me into every
relationship I had going forward, communicating my needs
clearly and kindly, setting limits around behaviors or dynamics
that weren't acceptable; and choosing myself and moving on if
my boundaries weren't respected.

They say "time heals all wounds," and never was that more
true than with my divorce. With the passage of time, plenty of
therapy, and refocusing on the new life I was building, I found
many of the issues I was afraid my ex and I would experience as
co-parents either never came to pass, or were quickly phased out
in favor of more cooperative behaviors. Though that period was
one of the most stressful of my life, it was also one of the most
hopeful. Because guess what else heals existing wounds, and prevents new ones from forming? Strong, healthy boundaries. (At
this point, I suspect all of you got that answer right.)

Clearing the Table

Setting Boundaries Around Food, Alcohol, and Table Talk

Brenna, a member of my online community, asked for help setting a boundary around her regular brunch meet-up with girl-friends. Their favorite spot had an extensive breakfast menu but was known for their huge variety of pancakes, each the size of a dinner plate. Brenna and her friends usually ordered one or two pancakes to split as "dessert" at the end of their meal, but after Brenna's recent Whole30, she knew that the extra sugar, gluten, and carbs would leave her headachy, tired, and cranky for the rest of the afternoon. The next time she went to brunch, she tried to opt out of the tradition—and was met with so much peer pressure and mockery that she gave in and ate her fair share.

"Help," she wrote to me. "I can't believe how snarky my friends got when I casually said no! I want to keep going to brunch, but I also need them to get off my case if I don't want the stupid pancake."

As I've mentioned, I began my career helping others set boundaries around alcohol, sugar, and the occasional brunch delicacy while leading people through the Whole30 program. When I asked Brenna for more details around her pancake problem, she said while she was *doing* the Whole30, it seemed far easier for her friends to accept her no. Having externally imposed rules and a time limit felt like a boundary safety net. Even if she did get some pushback from friends, she could always lean on "Hey, the rules are the rules, and I'm sticking to them for thirty days."

Over the years, I've seen that the real challenge actually occurs during the *other* 335 days of the year. Your friends are pumped to get their wine-drinking, pizza-eating, pancake-loving companion back—but what if you've figured out that wine, pizza, or pancakes are no longer serving you? Cue the peer pressure, snide comments, hostility, and attempts to sabotage, giving new meaning to the term "food fight." Here's the cold, hard truth, born from more than a dozen years of helping people identify and create their own personalized, sustainable diets: Often the people closest to you are the most likely to disrespect your boundaries around food and drink. Take Brenna's friend group: "My friends *encouraged* me to do the program," she said. "They knew I was unhappy with my energy and sleep, and that I hated how bloated I constantly felt. Yet the minute my Whole30 was over, they were saying, 'One pancake won't kill you' and 'We want the old Brenna back.' I don't get it."

I very much get it, and I want you to get it, too, because the boundary guidance in this chapter is important not just for those who do the Whole30 or eat gluten-free, keto, or vegan. It's for anyone with food preferences, health goals, medical needs, dietary sensitivities, or personal values around food or alcohol. It's for anyone trying to make peace with their body and weight and ditch the harmful influence of diet culture. It's for anyone who is working to improve their relationship with food, alcohol, and their bodies, who recognizes that boundaries would improve every single one of those dynamics.

That's *all* of us.

In my work, I've seen boundaries in these areas fall into three categories: food, alcohol, and table talk. While all three share some common traits, including the same kinds of emotional attachments; influence from diet culture, the media, and our families; and the defensiveness that can arise with any of these topics, they each have unique triggers and challenges, especially within our relationships.

FOOD: Like Brenna, we often find ourselves in situations in which we have to communicate our preferences or choices about food. We may want to set boundaries with ourselves or others around food that stirs up cravings, tanks our energy, disrupts our skin, unsettles our digestion, or causes other unwanted symptoms. Sometimes, we need to set a boundary around what someone else calls our food, like "unhealthy," "gross," or "bad." Or maybe we just want to say no—and it *is* okay to say no simply because you just don't like a certain food, even if that food is an American treasure, like pizza or ice cream. (I happen to not care much for either—don't @ me.) Once you see all the ways you *can* set healthy boundaries around food, you'll notice how far that simple practice goes to improving your health and self-confidence.

ALCOHOL: Like food, alcohol is "something we consume," but it demands its own category, both because of the addictive impact it can have on those who use it and the *intense* societal pressure to participate. Alcohol is the only drug in our culture that we feel we have to justify not using—and the societal pressures around drinking are intense at any stage of life, whether you're in college, a new mom, or starting a new job. Whether you never drink, are conscientious about when you indulge, or just want to keep your intake to a limit you believe is healthy for you, the phrases I'll share in the scripts in this chapter will help you "just say no" in all sorts of social situations.

TABLE TALK: These are situations tangential to food choices—for example, the amount or types of foods we choose to eat, whether or not we diet for weight loss, and how we talk about our bodies and other people's bodies. Table talk is a unique category because of the strong emotional attachments, insecurities, fears, and judgments we hold around bodies and weight. These conversations often happen while sitting around a table, preparing your lunch in the break room, or standing around at a party holding your plate. It's where others observe what and how much we're eating and how we choose to interact with our food, and it's a space where people feel deeply vulnerable, anxious, and defensive around their choices and their bodies.

While these situations are not specific to any one food or drink, these conversations can be triggering, damaging, and harmful to your mental health. Learning to set boundaries around not just what's on your plate or in your glass but what's said over those meals can go a huge way toward making mealtimes peaceful, enriching, safe, and healthy.

FRIENDS AND FOOD

You may be wondering why Brenna's pancakes-at-brunch scenario wasn't featured in the Friends and Neighbors chapter. Granted, there is overlap, but in my experience, food and drink fall into a category of their own when it comes to boundaries. If your new friends are going skiing and you say, "No thanks, I don't ski," it's unlikely they'll peer-pressure, ridicule, or judge you for saying no. But when you say, "I don't drink," or "I don't eat gluten," it can elicit a very different response. Eating and drinking (alcohol) have the potential to make people defensive and reactive the way few other shared activities do, so they get their own special category in *The Book of Boundaries*.

THE LANGUAGE OF FOOD

Setting any boundary can be difficult, but boundaries around food and your body have their own unique pain points and challenges. Yes, we all eat, but we all have different ideas about what's healthy, delicious, and appropriate to consume. That means it's hard to have a common language around what we're eating and drinking—from whether a particular food tastes good or bad to whether or not that food is health-promoting. Our relationship with eating, drinking, and our bodies evolved from our families and what was modeled for us by our parents. But were those relationships modeled in a healthy way? If your mom was always on a diet, you were told you couldn't eat dessert until you cleaned your plate, or certain foods like sugar or red meat were demonized in your household, that influences the way you see food and eating today.

Our relationship with food has also been heavily influenced by diet culture, which tells us that certain foods are good or bad, and hints (or says outright) that *we* are good or bad based on what's on our plate. Through diet culture, we've come to believe that our worth is tied to the scale, and the only reason we'd change our diet, give up a food group, or pass on a treat is to lose weight. You may have experienced eating enough as gluttonous or uncouth, while restriction was praised as admirable and healthy. As a kid, I certainly witnessed my female relatives squeezing their thighs in dismay and turning "you look too skinny" into the ultimate compliment. Those influences run deep, and can impact not only how we eat today, but the way we behave and communicate with others over a meal.

Food and alcohol are also common centerpieces when socializing. (Try giving up alcohol for a month, then count on your fingers how many of your invites or events revolve around drinking. I'd be shocked if you didn't need an extra hand or two.) And because our relationship with food is so deeply personal and often conflated with our worth, making changes to *our* diets can feel incredibly threatening to *others* in social settings, even if we do so without commentary.

Finally, habits are hard to change, and the more emotionally tied you are to the habit, the longer it takes to break the pattern. Our relationship with food is deeply related to the hyper-rewarding ingredients used in today's modern foods, the ways they've been marketed to us, and how reliant we are on food and drink for stress management, comfort, and self-love. The way we use sugar, carbs, and booze to numb, distract, relieve anxiety or boredom, and self-soothe makes these foods and drinks feel like security blankets—and the idea (for example) of taking that away can make us pull back, lash out, or both.

The good news is that by establishing healthy boundaries around your diet and body, you're both preserving your mental health and mindset *and* changing the culture that surrounds you. Imagine a universe in which nobody talks about other people's bodies, our food no longer has morality, and we're able to eat and drink as we please without anybody saying anything about it. The difference between that world and the world you're inhabiting today is (say it with me) *boundaries*.

DISRUPTING THE STATUS QUO

Lesson one: You can make people feel bad about what they're doing just by doing what *you're* doing. Food is such a sensitive subject, right up there with politics, religion, and the Oxford comma in terms of its potential divisiveness. (We *do* use the Oxford comma, don't we?) Simply turning down a "treat" or drink or asking for water instead of a glass of wine can feel like judgment to our social partners, who often experience our choices as if we're holding up an unflattering mirror to their behaviors.

Brenna's "No pancake, thanks" thus reflects on her friends' choice to *eat* the pancake (whether she meant it to or not), which can bring up feelings of guilt, shame, envy, defensiveness, and anger.

Instead of sitting in that discomfort and questioning what it means, however, it's easier for your friends, family, and co-workers to shove that back onto you by way of eye-rolling, taunting, guilting, or downright nasty comments. They think if they can get you to back down on your boundary, they'll feel better about their own choice—and it usually works. Once Brenna ate the pancake, brunch returned to its usual happy mood, where everyone was indulging together and nobody felt judged. But this only encourages Brenna's friends to keep pressuring, cajoling, and harassing, which leaves her and her shaky boundary perpetually eating pancakes she doesn't even want, and feeling like poop long after brunch is over.

Brenna's friends aren't mean girls, and neither are yours when they give you a hard time about eating (or not eating) something; there's actually a lot of fear and anxiety at the core of this response. Food and drink are at the heart of so many social interactions, and they've likely played a big part in the relationships you have with your co-workers, friend groups, and family. If indulging together is woven into that culture, it can feel disruptive and scary when someone changes that dynamic. Your friends may worry that you're outgrowing them, or that their choices reflect poorly on them. Your simple "No pancake for me" can signify the end of an era—your girls' Sunday brunch—and if *that* changes, it could impact the friendship and how you spend time together. What if you want to find a new, healthier brunch spot? What if you start going to the gym before brunch, showing up glowing and perky in your activewear? What if you make new, fit, beautiful friends and would rather do goat yoga and drink kale smoothies with *them* on Sundays? Your friends may fear that the bond that connected you may disappear altogether if pancakes are no longer something you share.

"PANCAKE" BOUNDARIES, EXCEPT WITH SUGAR, CARBS, AND BOOZE

While any food or beverage could potentially require a boundary for your own health, there are a few categories that are the hardest to set a boundary around:

- Sugary stuff like candy, soda, or chocolate
- Carby baked goods like bread, pancakes, bagels, muffins, cake, or donuts
- Salty, fatty shared indulgences like nachos, French fries, or onion rings
- Culturally significant dishes like pasta, babka, or enchiladas
- Alcohol

The societally encouraged "guilty pleasures" present the biggest boundary dilemmas, in part because of the way our modern world glorifies these foods and drinks. (No one gets up in arms if you pass on the green beans or herbal tea.)

Thanks to marketing and media influences, ice cream, chocolate, cake, nachos, wine, and beer are now synonymous with bonding with others, relieving stress and anxiety, and, as Donna and Tom say in *Parks and Recreation,* "Treat yo'self" culture. By the time we're done listening to everyone from McDonald's to Yes Way Rosé telling us how much we *deserve it,* it feels like saying no is an act of deprivation or punishment. In 2017, food, beverage, and restaurant companies spent $13.4 billion on advertising in the United States, and more than 80 percent of this advertising promoted fast food, sugary drinks, candy, and unhealthy snacks. Alcohol spends between $1 and 2 billion a year all by itself, convincing us that everything from mom life to brunch to watching football is just *better* with booze. Can you even break up with someone without ice cream, or parent without wine?

These associations are deeply ingrained in our culture, and though we know these foods and drinks aren't always health-promoting for us, there's a common understanding that if there's a *reason* we're indulging (like a birthday, work meeting, or the end of the week) and we're all eating them, the negative effects just, like, cancel out. (At least that's what my aunts always said at the holiday dessert table.) Okay, maybe not literally, but it certainly makes us feel better about taking the donut if everyone else in the break room has one, too, or accepting a third glass of wine if everyone else agrees to order another bottle.

Researchers in nutrition and dietetics say that eating behaviors are transmitted socially, and people's food choices are deeply linked to their identity. Even social media plays a role in influencing your choices—people who believe their social circles approve of eating junk food consume significantly more of it themselves. At our core, we all just want to belong, and everyone agreeing to eat the pumpkin pecan pie pancake is one way to reinforce that belonging in a social group.

As if that wasn't enough to explain why boundaries around chocolate and wine are hard, we also have strong emotional and often moral attachments to these foods, making us "good" or "bad" when we decline or consume them. (Thanks, diet culture.) If we eat the donut or have another glass of wine, we often say we're "being bad" or "naughty." Even if we say it in a joking fashion, we're really not joking. There's an underlying acceptance of these foods as universally bad, and that same morality and judgment sticks to *us* when we consume them.

The reason we give for saying no is just as anchoring: "No thanks, I'm being good tonight." Even if you don't explicitly say that, these connections are still burned into our social psyche. Because of this association, when we just say no, we can automatically put other people on the defensive. After all, if you're being "good" by declining the pancake, what does that make your friends who have forks in hand, ready to dive in?

DON'T JUSTIFY, EXCUSE, OR OVEREXPLAIN

Brenna didn't have a specific food sensitivity or health issue related to pancakes, but she was tempted to offer that up as a way of getting around the boundary conversation with her friends. "Should I just tell them I discovered I'm gluten-intolerant or something?" she asked me in our DM exchanges. In a word: no. This is deceptive, which is neither clear nor kind. Also, making things up as a means of avoiding setting the honest boundary doesn't actually strengthen your boundary-setting muscles. (Plus, people who have real allergies or sensitivities need to be taken seriously in a restaurant setting, and if too many of us pretend we have a serious reaction, those warnings won't carry the weight they should.)

If you *do* have a legitimate food sensitivity or health concern, you are certainly free to share that when setting boundaries around foods and drinks. Saying, "I'm pretty sensitive to gluten" or "Dairy makes my skin break out" can quickly remove any perceived judgment and bring the focus back where it belongs—on the limits you have every right to set around your body.

However, I'll caution you against leaning on this too hard for two reasons. First, you shouldn't have to offer up your personal health data for someone to respect your boundary. If you're talking to close friends or family, this may be a reasonable thing to share. But what about at a business lunch, charity event, or another setting where you may not want to disclose personal details? It's worthwhile to learn how to confidently say no to something that doesn't serve you without offering any excuse or reason whatsoever. And you should be able to expect that people will respect your choice simply because you've asked them to.

Plus, if you do offer a reason or excuse for your boundary, the other person may feel justified in offering "helpful" advice, or even posing a rebuttal. "Gluten makes me break out" might lead to "They have a gluten-free pancake on the menu," or "I just read gluten sensitivity isn't a real thing," or "Please, two bites will not make you break out." Now the situation is even more contentious, because you've told them a story they find flimsy, suspect, or unreasonable.

Also, what if *some* gluten is worth it for you—but these pancakes just aren't? It's a lot harder to explain saying no to the pancake but yes to your mom's chocolate chip cookies if you're leaning so hard on "I don't eat gluten because I'll break out." Of course, you're justified in saying yes and no to whatever you want, anytime you want (or don't want) it. But for all of these reasons, we're going to practice boundary language here that doesn't depend on personal details or excuses to be successful.

FOOD BOUNDARIES AREN'T JUST ABOUT FOOD

One last thing before we move into the boundary scripts themselves. Much like the pancake isn't just a pancake in Brenna's brunch situation, food boundaries aren't always just about the food (or drink). There are many problematic conversations or behaviors that tend to happen over and around food, where you may find a boundary is needed. Dieting, calorie counts, and weight loss are commonly discussed over food, and in a lot of families, so are bodies, especially related to weight or size.

Food is often a catalyst for body image issues, a trigger for disordered or addictive behaviors, and a tool of manipulation (especially targeting women). As many Whole30'ers have discovered, you may start to flex your boundary muscles over that piece of cake or glass of wine, then strengthen them further by asking others not to talk about their weight loss diet or comment on your body. The way I look at it, anything said at, around, or over the table is fair game when it comes to setting boundaries to preserve peaceful, healthy, happy mealtimes.

BREAKING THE CYCLE STARTS WITH YOU

"This pie is going straight to my thighs." "It's going to take forever to burn this off." "I'm saving my calories for wine." I've heard my aunts and cousins say stuff like this a hundred times during the holidays. It was passed down to them by their parents, and my young ears certainly picked up on the underlying messages: Calories are bad, staying thin is the goal, food is the enemy, and any body part that jiggles is unacceptable. I'm now trying to interrupt these toxic patterns for myself *and* for younger generations.

Here are some things you can do to help break this diet culture curse.

- **DON'T TALK ABOUT FOOD OVER FOOD.** This is one of the simplest and most impactful boundaries you can set for your mental health and the health of your social group—see page 246 for more.
- **DON'T TALK ABOUT OTHER PEOPLE'S FOOD CHOICES.** That also applies to comments about how much food is on someone's plate or your perception of their appetite.
- **DON'T ADD MORALITY OR JUDGMENT TO ANY FOOD OR DRINK.** Avoid referring to items on your plate or anyone else's as "good," "bad," "clean," or "junk."
- **DON'T TALK ABOUT YOUR BODY OR ANYONE ELSE'S BODY.** This is especially true if the comment is negative or disparaging, but it

applies even if you *think* it's complimentary (like "you look like you've lost weight"). Find something else to compliment.

- **DON'T REINFORCE DIET CULTURE.** Avoid making comments about food "going to my thighs," telling someone they're "good" for passing on dessert, or commenting that you'll "work this breakfast off" in the gym.
- **DO LEAD BY EXAMPLE.** Proactively set clear, kind boundaries when conversation topics turn triggering or harmful.
- **DO BE EXTRA-CAUTIOUS AROUND CHILDREN AND TEENS.** They're the most impressionable, and the most likely to be harmed by the modeling of diet culture.

Remember, a healthy boundary isn't about telling someone else what they can or cannot do; boundaries are always focused on *your* limit, and ultimately the actions you'll take to enforce that limit. Brenna wasn't telling her friends not to order the pancake, she was asking them to respect *her* decision not to be involved in said pancake. It's the same when you set boundaries at the table—you're not telling your companions not to have another glass of wine or never talk about weight loss, you're asking them to respect your decision to pass on the wine or not be subjected to that conversation.

When I reminded Brenna of this and offered her a few boundary scripts, she approached her next brunch differently. Before she and her friends even ordered, Brenna said, "Hey, there's something I need to say. Last time we were here, I said I didn't want pancakes, and it turned into a circus. We're not doing that again. If you want pancakes, order them. But if I don't, just let me pass, okay? I don't want this to be a big deal, because it's seriously not."

She said it was a little awkward, but they quickly moved on, and this time no one said a word when it came time to order the pancakes—they just ordered one and anyone who wanted to partake did. I followed up with Brenna a few months later, and she said this small change has made these get-togethers feel so much better—she no longer has to stress about doing something she doesn't want to do just to make her friends happy, and she said her friends don't seem to care who eats what anymore (or if they do, they're at least polite enough not to mention it).

FOOD, ALCOHOL, AND TABLE-TALK BOUNDARIES AND PREP TIPS

Before we get into the scripts themselves, I'm going to share some tried-and-true tips from more than a decade of helping people with their relationships with food, drink, and their bodies to help you navigate these conversations with grace.

DON'T REHEARSE DISASTER. Often, we build up these potential conflicts in our heads until we're having fights with people about things that haven't even happened. Approach these situations as if it's going to be easy-breezy, coming in with the confidence that you know what's best for you and believing that people will sense that energy and accept it gracefully.

DON'T MAKE A BIG DEAL OUT OF IT. The bigger a deal you make of your boundary, the bigger a deal it will feel to everyone. Instead of saying, "No, I know I always eat the pancakes but after my Whole30 I don't really want to keep eating pancakes, I know it's weird but you eat the pancake anyway, I swear it's not about you and I still *like* pancakes . . ." just say, "No, not today, thanks." You'd be surprised how often a simple, unexplained no is easily accepted.

DON'T QUOTE THE SCIENCE. The moment of communicating a boundary is not the time to reference the latest article about how alcohol marketing is destroying women's lives, even if that data did play a role in your decision. Keep your boundary clear and simple, and if anyone is curious about how you came to it, have that discussion at another, less potentially heated moment.

DON'T BE JUDGY. A clear, kind boundary isn't judgmental, but it might come across that way if you're looking smug while you set it. If your "No, I never touch the stuff" is accompanied by a pointed look at their glass and a face like you're sucking on a lemon, yeah, you might get some pushback. Remember, boundaries aren't about what other people choose to do, they're about what you choose to do and the limits you set around those choices. Mind your own business here.

DO CHANGE THE SUBJECT. You've already seen "change the subject" as a strategy throughout this book, but it's used heavily in this chapter. After you've set a boundary, changing the subject is an effective way to make it clear you won't continue the conversation your companion might be trying to have. It also gives that person a graceful transition to another subject, disarming any defensiveness or further lines of questioning they may have been tempted to let loose. When you see this in these scripts, bring up anything else unlikely to cause controversy—their job, your last vacation, the weather, or the latest Adele album (generally a safe bet).

Setting boundaries around food and alcohol is a great way to gain practice and confidence, strengthening your boundary muscles in preparation for more threatening situations. Plus, holding the boundary is perhaps easier in situations involving food and drink because whether or not you eat or drink something is always up to you—unless you trip and land face-first in a box of Krispy Kremes.

I've heard every excuse in the book.

SCRIPTS FOR SETTING BOUNDARIES AROUND FOOD

Setting and holding boundaries around specific foods or food groups helps you to feel your best (physically and mentally), affirms that you are worthy of making the choices that you know are best for you, reinforces the mindset that you are a healthy person with healthy habits, and teaches you to trust the signals your body is sending you. Potential challenges here include peer pressure, fighting against social norms, clever and insidious marketing, and your own emotional attachments to comfort foods or beverages. Still, a casual "No thanks" goes a long way, and I'll give you many phrases that no one can argue with.

> **I'm limiting my sugar intake right now, and I feel so much better for it. But it's my mom's birthday, and she's only eighty-five once, and I know I'll get pressured to eat the cake. (It's not even the kind of cake I enjoy.) How do I explain all of this?**
>
> **GREEN:** "No thanks."
>
> **YELLOW:** "Nope, I don't want any cake today, thanks."
>
> **RED:** "Oh, you can stop asking. I'm not eating cake." Change the subject or leave the room.
>
> *You can sub "cake" with "break-room donuts," "wine at book club," or any other food or drink you don't want to enjoy in the moment—the language I've offered here still applies. The important thing to note is that you don't even have to explain— you can just decline! If pressed, however, you could also add, "I don't need cake to enjoy the party," or "I won't feel good if I have cake, and that's important to me" to reinforce that you can participate just as happily no matter what you eat. It may also feel more comfortable if you already have something in your hands, like a plate with other food or a glass of sparkling water.*

JUST SAY NO

This is the chapter where you learn that "No" is a complete sentence. (Or make your mom proud and say, "No thank you.") You'll hear many iterations of this in this section, infused with phrases like "I'm not feeling it tonight" or "I just don't want any." It may be hard for other people to understand *why* you don't want a glass of wine/piece of cake/slice of pizza, especially if they always do, but that's where they should ask themselves, "Why am I getting so upset at what someone else does or doesn't eat?" The beauty here is that *no one* can argue with your taste buds if you're just not in the mood for cake.

My in-laws invite us to dinner but always serve pasta, even though they know I'm gluten-intolerant. Every time we go, I end up eating some to be polite, then paying the price afterward.

GREEN: (your spouse, to their parents) "Thanks for the invite. If you're making pasta, can you please buy the gluten-free kind? I can tell you some brands that Jordan likes."

YELLOW: (your spouse) "We'd love to come, but only if the meal is gluten-free, so Jordan can enjoy it. Can we help with recipe planning?"

RED: (your spouse) "No thanks—you know Jordan can't eat gluten, but you've not been willing to make accommodations for her. You are welcome to come here instead."

If your spouse is unwilling to have this conversation with their parents, take it on yourself, changing each statement to "I." In this case, the Red boundary is the consequence. Rather than get all the way to dinner and discover yet again that you / your partner can't eat, make it clear that until your parents/in-laws are willing to make the necessary accommodations, dinner at their place isn't happening.

My family is huge on "cleaning your plate." If I get too full to finish or I find the meal is upsetting my stomach, my mom guilts me into eating more by talking about poor children starving or how much money she spends on groceries. Do you have any strategies for me?

GREEN: "Mom, can you please just give me one small scoop? I'm not sure how hungry I am, and I can always take more."

YELLOW: "I don't like wasting food either, but I also don't like eating until I feel sick. I can put it in the fridge for you, or take it home to my roommate."

RED: "Mom, I'm done." Clear your plate and store any leftovers.

This often comes from an experience of scarcity, and it seems like your mom's intention is simply not to be wasteful, so try to avoid the need for this boundary by asking for a small portion or serving yourself next time.

I struggle with my family because I don't eat meat. In our Dominican culture where celebratory meals and events are centered on cooking pork four different ways, being pescatarian does not translate well! I usually just ignore the comments, but I'd rather find a way to address it directly, because my mostly meatless diet isn't going to change.

GREEN: "Oh, thanks, but I'm not eating pork anymore. Pass the guandules, please."

YELLOW: "No thanks, pork isn't sitting right with me lately, and I can still enjoy all of these other foods."

RED: "No, I'm good with my rice and beans with eggplant." Change conversation partners, step outside for a moment, or go sit at the kids' table.

I made sure these responses felt appropriate to the person who submitted this question, and she said they were perfect. None of these are super Red because it's important to honor your cultural heritage while upholding your own health-based choices. If there are pescatarian or plant-forward traditional dishes (like paella, lentil soup, or stewed okra), contribute or request those for the gathering, and make a show of eating and praising all of the family favorites that you do enjoy.

My twenty-two-year-old daughter has recently gone vegan. When she comes over for dinner, I make her a vegan protein source, but the rest of the family still eats steak or chicken. She is constantly making snide remarks about our meat-eating. I get that she's passionate and I'm supportive of her choices, but this isn't the way to influence people. How can I say this nicely?

GREEN: "I respect your decision, and I expect the same tolerance from you. You don't have to agree with our dinner choice, but please don't make it a subject of conversation."

YELLOW: "Let's not talk about our food while we're eating." Change the subject.

RED: "You are welcome for dinner, but only if you can eat without judging our meal. If that will be a challenge, please come by after dinner."

If your vegan friend or relative wants to talk about their choices or learnings, it's up to you as to whether or not you're willing to listen outside of mealtime. If you'd rather not, simply say, "I'm happy you've found what works for you. Eating meat works for me. I'm not going to debate this."

DON'T TALK ABOUT FOOD OVER FOOD

One of the most important boundaries I set around food is: "I do not talk about food over food." Conversations about what we choose to eat or drink, the amount we eat, and our feelings around food are always more loaded when the food or drink in question is right in front of you, with some folks consuming and you declining (or vice versa). Discussing the very food, beverage, or behavior some folks had been enjoying can immediately put others on the defensive, feeling judged or even shamed for their choice. It's simple enough to say, "Oh, I have a rule that I don't talk about food over food, unless it's to compliment the chef. Find me later and I'm happy to chat further." It's a pithy statement that might prompt some knowing laughter or nods, and you gracefully exit what could become a heated exchange in the middle of an otherwise lovely meal.

I've been avoiding gluten and dairy for a few months now, as they wreak havoc on my digestion. But at family dinners when I pass on the bread or ice cream, my mom calls me "orthorexic" and tells me she's worried about my health. It's frustrating, because this *is* about my health. How can I say that?

GREEN: "Mom, I know you care about me, and those foods don't make me feel good. I'm leaving them out because that's what is best for my health, and I'd love your support here."

YELLOW: "I am paying attention to what I'm eating, and my mental or physical health has never been better. Please stop making comments like that. It's not helpful, and you're not my doctor."

RED: "Mom, I trust myself to make the right decisions for my health. If you can't respect that, I'm going to stop coming over for dinner."

You could also ask (outside of the meal), "Mom, do you feel like our bond or time together has changed now that I've changed my lifestyle?" She may be feeling judged or sad that you aren't eating her cookies anymore, and opening that conversation could bring you closer together and open new doors to gluten-free alternatives or bonding over Scrabble instead.

SCRIPTS FOR SETTING BOUNDARIES AROUND ALCOHOL

Boundaries around alcohol are a necessity for some. Much like I had to set boundaries around any drugs I was exposed to during my own recovery, for many, alcohol is a triggering and dangerous substance and firm limits must be established to stay safe and healthy. For others, boundaries with alcohol are about being in touch with your body, respecting your health goals, and bucking stereotypes like "You can't have fun without beer" or "Mommy needs a glass of wine once the kids go to bed."

Take it from me, setting boundaries around alcohol will make you feel like a badass. You're standing your ground, doing it your way, and setting an example for others. You don't *need* to drink to close the sale, celebrate the event, or deal with stress, and the more you stick up for yourself here, the easier it will be to stick up for yourself in other areas of your life.

I'm in my early twenties and love going out with friends, but I don't drink. My friends are supportive, but how do I respond to pressure from others at the bar who get way too pushy about buying me a shot or having "just one beer" with them?

GREEN: "No thanks, I'm good with water."

YELLOW: "Nope. I'm not drinking right now."

RED: "I've said no three times in a row. I think that's pretty clear." Walk away.

If you're sober and comfortable saying, "I don't drink" or "No, I'm in recovery," please say that—ideally holding direct eye contact. It helps normalize not drinking in social environments, may prevent the other person from pressuring someone around alcohol in the future, and encourages others who witness the exchange to hold their healthy boundaries, too.

THE POWER OF "RIGHT NOW"

In September 2018, I decided to take some time off from alcohol. I wasn't drinking much, and never to excess, but I still wondered if my life could be even better without any at all. So I took an indefinite break, and adopted the phrase "I'm not drinking right now" when people offered me alcohol in social settings. At first, I added "right now" for myself, only because the idea of *never* drinking again felt too restrictive. But I immediately noticed an unexpected power in those two little words. They reduced all defensiveness in my conversation partner, because "right now" implied I used to drink and I might drink again, which felt less judgmental than hearing a flat "I don't drink." The words "right now" also implied that this was a thoughtfully made decision on my part, which, I noticed, led to far less peer pressure or pushback than I otherwise would have received. Also, people rarely asked why, which I found interesting because during other periods of sobriety when I'd say "no thanks," people *always* asked why. So steal my hack: Add those two little words and discover how they can pave the path for a more graceful no. (By the way . . . four years later, and I'm *still* not drinking right now.)

I'm not a big drinker—never have been. When we go out or are with friends, my new boyfriend teases me about being his "designated driver" and otherwise calls attention to the fact that I'm not drinking. Saying no doesn't make me uncomfortable—his behavior does!

GREEN: (at home) "Hey babe, can you lay off the DD jokes tonight? It's easier for me if you don't call attention to the fact that I'm not drinking."

YELLOW: (aside, at the event) "Hey, can you please chill on the commentary about me not drinking? I'm fine ordering water, but you're making it a big deal."

RED: (right on the spot) "Ben, give it a rest or I'll see you at home." Go talk to someone else.

The trouble with setting boundaries around alcohol in the moment is that as your companions continue to consume, they're less likely to be respectful. Hopefully the Green or Yellow sticks, or it may turn into a "You can catch an Uber home, we'll talk about it in the morning" situation.

I'll have a beer with co-workers, but there's always pressure to have more, and sometimes they just hand me another one. Should I go to the bar and order sparkling water and lime, then pretend it's a vodka soda?

GREEN: "No thanks, I'm good after this one."

YELLOW: "Don't waste your money—I'm not drinking another one."

RED: (if they bring you one) "I said I was good." Leave it on the table.

Please don't pretend your water is vodka. One, that's not clear or kind; two, it feels inauthentic, which will leave you less confident; and three, hiding like this isn't strengthening your boundary practice. If it's more comfortable to have a drink in your hand, just be clear about what it is: "I'm good sticking to sparkling water for the rest of the night."

NO EXCUSES

Think twice about making excuses for why you don't want another drink, even if they're true. Saying, "I can't, I have to work out tomorrow" or "I can't, I have to do some yardwork in the morning" can feel to others like an invitation to "fix" your problem so you can imbibe tonight. Your conversation partner might say, "I'll hit the gym with you tomorrow—that way we can enjoy tonight and you'll have company," or "I'll come help you with yardwork—we'll be done in half the time so you can stay out later tonight." It's far more effective to be clear and let your "no thank you" stand alone—and it's great practice for standing up for yourself in other areas of boundary-setting.

I love going out for drinks with friends, but my friends still like to party like we're back in college. To be honest, that's not fun for me anymore, but I still want to see them. How can I walk this line?

GREEN: "I'll come out for a few hours, but I'll probably head out early." Leave whenever you're ready.

YELLOW: "I can't wait to see you tonight, but once y'all start dancing on tables, I'm out."

RED: "Are you having drinks tonight, or are you having *dranks*? If it's dranks, I'll catch you another time."

Basically, you're sharing the consequence up front, either gently or very clearly—"I'm in unless you start getting too drunk, at which point I shall Irish goodbye and slip out the back door." The key here is communicating the boundary in advance. Before you get to the bar, before your friends pressure you to stay out too late, before they're dancing on the tables, tell them what you're comfortable doing, then go enjoy yourself within the limits you've set.

Anytime I decline a drink, someone invariably asks me why. Sometimes I'm comfortable sharing, but sometimes I'm not. How do I reply kindly if I'd rather not share?

GREEN: "I just don't want one."

YELLOW: "It's a personal decision." Change the subject.

RED: "I'm not going to answer that, and you should not be asking." Change the subject.

If you're in recovery, you may or may not be comfortable sharing that—and people's reasons for asking can range from considerate to invasive. If you're not comfortable with sharing more, use one of the boundaries above. If you don't mind answering, you could say, "I'm in recovery, actually. But just so you know, not everyone is willing to share that. In the future, it's best if you just accept when someone says they don't want a drink, and don't ask why."

KISS

One thing that no one can argue with is your personal preference. (I mean, they can try, but it's not like they can climb into your body to evaluate the truth.) Here are some "keeping it short and simple" phrases you can use when you're pressured to enjoy a food or beverage you're just not into. (These also come in handy when you don't feel like explaining that dairy makes your digestive tract revolt.)

- "No thank you."
- "I'm solid, thanks."
- "No thanks, I'm good."
- "No thanks, I'm not hungry right now."
- "That looks delicious, but not tonight."
- "I'm just not a donut/pizza/beer/ice cream/cake person."
- "I might be the only one, but I'm not that into ice cream."
- "Macarons just aren't my thing."
- "I'm not eating sugar/drinking/eating gluten right now."
- "I'm taking a break from bread/alcohol/dairy."
- "Gluten/alcohol/dairy just doesn't agree with me."
- "I'm not into beer/pizza/cheesecake, thanks."
- "I'm just not feeling it tonight."
- "I don't drink."

SCRIPTS FOR SETTING BOUNDARIES AROUND TABLE TALK

As you'll recall from Charley's example in Chapter 1, sometimes even the people we love will say things about our bodies that make us anxious, unhappy, or insecure. Much like with alcohol, setting limits around the kind of diet, weight, and body talk you will and will not be present for can be a necessity. If you have a history of disordered eating, diet talk can be incredibly triggering and detrimental to your recovery. Even if you don't have experience with disordered eating or body image issues (who, tho?), I don't believe it's healthy for anyone to bring up body weight or food choices, especially if those conversations happen over a meal. We get enough reminders that calories should be counted, smaller is better, and worth is tied to the scale just by existing in our culture—we don't need to hear any more of it over a delicious dinner.

Often, these types of potentially triggering conversations occur without anyone consciously choosing to bring them up; they're ingrained in our social dynamics, especially in women. By clearly communicating your own limits here, you'll not only preserve your healthy relationship with food and your body, but you'll be helping others become more aware of how often they focus on calories, weight loss, or their bodies. In fact, your boundaries here could very well be the first step toward helping your social groups find other ways to talk about food and health.

My relatives are always commenting on my body—especially when I've lost weight. They speculate openly about how much weight I've lost and make comments about my food with respect to "keeping the weight off." I find this uncomfortable and often triggering. How can I communicate this when they've never even heard of "diet culture"?

GREEN: "I know you mean well, but I'd rather not discuss my weight. Don't you love this sweater, though? / Did you hear about my promotion? / I did just finish my first 5K, though!" (Direct them to something else to compliment.)

YELLOW: "Please don't talk about my body or my weight in front of me. Comments like that make me uncomfortable." Change the subject.

RED: "I've asked you not to comment on my body. If you won't respect that, I'm going to head out." Leave the room or gathering if needed.

For people who have been deeply entrenched in weight loss/diet culture, "You look thinner" is the ultimate compliment, and they might not understand why you're not taking it that way. If they push back by saying, "No, it's a compliment!" you can explain that regardless of how they meant it, you don't want to hear any comments about your body, period. If you want to share more of your perspective or personal experience, do so after the meal. Just remember, people don't need to understand your boundary in order to respect it.

I dread Thanksgiving. My mom and aunts are always dieting, and when I prepare a healthy, balanced plate, they make "helpful" comments about how much or what I'm eating. It's ruining the holiday, so what can I say?

GREEN: "I don't want to talk about what's on my plate today. I'm very happy with my meal." Change the subject.

YELLOW: "Please don't comment on what I'm eating, or I'll take my plate elsewhere."

RED: "If you can't mind your business when it comes to what I eat, I'll start celebrating Thanksgiving with my friends, because this isn't fun for me."

The holidays are hard enough, for so many reasons. If diet, body, or food talk is taking you out of gratitude mode, swing by after the meal, host a Friendsgiving instead, volunteer, or opt outside and celebrate on the trail.

My roommate is super health-conscious. Every time I cook a meal or order takeout, they find something to say about it

under the guise of being "helpful"—how my salad isn't actually healthy because of all the fat, or that white rice will spike my insulin. I'm tired of them inspecting and judging my food choices, especially as I haven't asked for advice. How do I approach them?

GREEN: "I'm fine with what I've chosen, actually, and I'd rather not talk about it." Change the subject.

YELLOW: "Ooh, let me stop you there—I just want to eat without commentary, okay? Thanks."

RED: "Blake, my food is not your business, and I'm not asking you for advice. Please stop."

Another Red boundary might be, "You may think you're being helpful, but offering unsolicited opinions on someone else's food comes across as judgmental, and it's putting a real strain on our relationship." I guarantee you're not the only one they're doing this to, so you're doing everyone else in your roommate's social circle a favor by speaking up.

Every time I bring in the lunch I've packed for myself, everyone at work makes a big deal about my "weird diet food" and how I'm probably judging their Diet Mountain Dew. Help me eat my lunch in peace?

GREEN: "Why is my lunch always a topic of conversation? Y'all are making me want to eat in the car."

YELLOW: "Can we please stop talking about our lunches and eat in peace?"

RED: "I'm going to finish lunch at my desk. If you think we can have one meal together without the running commentary, I'll join you tomorrow."

This behavior often comes from other people's defensiveness or guilt around their behaviors, but they might also be curious about what's prompted the shift for you. You can always set a boundary that you don't talk about food over food, but then offer, "If you want to know why my lunches have changed, find me this afternoon and I'll tell you all about it."

My mom and other family members are always talking about food and weight in front of my children, especially when the kids ask for seconds or reach for dessert. I want my children to grow up with a healthy relationship with food and their bodies, and I don't want to expose them to unhealthy diet talk. How should I explain this to my mom?

GREEN: (ahead of the meal) "Please don't talk about dieting or weight in front of the kids, and don't comment on their food choices, either. We are working hard to remove morality from food and not let diet culture seep into our table talk."

YELLOW: (in the moment) "Oops—Grandma, remember that Jack and Ellie can trust their own hunger and know their bodies best. Kids, if you want more, go right ahead."

RED: (in the moment) "Again, no. This isn't a healthy way to talk about food or our bodies. Please change the subject or the kids and I will excuse ourselves and go for a walk."

Outside of the meal, you may have to flesh out your boundary even more. Say something like, "Talking negatively about your body or weight also negatively impacts the kids' mental health. You may not even realize you're doing it, so I'll call you on it if it comes up."

LOVING THE LIMITS THAT SET YOU FREE

It was the summer of 2019, and Whole30 was planning our annual Certified Coach Summit—an in-person retreat with educational workshops, movement sessions, and plenty of opportunities to socialize. I had been doing my "not drinking right now" experiment for almost a year by then, and had realized so many unexpected benefits, including how much more present and connected I was in social settings, and how little anxiety I experienced heading into big events, knowing that was one decision I wouldn't have to agonize over.

I sent an email to my executive team with a wild proposal— what if we made the entire summit 100 percent alcohol-free? I thought of the tremendous benefits it might bring to coaches during this intense period of connection and community—better sleep, more energy, less anxiety. Plus, Park City is at high altitude, which can wreck someone coming from sea level even before the wine starts flowing. It was a risk, for sure, but I liked the idea of putting our stake in the ground and giving people a healthy foundation with which to start their long weekend.

The team loved the idea, so I pitched it to the coaches in an email. I wrote: "In a conscientious decision to build community, provide a safe space for socializing, and to help people foster authentic connection, this year's Coach Summit will be an alcohol-free event. We want everyone attending this week's events to engage openly, honestly, and vulnerably with one another. We want everyone truly connecting and committing to being fully present, toasting your accomplishments and our shared community with whatever fabulous herb-and-citrus-infused mocktail you've created for the occasion." (Yes, we had a full mocktail bar!)

I nervously awaited the replies, wondering how many of our coaches would be upset or disappointed. It turns out . . . none of them. Not a one. The email replies I received back ranged from enthusiastically accepting to deeply grateful. In talking with coaches during the event, I learned that many of them didn't want to drink but probably would have, if everyone else was. Because boundaries are *hard,* and peer pressure is real, and they didn't yet have the words to say no with confidence.

I'm not telling *you* not to drink, eat the cookie, or talk about your pant size. I am saying that your relationship with all of these things will be better, healthier, and more peaceful if you spend some time thinking about where you might benefit from some healthy limits and start establishing them clearly and kindly. I promise the self-confidence you build here will carry over into every area of your life, helping you identify the limits that are right for you and allowing you to set and hold them with confidence.

Handle with Care
Setting Boundaries Around Sensitive Subjects

A woman named Heather messaged me over the summer, asking for some emergency boundary help. "My father died quite suddenly last week," she wrote. "He was extremely social and had a huge network of friends, and they kept in touch regularly. Now that he's gone, *everyone* is calling and texting asking how I am, wanting to express their condolences, or to share a memory of my dad. I'm devastated and need time by myself right now— but I feel like I *should* respond to these heartfelt messages, so I need some boundary help. I don't usually reach out to strangers on the Internet, but I'm too emotionally zapped to think of anything to say to my dad's friends besides PLEASE STOP."

Dear Heather (and everyone else): Yes, you can and should set boundaries around your grief. And your health status. And your divorce, relationship status, sex life, family planning, identity, religious convictions, trauma, and anything else that other people attempt to insert themselves into—well-meaning or otherwise. This chapter is all about navigating boundaries around difficult subjects, which, it turns out, are like those Russian nesting dolls— challenges within challenges related to subjects that are already (you guessed it) challenging.

While sensitive subjects can come up with family, friends,

neighbors, or co-workers, they deserve their own chapter—not just because of their delicate nature, but because these boundary violations can happen *anywhere*. These are the boundaries violated by the woman in line with you at the grocery store who reaches out to touch your hair; by the trying-to-bond parent at your kid's school play saying, "Don't you want another baby?"; or by the guy sitting next to you on the airplane thanking you for your service, then asking under his breath, "Did you ever kill anybody?"

Some of the people who ask questions like these—the people who seem to have a unique ability to touch our most sensitive buttons and to make us deeply uncomfortable—are coming from a truly innocent place, until someone (maybe you) points out how problematic their questions or actions are. But people can also be deliberately passive-aggressive, revealing learned behaviors and influences from the patriarchy, misogyny, white supremacy, and other systems of oppression. And occasionally people are just plain aggressive—as if they want to remind you that they can and will insert their preferences over yours any damn time they please, even when you're at your most vulnerable.

The Red boundaries in this chapter were especially designed for them.

NOT SO INNOCENT

There are some subjects that always feel safe to discuss, no matter the company. Take the weather: It's rather uncontroversial, a common experience, and (as long as you don't mention global warming in the wrong crowd) generally unproblematic to bring up. There are other subjects that have been woven so tightly into our moral fabric that they may *feel* unproblematic, but are anything but.

For instance, "Do you have kids?" A common get-to-know-you question heard at social gatherings, work events, and even job interviews. For many, the answer to that is a simple yes or no, and conversation moves on.

But for so many people, fertility issues, miscarriages, health challenges, relationship issues, or financial constraints make this a loaded and painful question. Imagine asking someone who's just suffered their third miscarriage, "So, when are you two gonna have kids?" You'd never do it if you knew that the person you were talking to was in emotional or physical pain. But that's the point . . . *you never know.* There are a dozen questions of this nature, from "Are you going to get married or what?" to "Have you lost weight?" to "Why are you still single?" and every single one of them could be hugely, if invisibly, triggering.

Now I'll say what you might be thinking: "Anything is a potential trigger, Melissa." Yes, that's true. You could ask someone about their long-term partner and discover they just broke up, or invite a neighbor to meet you at the dog park and find out that their dog died last week, or mention how much you love ice cream and learn about someone's best friend who died in a traumatic ice cream cone–related incident. You cannot possibly avoid *every* sensitive subject, because you're not a mind reader. But here are some general areas of inquiry that are best to avoid without an invitation (you'll find scripts for all four of these later in this chapter):

- **CHILDREN:** Do you have any kids? Do you want kids? Can you have kids? How many kids do you have? Will you have more kids?
- **RELATIONSHIP STATUS:** Why are you single? Do you have a boyfriend (assumptive on many levels)? When are you two getting married? What's your age difference?
- **HEALTH OR ABILITY:** Have you lost weight? Have you tried (x) treatment for your condition? What happened to you? What's your disability? Can you still (insert activity)?

- **RECOVERY:** Do you miss (alcohol, drugs, gambling)? What was your rock bottom? Tell me your wildest story. Do you think you'll ever go back to it?

Not only can questions about sensitive subjects unknowingly cause harm, but unsolicited stories can also upset or trigger others. I recently posted on social media that I was considering selling my beloved motorcycle. The older I got, the more uncomfortable I became with the level of risk involved, but I still wasn't sure I was ready to give it up. You wouldn't believe (or maybe you would) the number of unsolicited stories I received about gruesome motorcycle accidents. "This person died, my brother lost his leg, my friend never walked again . . ." Excuse me, but I wasn't asking for your horror stories, and if I wasn't nervous about riding before, now I'm positively out of my mind with fear and anxiety. THIS IS NOT HELPFUL.

That goes double if a person is pregnant, by the way. There's a special circle in hell for someone who tells a pregnant person a birth-related horror story. Just sayin'.

BE KIND

The point of this chapter is twofold. First, I want to help those who are dealing with challenging seasons or situations learn where and how to set boundaries to keep themselves safe and healthy. Second, through these examples, I hope to point out that some things you say or ask may be more problematic than you realized. When we know better, we do better, and after reading this chapter, hopefully you'll think twice about sharing some of these questions or stories uninvited. You never know what people are struggling with, and I'm assuming that the last thing you want is to add to anyone's stress during an already difficult time—even if they are a total stranger.

THE RING THEORY

Though Heather wanted to offer her father's friends comfort and support through their grief, she had no capacity. Her own grief was so overwhelming, she knew she wasn't ready to take on anyone else's. Though she had asked her husband to run interference and let people know that she needed time and space to process her loss, after about a week, the texts and messages started pouring in again. "It seems like people think I've had *enough* space," she wrote to me. "I understand they're grieving and looking for connection, but right now these messages just feel intrusive and demanding."

The Ring Theory was first developed in 2013 by psychologist Susan Silk and her friend Barry Goldman. It helps people understand what to do in times of crisis. Picture a small circle, with a number of concentric circles around it. If the crisis is happening to you, you're in the very center circle. The farther away you are from the center of the crisis, the farther out you sit in the rings.

In the case of her dad's passing, Heather, her mother, and her siblings are in the center of the ring, as they are the most closely affected. Other family members (like Heather's husband, aunts, and uncles) and her father's closest friends would sit in the next concentric circle. Other friends and co-workers might sit in the next circle out, and casual acquaintances would sit in the outermost circle.

In Silk and Goldman's Ring Theory, grief (or complaints, anger, frustration, or as Silk calls it, "kvetching") flows *out* from the center of the ring, whereas comfort—and only comfort—flows back *in* toward the center. That means that Heather can do or say anything she needs to process her grief, whether that's accepting comfort or support from those in outer rings, sharing her anger or frustration with them, or simply closing them out because that's what *she* needs as the person in the smaller circle. Those in the larger rings outside of Heather's should not expect or demand that she help them process their feelings. They shouldn't share unsolicited memories, offer advice, express despair, or center themselves in any way to anyone closer to the crisis than they are. They can only express those feelings to the members of circles farther out than their own.

Grief flows out, comfort flows in.

This doesn't just apply to grief; this theory can be applied to any crisis, whether that's death, trauma, illness, injury, miscarriage, or divorce—all subjects you'll find within this chapter's boundary scripts. If your sister has cancer, you (and her children, spouse, and parents) sit at the center of the ring and have zero responsibility to comfort her friends or co-workers. If you are divorcing, your parents don't get to dump on *you* how devastated *they* are. And as I shared with Heather, she has no obligation to answer a text, listen to a story, or offer consolation to anyone outside of her tiny center circle—now or in the future.

Ring Theory made Heather feel much better and gave her confidence to set additional boundaries to preserve her alone time and claim the space she needed to process her feelings. This brings us to the second reason I'm sharing the Ring Theory here: Understanding your role in any crisis will make you more comfortable setting the boundaries you need to keep yourself safe and healthy *and* should help you to be more understanding when someone in the center of the ring sets a boundary when you're in an outer circle. As you'll read in Chapter 11, one of the biggest benefits of becoming comfortable setting boundaries is that you'll be better at recognizing when one is being set with you, and have the tools and perspective to respect that boundary with more grace and understanding.

USING BOUNDARIES AS A TOOL FOR TEACHING

Nearly every boundary conversation I include in this chapter offers the person setting the boundary the opportunity to educate their conversation partner about why their query, comment, or advice was harmful—regardless of that person's intention. Explaining why certain questions and comments can be painful, triggering, or more invasive than intended goes a long way in defusing their line of inquiry or action. Explaining why something is harmful also helps other people change their behavior so they don't make anyone else feel uncomfortable in the future. Let's talk about why you might want to take this extra step.

If you're in a comfortable place with your situation—like I am in my recovery—you are probably feeling confident and grounded enough to field a potentially triggering question and to explain exactly what makes that question so problematic. When people ask me, "Do you miss doing drugs?" I'm comfortable replying, "That's not a polite question to ask someone in recovery. It can be incredibly triggering, especially if they're newly sober and not yet steady on their feet. You're asking me to go back and revisit my using days, and I'm sure you can see now how that could be painful." Or I might say something like, "I don't mind answering this because I've talked about my recovery publicly and I've invited questions, but just so you know . . ." and finish the thought about not asking this question of others unsolicited.

When I do this, I both set the boundary for myself ("That's not a polite question to ask me as someone in recovery") and help this person not make the same mistake with anyone else. Often all it takes is for one person to point out how a question can be potentially harmful to make the person asking it think twice before asking it again.

That said, it is not your responsibility or obligation to educate while you set a boundary.

There are many reasons why you may not feel like explaining to someone in the moment why their behavior is hurtful to you. Maybe, like Heather, your situation is fresh and painful, and all you can say is, "Please don't." Often, the person who made the faux pas is embarrassed, and educating them further (especially in a public setting) may bring on defensiveness or anger. Maybe you're disabled, trans, or Black, and understandably tired of providing free labor to advocate for yourself and your communities. Maybe in the moment, you don't feel like the education will be appreciated or well received—in which case, save your breath, set the boundary, and walk away.

The reason we set boundaries is to keep ourselves safe and healthy. Only you know the most effective way to do that in any given moment. I've offered you the words you'll need to help educate other people about why respecting boundaries around sensitive topics is so important, but as always, do what feels right to you at the time.

IMPACT VS. INTENTION

As we talk about these sensitive subjects, it's important to center impact over intention. Whether someone shared a microaggression (a communication that contains harmful bias or connotation), asked an insensitive but well-meaning question ("When are you two gonna have babies?"), or made a harmful assumption (like telling someone they're in the wrong bathroom), the focus of these boundary statements is to point out the *impact* of that person's actions, and not to get stuck on their *intentions*. Think of it like this: If I accidentally rear-end you with my car, my intention was good— I didn't mean to run into you! But I still hit your car, and that action has a clear and definite impact on your health, safety, and property. When you set a boundary in sensitive situations, many people will fall back on their intention ("I didn't mean anything by it") and expect a pass. While you can certainly acknowledge their good intentions, the boundary will be most meaningful when you clearly spell out that the *impact* of their words or actions was harmful—and, if you choose, exactly *how* it was harmful.

I've discovered in my work that boundaries around sensitive subjects can be grouped into three main categories: limits to preserve our mental and physical health, limits we set during public encounters, and boundaries we might need to set and hold in various stages of life.

MENTAL AND PHYSICAL HEALTH: These are boundaries you'll set to preserve your mental health, protect your privacy, and ensure that conversations don't head in a direction that would trigger pain, anxiety, or unpleasant memories. You'll find boundaries around addiction and recovery, illness or injury, gender identity, and trauma in this section.

PUBLIC ENCOUNTERS: These are boundaries you find yourself needing to set when you're in a public setting, often surrounded by other people. In these situations, you feel the need to set a boundary around inquiries or statements that could be offensive to you or others present. Most of the time, we set boundaries with people in order to strengthen our relationship to that person, but these "public encounter" boundaries are often set with people we'll never see again. Still, they're critical. These are the boundaries we set around the casually racist statement a stranger makes at a party, an uncomfortable personal question asked of you by a shop clerk, or the handsy uncle you meet at your friend's wedding. You set these boundaries not because you value your relationship with those people, but because sticking up for yourself and what's right is important to you.

LIFE STAGES: Here, you'll find boundaries to help you navigate sensitive life stages and changes. These are the questions people often pose "innocently," but which have the potential to be quite painful. The scripts I offer in this section encompass your relationship status and progression; education and career path; pregnancy and family planning; and coping with death and divorce.

SENSITIVE SUBJECT BOUNDARIES AND PREP TIPS

Before we dive into the scripts, I want to offer some gentle advice for setting and holding boundaries in what might prove to be some of the hardest times of your life.

PROTECT YOURSELF FIRST. I know you care about other people's feelings, and that compassion is admirable. But nobody's feelings are worth sacrificing your own health and safety. Now more than ever, you need clear, kind boundaries. You have enough on your plate, and if people don't understand, or if they react poorly to you setting a limit, that is very much not your problem.

AUTOMATE YOUR BOUNDARIES. If you know you'll be facing insensitive questions or an influx of attention, automate your boundaries as much as possible. Hold your arms protectively over your baby bump to send the vibe "don't touch," or wear a pronoun pin that says "they/them." Automation may also include asking other people to communicate your boundaries for you. Have your spouse tell his family ahead of time, "Please don't ask us about having a baby again, and no, we don't want to talk about it further right now," or hand your phone to your best friend and have her reply to messages of consolation so you don't have to read them.

BE AN EFFECTIVE BOUNDARY PROXY. If your sister has cancer, your husband just had a life-changing accident, or your best friend is transitioning their gender, talk with them about what information they're comfortable sharing and with whom. That will allow you to hold the boundaries *they* wish to set (or set them yourself as their proxy), even if you have other opinions. Know that by being an effective advocate, you're taking the burden off of your loved one and demonstrating that they can trust you to keep them safe and healthy.

EDUCATE WISELY. If you do choose to use your boundary-setting as a teachable moment, consider the context. If you're setting a boundary with your boss, you may want to separate the boundary ("I'd rather not talk about it") from the education, and speak with them at another time, when co-workers aren't present. If you're tempted to speak up as an ally, ensure the harmed person feels safe enough for you to say something—you don't want to make the situation worse. When in doubt, simply state your boundary and change the subject or walk away.

PRACTICE, PRACTICE, PRACTICE. When I first started talking publicly about my addiction and recovery, I'd get flustered when people would ask me invasive questions about my history or use. Either I found myself getting mad, or I'd answer their questions automatically (and then get mad at myself for over-sharing). I spent time with my therapist discussing how I could share my story in a calm and grounded way, and what my limits were around what I would and would not discuss. If you're in a season where you know you'll be in these types of situations, write down a few scripts of your own (or borrow what I'm offering here) and practice them out loud, until responding in this way feels comfortable and grounded.

BE PREPARED FOR THEIR "FEEL-BADS." Once someone understands how their well-intentioned question was actually harmful, they may now expect you—the hurt party—to comfort *them* because they feel so bad. You don't have to do this. In fact, trying to "fix" their discomfort only gets in the way of their growth, and may rob them of an important life lesson.

It's not clear or kind to pretend what they did wasn't hurtful, to say "It's okay" if it wasn't, or to dismiss the impact by saying, "I know you meant well." They can mean well *and* still cause harm. You can acknowledge that, accept their apology, and move on.

> ## It's okay for people to feel bad when they do something that causes harm.

Ultimately, Heather decided to copy and paste the same response to everyone who reached out to her following her father's death. It said, "Thank you for checking in. I'm doing okay, but I need continued time and space to process how I'm feeling. I'll let you know when I'm ready to talk—and I don't know when that will be. Thank you for understanding and not reaching out again until I'm ready." Composing that message felt like a relief, and once she sent it out, she stopped feeling a need to respond to anyone's follow-up message. This granted her the space she needed to work through her feelings, without pressuring her to share that space with those in outer circles.

I hope the scripts in this chapter help you navigate your own difficult seasons or challenging situations with the same grace, ease, and comfort.

SCRIPTS FOR SETTING BOUNDARIES AROUND MENTAL AND PHYSICAL HEALTH

Setting boundaries around your mental and physical health will help you work through the challenges you are facing with less risk of feeling triggered, having your privacy violated, or having your identity questioned. It's up to you to determine your own comfort levels here. How much are you willing to engage? What are you willing to share in the name of creating a closer relationship, and at what point should you enforce a consequence if your boundaries are not being respected?

If possible, work with your therapist or counselor on specific boundaries that might be helpful for you to set so that you're prepared when the need arises. A professional might be able to help you identify situations that you hadn't even noticed were draining or triggering to you.

I'm navigating a chronic health condition and as a result, I'm constantly receiving unsolicited advice about trying this treatment or that diet, or "positive-thinking" my way to healing. People mean well, but they're just adding more stress. I need some words at the ready for the next time this happens.

GREEN: "My treatment team has a good plan, and we don't want to start incorporating random advice, but I appreciate you wanting to help."

YELLOW: "Thanks, but I'm not looking for advice outside of my own healthcare team right now."

RED: "It's insensitive of you to continue to share unsolicited opinions about my condition. I will not receive your suggestions again."

My first two boundaries here include some form of gratitude, because you can assume the advice people are sharing with you comes from a place of care, frustration at seeing a loved one hurt, and a genuine desire for you to feel better. The Red boundary is for folks who don't take the hint; who like to wellness-gaslight you by insinuating if you'd only do this one thing (go gluten-free, manifest more, or work harder to process your trauma) you'd be healed; or who try to sell you their MLM supplement or essential oil as part of their offer of "sympathy."

I'm often misgendered in public, from cashiers calling me "sir" to co-workers or acquaintances struggling to "remember" that I use they/them pronouns. I'm never quite sure how to handle it respectfully but firmly. Can you help?

GREEN: "Oh, I'm not a 'sir' or a 'ma'am.' I use they/them pronouns."

YELLOW: "I use they/them pronouns. Please remember that when you're talking about me."

RED: "You continue to misgender me, and it's starting to feel deliberate. That's disrespectful and unkind, and if it continues I'll shop elsewhere / I'll speak to HR / I'm going to leave."

You may need to remind people several times of your pronouns and identity, especially if they're used to thinking of you in different terms. Only you know when it's appropriate to escalate from a Green response to a Yellow or Red one. You also may decide it's not worth correcting the cashier at Target that you'll never see again, or you may choose not to correct them for your own safety. Only you know where and when you need to set a limit.

PRONOUN ETIQUETTE

I asked queer educator and activist Dr. Dolly Jaye Jenkins (they/them), to help me share the basics on pronoun etiquette. Here are a few things to remember, so folks don't have to set these boundaries with you:

- **Never assume gender based on how someone looks.** In fact, never assume gender, period.
- **Avoid gendered terms like "sir/ma'am" or "ladies and gentlemen" when addressing people or groups.** When talking to a group, you could use a number of gender-neutral terms like "Hi, y'all," "Welcome, everyone," "Hello, party people!," or "Good morning, Miami!"
- **If you're referring to a stranger, don't guess their gender.** Instead, use a descriptive term, their occupation, or their name. This sounds like, "Can you hand that to the cashier?" or "Oh, that's Brooks! Brooks came with Christine."
- **When introducing yourself, volunteer your own pronouns.** You can also ask, "Do you want to share your pronouns?" But please don't *insist* that someone share, as it might mean outing themselves in a space, time, or environment in which they're not comfortable or feeling safe.
- **Alternate with multiple pronouns.** If someone uses multiple pronouns like "they/she," it's generally best to use both when you refer to them. "This is my friend Kim. They are an artist; her work is so vibrant." You can also ask them, "Do you want me to use one pronoun more than the other?"
- **Be considerate of pronoun changes.** When someone shares with you that they are going by new pronouns, thank them for telling you and start using them immediately—with one caveat: Ask if there are any spaces or people where you *shouldn't* use those new pronouns in order to avoid outing someone (especially if this is a recent change).
- **If you use the wrong pronoun, quickly correct yourself.** "Jamie has the best style. He—I mean, *they*—have a great Instagram feed." Don't follow it up with a lengthy apology. That forces the person harmed to expend energy reassuring you, and could drag out an already uncomfortable situation.
- **Make the damn effort.** If you can remember Mary-at-the-office's new last name when she got married or the pronouns for your neighbor's Labradoodle, you can wrap your head around this pronoun change, too.

My sister is going through cancer treatment. Friends and relatives are always asking for details. "How is she doing? What do her doctors say? Has she lost her hair?" They mean well, but I won't share beyond what my sister is comfortable with—and as it's so early, she'd rather not say anything at all. How can I explain that gently?

GREEN: "Thank you for asking. Yes, she's in treatment and doing her best, but I don't have any update to pass along yet. I'll let her know that you were asking after her."

YELLOW: "She's doing her best right now. She's asked me not to share details of her medical treatment, but thank you for asking about her."

RED: "I can't share anything further right now. Thank you for respecting her privacy."

I can imagine you'll be fielding "How is she doing?" a number of times, so think of yourself as your sister's boundary proxy. Talk to her first and ask how she'd like you to answer when people inquire—does she want you to keep it positive and general, like "She's doing her best," or would she prefer if you were more specific and truthful about her current condition— "Chemo has been hard"? How much is she comfortable sharing, and with whom? (The Red boundary here is for anyone who feels entitled to more information than your sister is willing to share.)

I've recently been through something traumatic, and my friends are trying to be supportive. But once I start to talk, they try to empathize by telling me a traumatic story from their own lives. I know they're trying to make me feel better, but this just makes me feel dismissed and invalidated. Can I set a boundary around the way my friends listen?

GREEN: (before the conversation) "I really just need you to listen right now. You don't have to say anything, just let me talk and tell me it'll be okay."

YELLOW: (mid-conversation) "Oh, can you please not share your own story right now? It's hard not to feel dismissed when you do that. I really just need to get this out with someone who cares."

RED: (mid-conversation) "It seems like you're struggling to listen without inserting your own experience, and that's not helpful for me. Let's talk another time."

If this script makes you realize that you've been intruding on others in this fashion, don't beat yourself up—but do allow that to shape how you respond moving forward. While it may seem empathetic to share your own similar story ("Look, I've been there, too!"), what it actually does is center you in the conversation, instead of allowing you to be there for your friend. The best way to be empathetic here is active listening, reflecting back what you hear your friend saying, and then asking how you can best support them.

I'm a young, healthy-looking woman who also has multiple sclerosis. I sometimes use a walker to get around, but when I park in a disabled spot or use my walker, I'm often met with invasive questions from strangers like, "You don't look disabled" or "What happened to you?" My diagnosis is none of their business, so what should I say?

GREEN: "I am disabled, and just so you know, some disabilities aren't as evident as others. It's best not to make assumptions."

YELLOW: "I am disabled, yes, and I'd rather not get into the details of my personal medical history."

RED: "I will not be justifying my disability to you."

You may have noticed that in this case, the educating comes with the Green boundary, not the Yellow or Red ones. As a member of an often marginalized group, you don't always have to be the one to educate others. Feel free to say, "I may not look it, but I am," and let someone else (like a friend) ally for you by explaining that disabled people don't "look" any certain way, and it's rude to question someone's lived experience.

My husband is in the military and has served several tours over-seas. Often people (strangers, even) will ask him questions like, "Did you have to kill people?" or "What was it really like over there?" These questions are so invasive, especially as he's already dealing with PTSD. He never knows what to say, and sometimes he (understandably) reacts with anger in the moment, then feels bad later. What should he say in these situations?

GREEN: "Please don't ask me to revisit my time there. I'm happy to be back home with my family now, and I'm focusing on that."

YELLOW: "Do you know how many vets come home from service with PTSD? Lots of us. Maybe most. Please don't ask those kinds of questions."

RED: "I'm going to pretend you didn't just ask me that."

I've heard from firefighters, police officers, EMTs, and health-care workers on the front lines of COVID—anyone who is intimately involved in what can be dangerous, life-threatening work—that they are often asked to trot out stories of trauma like a party trick. It is not appropriate to treat the courageous and essential work done by members of the military, fire and safety, and healthcare fields as entertainment. For individuals asked to tell stories or to discuss experiences they'd rather not rehash, practicing responses like those offered here allows you to keep a cool head in the moment, even if your anger or frustration is understandable.

SCRIPTS FOR SETTING BOUNDARIES DURING PUBLIC ENCOUNTERS

Setting boundaries in various social settings, often with people you don't know well or will never see again, is different from establishing boundaries with friends or family members. With people you're close to, the boundary is meant (in part) to maintain a healthy relationship with that person. Here, you'll find boundary scripts that serve one purpose: keeping you safe and healthy.

You may feel as if even the Greens are a little firmer than in other chapters, but that's intentional. You have one opportunity here to set your limit, and a stranger's hurt feelings aren't as important as your own mental health or physical safety.

Sometimes people—co-workers, acquaintances, or people I meet at events—ask me personal questions that I just don't want to answer. (Examples: "How much money can you make doing that?" or "How old were you when you lost your virginity?" Yes, that happened at a networking event.) I never quite know how to respond politely. Can you give me some ideas?

GREEN: "I'm not going to answer that, but . . ." Add something nonspecific, like "It depends on your level of experience and where you're working" or "Virginity is a social construct anyway."

YELLOW: "Wow. I'm not gonna touch that one."

RED: "You know, I don't think that is anybody's business."

People ask me deeply personal questions often, and I find I can usually stay Green here pretty easily. If they ask why my ex-husband and I got divorced, for example, I'll say, "That's not something I'm going to answer. Relationships are hard, and sometimes you just can't make them work." The good news is that holding this boundary is easy, because it's 100 percent up to you as to whether or not you reply.

CAN I ASK YOU A PERSONAL QUESTION?

I *really* hate this opener, and from what I've heard from my community, you do, too. If you say yes to be nice, you've opened yourself up to a question you may not feel comfortable answering—but now there's pressure, since you've already agreed to hear them out. (And if you say no, you may look like a jerk.) Here's what I say whenever I'm confronted with this one: *"Go ahead and ask, and if I'm not comfortable answering, I'll tell you."* Of course, "personal" can mean anything from "Did you have a natural birth?" to "You're tall like me, where do you shop for pants?" so hear the person out before you decide whether or not to answer. Set the expectation up front that an answer isn't guaranteed. Remember, it's not other people's jobs to guess your boundaries. I never fault anyone for asking me anything, because I know it's my responsibility to set and hold the boundaries that are right for me.

I'm attending a wedding where I've been told the family members are "big huggers." I don't enjoy being hugged, especially by strangers. How can I make this not awkward?

GREEN: Approach people with your hand firmly extended, to indicate you prefer a handshake.

YELLOW: If someone moves in for a hug, step back with your hands up and say, "Oops, I'm not a hugger—it's great to meet you."

RED: Physically step away and say, "Please don't." Then introduce yourself from an appropriate distance.

I've heard this discussed often in neurodivergent communities I follow on social media, and I'm always conscientious about this when I meet people for the first time. You can be a good boundary accomplice by saying, "Nice to meet you! Do you want a hug, handshake, or just a hello?" If anyone accuses you of being impolite for refusing physical contact, politely point out that touching someone after they've specifically asked you not to is actually the rude thing here.

My parents and I are firmly estranged. In social settings when families come up, I'll mention we aren't in touch. Often I'm told "family is everything," or that when my parents die, I'll feel awful for how I've treated them. I don't want to lie about my relationship with them, but I also don't want unsolicited feedback about it. Help?

GREEN: "I'm glad you and your family are close. I'd rather not talk about mine anymore."

YELLOW: "Respectfully, it's not / I won't, so let's move on."

RED: "You don't know my family, and that feedback isn't welcomed."

You don't have to share anything about your family history in these responses, but I have a girlfriend who replies, "Huh. So even though she beat me throughout my entire childhood, you think I'll regret not trying harder?" There is shock value in setting a boundary that way, but it's not always effective, and may not be kind. Still, after the second or third boundary violation, a strong statement like that can be satisfying to deliver.

I work in retail, and a customer just asked me if I'm expecting. I'm not, and I was completely embarrassed in front of the other people in my line. The customer apologized, but I didn't know what to say.

This isn't really a boundary situation, because that customer isn't going to ask that question of you again, and you'll likely never see them again, either. However, here are some things you could say in the moment besides "It's okay." Because in this case, it's super-duper *not* okay of them to have asked that.

- "I'd like to pretend you didn't just ask me that."
- "Wow, I can't believe you just asked me that."
- "It's never okay to make assumptions like that."
- "I'm not, and I hope you never ask that question again unsolicited."
- "No, but you've just made me really uncomfortable."
- "Unless you see a baby coming out between someone's legs, you should never ask that question."

You'd think by now people would know there are some comments you shouldn't make, ever. Don't ask a person if they're pregnant. Don't ask someone if they've lost weight. Don't assume anyone's gender out loud. But these situations still come up, and I want you to have the words to respond clearly and kindly. (In this case, it's particularly kind of you to give this sort of constructive feedback because it will hopefully spare another person from being asked in the future.)

Sometimes in my everyday life, I'll bear witness to a stranger saying something low-key racist, homophobic, or ableist (usually proceeded by "I'm not trying to be racist, but . . ."). I want to

call it out as an ally, but I don't know what to say that won't embarrass or anger the person making the comment.

GREEN: "Ouch. Just so you know, that's actually a problematic statement. I think it's best if we move on." Change the subject.

YELLOW: "Ooh, stop—what you just said is not okay, and it's best if you don't continue."

RED: (if they respond poorly) "I'll excuse myself now, because I'm not interested in hearing you double down on why it's perfectly okay to share racist sentiments."

If they indicate a desire to understand, feel free to educate as to why what they said is problematic—that's a best-case scenario. If it's clear they don't actually care about the impact, then make your limit clear—you won't let comments like that go unchecked, and you'll remove yourself from the situation before you'll be a party to those kinds of sentiments.

BYSTANDER INTERVENTION

What if you (a person of privilege) witness the harassment of someone due to their race, color, gender presentation, sexual identity, religion, size, or ability level? Think about "ally" as a verb, not a noun. To be truly effective, you need to take action (as we discussed in Chapter 3). Here are the "5Ds" from Right to Be, a nonprofit that offers Bystander Intervention Trainings to teach people how to stop harassment.

- **Distraction:** Derail the event by interrupting it, engaging only with the person who is being harassed. Ask them for directions, absentmindedly walk between them and the harasser, pretend you know them, or "accidentally" drop your water on the ground near them.

- **Delegation:** Ask a third party (someone with you, a stranger who is also looking to help, or a nearby employee) to provide the distraction so you can check on the person's well-being.
- **Document:** If someone else is already helping the person being harassed and you feel safe, take notes, photos, or video of the interaction. Then ask the person being harassed what (if anything) they'd like you to do with your documentation. Never post or share without their permission.
- **Delay:** If you can't act in the moment, offer the harassed person support after the fact. Ask if you can walk with them or sit with them for a moment, offer to stay if they want to report the incident, and validate that what you witnessed was not okay.
- **Direct:** If appropriate (you and the person being harassed are physically safe, it does not feel like the situation will escalate, and the person seems as though they'd welcome the help), address the harasser directly. You can say, "Stop harassing them," "Leave them alone," or "That's racist, and you need to leave." Keep it short, and immediately shift your focus to supporting the harmed person.

These bystander intervention tips can apply to a variety of circumstances, whether you witness harassment at work, in a grocery store, or at the bus stop. For more of Right to Be's Bystander training resources, visit righttobe.org.

Sometimes I'll overhear someone make a sexist, racist, or otherwise offensive comment couched in humor. If I react, they tell me it's "just a joke," like it's my fault they said something offensive. I'm over letting things like that slide under the guise of comedy. What do I say?

GREEN: "Huh, I don't get the joke. Which part of that was meant to be funny?"

YELLOW: "I don't find it funny, and I think you know why."

RED: "It's not funny, it's just sexist. Please excuse me."

People love couching their microaggressions in humor, but the impact is just as harmful regardless of the supposed intent, and you're right to call them out. If the person making the statement was really trying to make you laugh, telling them "but it's actually not funny" should put a quick end to it.

SCRIPTS FOR SETTING BOUNDARIES AROUND LIFE STAGES

These are some of the most common boundary questions I've received throughout the years, which is why this section is a little beefier than others. It seems like at *every* phase of life, you will inevitably be asked by a stranger, acquaintance, or even a loved one why, when, or how you're going to proceed. Too often, other people demand the deeply personal details of where we are in our lives. We don't owe anyone answers, especially if we are struggling with those same questions ourselves.

You'll see many opportunities for education here, if you are in a safe enough space to explain exactly why the inquiry is intrusive and harmful. Or you can simply set the boundary that this isn't something you want to talk about, and walk away.

My boyfriend and I just quit our corporate jobs to travel the country in our van for a year. We have enough saved to make it work, and hope we can connect with sponsors to extend our trip for even longer. My family has a *lot* to say about this, though, none of it positive. How can I tell them (nicely) to butt out?

GREEN: "I get that this doesn't make sense to you, but we're so excited about this next phase. We're not asking anything from you but to be supportive—or at least keep your opinions to yourself if you're not as excited as we are."

YELLOW: "Oops—let me stop you. We're not looking for feedback here, and I'd rather not hear your negativity right before we leave."

RED: "How about you text me when we can have a conversation that doesn't include your disappointment in my life choices? Until then, I'd rather just not talk."

This is the perfect example of "you don't have to understand my decision to respect it." And of course it doesn't apply only to #VanLife; you don't have to take criticism or field your family's opinions on any of your choices, from the job you take to who you marry to where you live. You're not asking your family for money, advice, or even false enthusiasm—your very reasonable boundary is simply "I won't stand here and let you pee in my Cheerios."

My partner and I have been together for two years, and due to past relationship trauma, he's hesitant about getting married. I'm not in a hurry and happy to continue to work with him on our relationship, but the pressure from other people is making things worse. Every time someone asks, "When are you going to pop the question?" he gets anxious and uncomfortable, and I get embarrassed. Help?

GREEN: "Oh, we don't like that question. I'll let you know if we have anything to share." Change the subject.

YELLOW: "Honestly—we both wish people would stop asking. Neither of us appreciates that kind of pressure."

RED: "Last request—don't ask us that again." Move on however you can.

If you have an opportunity to speak with family or friends in private, you can share some context, but don't throw your partner under the bus. "I know you just want me to be happy, and I'm telling you I am. You continuing to pressure us isn't helpful, and it makes me anxious about spending time with you. For the good of our relationship, please give it a rest."

We want kids more than anything, but I've had two miscarriages, and fertility treatments haven't been successful. The question "When are you going to have kids already?" makes me want to cry. I know people mean well, but they don't understand how hard that question can be. How can I respond (other than bursting into tears)?

GREEN: "If only you knew how much we pray for that. I'd rather not talk about it, thanks." Change the subject. Or "I'm sure you mean well, but I'd rather not talk about it." Change the subject.

YELLOW: "That's actually a sensitive subject. Please don't ask again." Change the subject. Or "We're not comfortable talking about that." Change the subject.

RED: "I need you to know that question can be incredibly painful. You have no idea what people might be going through, and if you did, you wouldn't be asking. We're not going to discuss this further." Or "That's not a question you should be asking people. Excuse us, please."

I'm giving you options here because you might not want to hint at your own situation, or you might not be prepared for the invasive questions ("Why, what's happening?") that might follow. Feel free to reply to any follow-ups with "As I said, we're not talking about that now."

My spouse and I have decided we don't want kids. We're comfortable sharing that with people, but whenever we do, we're told, "You'll be sorry" or "You'll regret this choice, and then you'll be too old to do anything about it." Rude, right? What could we say that isn't super snarky?

GREEN: "Oh, no thank you—we're not looking for outside opinions on that decision." Change the subject.

YELLOW: "Oops, let me stop you there—we're not looking for your input. It's *our* decision."

RED: "Please don't." Excuse yourself, or change the subject.

Depending on your relationship with the person questioning your decision not to have kids, you might also clap back with humor: "I'll remember you said that when we're at our adults-only resort in Maui next month," or "I'll remind you of this conversation when you start complaining about how expensive college is." I wouldn't call that snarky, but my tolerance for snark is higher than most.

I'm eight months pregnant, and all anyone wants to do is provide unsolicited baby advice. It's overwhelming, and I'm already anxious enough. People mean well, but how can I politely say, "Zip it"?

GREEN: "Oops, let me stop you there! I appreciate the intention, but I'm not looking for baby advice right now."

YELLOW: "Ooh, nope! No baby advice or birth stories, please. I'm not seeking input outside of my own healthcare team and partner."

RED: "Whoa, stop. I will not listen to your story." Excuse yourself.

During my own pregnancy, it felt like people only wanted to share birth horror stories with me. No one ever said, "Oh, my friend just had a baby, and it went exactly as planned"; it was always, "Make sure you look out for this / be prepared for that / know about this risk." (WHY?!) You may have to repeat yourself very directly here, but it's worth preserving your mental health as you head into your own birthing experience.

My spouse and I recently left our faith, and it's created a huge scandal amongst our families, friends, and community. We're barraged with questions like, "Why did you leave?" or "What do you believe in now?" We know the answer to the first question, but it's really nobody's business. And honestly, we're still figuring out the second question ourselves. Plus, if we actually answer either of these, people will see it as an invitation to try to change our minds. Can we just say, "That's none of your business?"

GREEN: "That's between us (and God), and we're asking you to respect that."

YELLOW: "We don't want to talk about it, nor will we let you argue with us about it. Please don't bring it up again."

RED: "If you continue to try to force your beliefs upon us, we're going to leave/hang up/stop opening your emails."

P.S. You can totally also say, "Respectfully, that's not your business." I don't understand why people think bullying, harassing, or condemning someone is an effective way to bring them back into the fold. Having spoken to many friends about their crises of faith, I know that you've likely been through your own hell and back considering this decision. Take every step needed to protect yourself from outside opinions—even your own fami-

lies'—as you figure out what this phase of your faith means for you.

I'm in the process of a divorce, and my parents aren't at all shy about telling me what a huge mistake I'm making, and how a divorce is going to ruin my kids' lives. (As if I'm not already stressed out of my mind worrying about that.) I need them to butt out, because they're not helping. Help?

GREEN: "I know you care about me and the kids, but this decision is mine, and I'm asking for your support, not your advice."

YELLOW: "Your opinions here are not helpful or welcomed. If you can't just be supportive during this difficult time, I'm going to stop talking to you about the situation."

RED: "This is not a topic I will be discussing with you." Change the subject, hang up, or walk away as needed.

A word of caution—you may need to set a boundary on behalf of your kids here, too. Even well-meaning grandparents who make comments like "We really hope your mom and dad don't get divorced" can be incredibly harmful to little ones. Set whatever limits are right for your family.

My mom's health is rapidly declining, and I'm her primary caregiver. My husband and I are talking about next steps, but everyone has an opinion about what we should (or should not) do to care for her. This is an incredibly difficult time already, and I don't need outsiders making me feel worse about this decision.

GREEN: "This is already a difficult decision, with no easy answers. Unless you're her doctor or my husband, I'm not looking for advice."

YELLOW: "Respectfully, please don't offer unsolicited opinions about my mother's care."

RED: "I will not listen to your opinions on this." Walk away.

This boundary is the bare minimum for preserving your own health during this stressful time. Don't feel at all guilty or bad about protecting your space and energy right now. Automate this by not discussing your mom's health or care with anyone outside of your immediate circle. You can simply respond to inquiries with, "She's doing as well as can be expected. Thank you for asking about her—I'll let her know I saw you."

LOVING THE LIMITS THAT SET YOU FREE

After I had a concussion, I spent three years navigating post-concussion symptoms. (I still get flare-ups during times of significant stress, heavy travel, or overexertion.) I knew nothing about head injuries before I sustained one, and I've shared about my experience quite a bit on social media in the hopes of helping people navigate their own head injuries or offering better support to loved ones with concussions.

Once I started sharing, people inevitably had one question: "How did it happen?" For a while, I told the full truth: I was playing laser tag with my son at a fun center, and during the game, I was either hit in the head by another player's gun or somehow knocked into a concrete pole—I'm not exactly sure what happened. But I soon realized that people's well-meaning responses after my disclosure were setting my mental health back.

"Oh, whew, that's not so bad, then!" (Except it was, because it was three months later and I still couldn't travel, hike, or speak in public.) "Wow, and you're still experiencing symptoms?" (Yes, but now I wonder if you think I'm faking, exaggerating, or being dramatic?) "Imagine what race car drivers or football players go through." (Yes, their injuries are so much worse, and I imagine they suffer even more, but I'm still in constant pain, so can we not compare?)

These types of comments were well intentioned, but I was still processing my injury and its impact on my life, and I recognized after a therapy session that I needed to set some boundaries here. So I adopted a "pre-Green" strategy, telling people, "I had an accident." I wasn't establishing a true boundary in that I wasn't setting a clear limit around what I would and would not share, but it was a half step toward one, in that it let me share as I was willing without inviting additional questions. Furthermore, because I wasn't going into detail, the comments around the accident seeming "not so bad," or the questions about why I still had symptoms basically disappeared.

In these most sensitive of subjects, you may find this "pre-Green" response a helpful bridge into having to set an actual boundary, while still setting a limit around your interactions. For example, you might answer "How did your loved one die?" with a pre-Green boundary like "It was quite sudden, and we're all still in shock," or "We were lucky to have time to say goodbye, and he passed peacefully." (It's unlikely anyone will be tactless enough to follow up with "No, but what did he *die of*?")

If we practice the idea of "minimum dose, maximum effect" (see page 54) when it comes to boundaries, you may be able to expend even less energy with a carefully crafted half response. And during this most difficult season, if it works and creates less stress for you, I'm all for it.

CHAPTER 10

Gifts to Future You

Setting and Holding Boundaries with Yourself

In October 2020, the country was gearing up for a contentious election, COVID was raging, and I was deeply invested in the social justice efforts dominating the news. I was struggling to maintain a healthy relationship with social media, as it felt like the world was nothing but people arguing, sharing misinformation, getting sick, and dying. I would get ready for bed every night outraged about something, venting to my husband about how unjust and unbalanced things were. After the third night in a row of feeling overwhelmed to the point of tears, he staged an intervention: "Babe, I think you need to get off Twitter."

I immediately pushed back. "How else will I know what's going on? I have an obligation to stay involved." He replied calmly, "How up-to-date do you need to be at ten o'clock at night?" He was right. My habit of checking social media "one last time" before bed was making me anxious, angry, and unsettled, which impacted my relationship with my spouse, my mental health, and my sleep. I immediately set a boundary with myself: "No checking social media in the hour before bed."

Boundaries are designed in part to help you create, maintain, and preserve healthy relationships. Sometimes, the relationship that boundary preserves is yours with yourself. Self-boundaries are in their own unique category, for two reasons. First, since you're only talking to yourself, respect for that boundary depends on one person and one person only. This can be a blessing and a curse. It's certainly easier to uphold a healthy limit if you decide it's in your best interest, but not everyone responds to internal expectations the same way.

RESOURCE: *THE FOUR TENDENCIES*, BY GRETCHEN RUBIN

In her book *The Four Tendencies,* my friend Gretchen Rubin outlines a fabulous framework for determining how people respond to internal and external expectations. She breaks down our response instincts into four types: Upholder, Questioner, Obliger, or Rebel. You can find out more and take a free quiz to discover your own tendency at quiz.gretchenrubin.com, unlocking insights and strategies that will work best for you when setting and holding self-boundaries.

- **Upholders:** Someone who identifies as an Upholder responds to internal expectations remarkably well. I'm an Upholder, so if you tell me to do something (like start a thirty-day dietary experiment), I can just do it, and it's easy. And when I say I'm going to do something (like not check Twitter before bed), I also just do that, and it's easy.

- **Questioner:** If you identify as a Questioner, you'll respond well to external expectations if they make sense to you (that is, if they align with your internal expectations). You ask a lot of questions and need to be convinced of the benefits before you sign on, but once you do, you'll get it done.

- **Obliger:** If you identify as an Obliger, you don't respond well to internal expectations. You really need external accountability to make things stick, even if what you're trying to achieve is something you want for yourself. (Obligers are the most common tendency—what you'd think of as "people-pleasers.")

- **Rebel:** If you identify as a Rebel, you don't respond well to outer *or* inner expectations. If someone asks or tells you to do something, you resist. You don't even want to tell yourself what to do; you'll resist expectations imposed from within as vigorously as those imposed from the outside.

No one Tendency is better than any other, but knowing your Tendency (and working with it, not against it) can help you find the right language and approach to solidify new habits, lose bad ones, and set effective boundaries with yourself.

Understanding that we all respond to internal expectations differently, it's easy to see that self-boundaries may be a real challenge for some people, especially those who rely on external expectations for accountability. But there's another reason certain people find self-boundaries especially difficult, and that has to do with what happens when you violate your own boundary. Think about it—what *does* happen? It's easy to see if you're setting a boundary with someone else. If you set a limit around smoking inside your home and Uncle Joe walks in and lights up, the *consequence* is that you ask him to put it out or go outside—and he does. But if you've set a boundary with *yourself* that you will not smoke inside your house, and on a rainy day you break your own boundary and smoke inside, no one is going to make *you* go outside. The consequences of violating the boundaries we break with ourselves feel less important, obvious, or relevant when they're imposed on us by us, especially when you're the only one who decides if you want to enforce the boundary in the first place.

Maybe you try to manufacture a consequence, like "Every time I smoke inside, I'll put $20 in the jar." Except you're smarter than that, aren't you? You'll know the $20 penalty is wholly unrelated to the behavior you're trying to regulate—and that makes it feel more like a punishment than a consequence. Nobody likes the idea of punishing themselves . . . and again, who's gonna enforce it? It's harder for us to change or adapt our behavior when the consequences feel airy, negotiable, or irrelevant, especially when instant gratification is right in front of us.

Self-boundaries come up again and again for a reason, though. Setting boundaries with yourself can happen in an instant, don't require anyone else's cooperation, and can make your life infinitely happier, healthier, calmer, and more productive. So, let's devise some strategies for setting and holding boundaries with yourself.

LOOK FOR PAIN POINTS

The fastest way to spot a need for a self-imposed boundary is to look for pain points. What are the areas of your day that are stressful? The times when you feel reactive? The circumstances that provoke or worsen anxiety, or otherwise don't feel good to you? Sometimes those closest to you can "helpfully" point those out, as my husband did with me that night after another round of doom-scrolling. I put "helpfully" in quotes because at first you may feel defensive or angry at their observation. Consider that defensiveness another flashing neon "BOUNDARIES" sign with an arrow pointing in your direction.

Start paying attention to those moments throughout your day. Here are some questions you can ask yourself:

- Is there one particular part of my day that feels the most stressful?
- Is there one piece of technology or social media that provokes the most anxiety?
- Is there a habit I really want to start, and that I know would benefit me, but I just keep blowing it off?

- Is there a habit I'm stuck in that I know isn't serving me, but I don't know how to stop?
- Is there a goal that I'm working toward that could be furthered if I just set a limit?

I'll identify boundaries in this chapter according to two broad categories: stressful situations and habits and goals. You'll notice "technology" plays a role in both of these categories, which is why I'm not pulling it out on its own. In fact, you'll find a ton of overlap even in the two categories I've outlined; setting a boundary around a habit or goal often also helps with your stress levels, and vice versa. In both sections, you'll also be reminded of boundaries that you've set with others (like alone time or not caving to the pressure to drink) that could be reinforced by setting a boundary with yourself, too.

RESOURCE: *TINY HABITS* BY BJ FOGG

Think of setting a self-boundary as a first step in establishing a new healthy habit or eliminating one that isn't serving you. Not every habit change starts with a self-boundary—sometimes we just decide we want to start running or flossing our teeth. But once you identify and set a self-boundary, as I did with my late-night Twitter sessions, you'll need some kind of strategy to keep it in place. That's where the book *Tiny Habits*, by PhD and Stanford behavioral scientist BJ Fogg, comes in. You'll see tips from *Tiny Habits* and Fogg's twenty years of research (most of which I've used myself) sprinkled throughout this chapter, including the "short and simple" strategy for automating self-boundaries; environmental changes you can make to support your efforts; and thought exercises that will lead you from self-boundary to healthy habit in no time.

STRESSFUL SITUATIONS: These are boundaries you'll set with yourself to ease your stress, avoid unnecessary conflict, and improve your health. They may involve the ways you communicate; how you interact with technology; how you spend your money or time; or self-care behaviors you're committing to for your mental health. While setting boundaries around some stressful situations may involve other people (and communicating your boundary with them may also be appropriate), you will likely discover that focusing solely on *your own* behavior can have a powerful impact on your stress levels.

HABITS AND GOALS: These are boundaries you set with yourself around healthy behaviors you want to start or maintain, or behaviors you know aren't serving you or are hindering your goals. Examples include setting boundaries around your fitness routine, spending habits, alcohol consumption, or career aspirations— boundaries that are often tied into larger goals like "run a 10K" or "buy a house by the end of the year."

Going back to my Twittering, had I just asked myself the first question—"Is there one particular part of my day that feels the most stressful?"—I would have seen that, yes, the hour right before bed was feeling awful. The natural follow-up question would have been, "Well, what am I doing differently?" and the answer would have jumped out at me. Happily, the next night I went to bed with my book instead of my phone, drifted off to sleep feeling calm and peaceful, and the evening was perfectly pleasant— outside of my husband doing the "told you so" dance. (I was grateful, so I let him have it.)

FIND YOUR LIMIT

When it comes to self-boundaries, the YCDI policy applies here perhaps more than anywhere else. You can (and should) set the boundary that works for you, because you're the only one it has to work for. If you also find yourself doom-scrolling at night, the right boundary for you might be to remove Twitter from your phone altogether, keep your phone in the bedroom but listen to a restful meditation before bed, or try therapy to help you process what you are reading in the news more effectively. I found the behavior that served me best involved keeping up with the news during the day, but limiting my consumption in the evening. (I was also in weekly therapy. Have I mentioned how much I love therapy?)

The key here is thinking creatively to identify the boundary that works best to eliminate or marginalize your particular pain points, then set those clear, kind limits around what you will or will not do to support those needs. It doesn't have to be a solution that worked for someone else, although that's a great (and easy) place to start. Stay committed to exploring options until you land on the one that works best for you.

AUTOMATE THAT SELF-BOUNDARY, TOO

The best way to automate self-boundaries is by keeping them as short and simple as possible. Ask yourself if there is *one thing* you could do that would make holding your boundary effortless, applying a tried-and-true principle from habit research that says the more difficult or complicated you make something, the less likely you are to do it (and vice versa). In the case of my Twitter fixation, if the phone wasn't in my room, I couldn't mindlessly pick it up, so that was the shortest, simplest route to a boundary. If you decide to cut your wine consumption to nights out, set a boundary that there will be no alcohol in the house—ever. If you're struggling not to check up on an ex, preemptively block them on all social media so you can't go down the Instagram rabbit hole. Taking the simplest or shortest route when you're thinking about setting self-boundaries makes it harder to disrespect your own limits, and makes it near effortless to uphold them.

REFRAME YOUR CONSEQUENCES

This is perhaps the most important aspect of self-boundaries, because consequences aren't as natural or easily enforced when you're talking to yourself. What would happen if I *did* pick up my phone and doom-scroll in the bathroom right before bed? Upon first glance, it would be easy to say, "Well, nothing." I could hide it from my husband, my phone wasn't going to punish me with an electric shock, and realistically, I could keep breaking my own boundary night after night with zero consequences. Right?

Except there *are* consequences. You just have to think more about Future You and the way these behaviors are affecting your life in the short and long term.

If I disrespect my own boundary (I will not look at my phone in the evening), I'll continue to spend my nights feeling anxious, angry, and frustrated. I might start picking fights with my husband or trying to draw him into my stressful energy. I'll have a harder time falling asleep and have less restful sleep. Eventually, that would start to catch up with me. Bedtime would start to feel like a tense and contentious time in our household, and I'd be under-slept and not well rested, which would make me feel cranky and stressed through the rest of my day. If this goes on long enough, I'll hit an emotional wall and require an entire weekend of rest, apologies, and a social media detox just to center myself again. (I've been here before.)

Those are the consequences of breaking my own boundary:

the energetic drain on Future Me; the strain that puts on my mental health, relationships, and work life; and how awful I'll feel if I don't hold this one simple boundary for myself.

When I put it in terms like that, it was easy to connect the boundary violation with the very real consequences, and a lot harder to justify peeking at my phone "just this once." In each of the boundary "scripts" I share here, I'll help you tease out the potential consequences, to get you thinking bigger-picture about why these boundaries with yourself are so important to your health and happiness.

FREEDOM!

A reminder: Keep in mind the ultimate benefits of boundaries. The cover of this book says, "Set the limits that will set you free," and that's what self-boundaries are about—freedom! Freedom from stress, anxiety, and anger, and the freedom to feel happy, healthy, peaceful, and grounded. Setting boundaries with yourself is another path to that sense of freedom—in my case, the freedom from feeling chained to my phone during what should have been a peaceful part of my day. If you ever feel stuck trying to establish a self-boundary, ask yourself, "What do I need freedom from (or the freedom to do), and what are the guardrails I can establish to create or preserve that freedom?"

BOUNDARIES WITH YOURSELF AND PREP TIPS

Setting boundaries with yourself may not always feel simple or clear, and as we'll discuss, they may not instinctively feel kind, either! The way you consider, frame, and enforce them may take some practice. If healthy boundaries haven't been effectively modeled for you by your parents, friends, or partners, you may find yourself challenged by your own ideas around boundaries as an act of self-care. As with any boundary practice, it is a *practice*; the more fluent you become in the language of boundaries with others, the easier it will be to spot opportunities to set a boundary with yourself.

ACKNOWLEDGE BARRIERS TO SELF-BOUNDARIES. There are a variety of factors that may make setting boundaries with yourself more challenging—notably, stress and mental health issues. When I'm in a period of seasonal depression, it's so hard to uphold commitments to myself, even if I want to. And under periods of intense stress, your body's biology may steer you to numbing, distracting, or coping mechanisms like sugary foods, alcohol, or bingeing TikTok videos—which you know aren't healthy, but have a hard time resisting. A neurodivergent condition like ADHD, autism, or acquired brain injuries (like my concussion) also factors into concentration, time management, and organization, and how you navigate temptation, reward, and self-boundaries. A therapist can point out the ways in which these factors might affect your behaviors, encourage you to develop grace and compassion for yourself, and help you identify the right boundaries for your particular context and goals.

REFRAME YOUR INNER REBEL. You might notice (especially you Four Tendency Rebels) that self-boundaries can start to feel restrictive or punitive instead of empowering and liberating, which is their intention. If you notice that you're feeling restricted when setting a self-boundary, return to the way you've framed the consequences of not respecting your boundary. Not having wine on Wednesday isn't a punishment, it's an act of self-care—a gift from Present You to Future You to ensure you have a restful and relaxing evening, a good night's sleep, and that you awaken feeling clearheaded, energized, and positive. Setting that boundary actually sets you *free* from the major limitations imposed upon you by drinking on a Wednesday night. Reminding yourself that boundaries are an act of defiance against harmful societal systems or expectations can also help—if media, society, culture, and marketing efforts are all pushing you *toward* a behavior that doesn't actually serve you, it's a radical (dare I say *rebellious*) act of self-care to stand up for yourself and say no.

RECRUIT HELP. If you're an Obliger or a people-pleaser, you rely heavily on external accountability to make change stick—but self-boundaries are between you and you, and may prove extra-challenging to hold. If you're struggling to respect your own self-boundaries, lean into your tendency and recruit some external support. Tell your husband, "I'm not checking my phone before bed, so if you see me on it, remind me how much better I'll feel if I put it down." Share your self-boundary with friends, family, or your therapist so you'll have someone cheering you on and holding you accountable, even if the boundary has nothing to do with them. Talk about it on social media as a way of connecting with others who share the same goals. You can also support your self-boundary by setting supporting boundaries with others, like asking your friends not to bring wine when they come over for dinner next Tuesday.

TRY, TRY AGAIN. Trauma, especially in childhood, can trick you into thinking you can't trust yourself, and that you aren't worth keeping promises to yourself. It can disconnect you from your own body so thoroughly that you may still struggle to know what you really want or need. If that is your context, self-boundaries will challenge those beliefs, help you prove to yourself that you can trust your own experience, and demonstrate that you are worthy of exploring and setting these helpful limits. Still, it can be hard to break self-sabotaging patterns, so show yourself grace. If you set a boundary with yourself and find you're struggling to hold it, talking with a friend or therapist, journaling, or engaging with an online support group can help. Boundaries are a practice, and you won't always set the right limit for yourself on the first try. Stay committed to the process, use the tools in this chapter to help, and speak kindly to yourself along the way. I promise if you've made it this far, you're already doing a fantastic job.

SCRIPTS FOR SETTING BOUNDARIES WITH YOURSELF IN STRESSFUL SITUATIONS

These scripts won't include the signature Green, Yellow, Red— just several boundary examples, consequences if your boundary is not upheld, and the freedoms that boundary will bring. (Note: I'll always share the shortest and simplest boundary *first*.)

Since you're only talking to yourself, I can't see a reason for your boundary language to escalate—to be honest, that *would* feel like punishment! Instead, if you find you're not respecting your own boundary, revisit the pain points, the potential fixes, and the consequences *and* freedoms associated with that boundary, and adjust as needed until you find the right fit.

Here, you'll find a variety of commonly stressful situations, example boundaries you might set as a result, and the potential consequences and freedoms associated. Remember to apply the YCDI principle as needed.

I've found myself flopped on the couch scrolling through Netflix every night. I end up staying up way too late, blowing off other things I need to do, or both. What's my boundary here?

BOUNDARY: I will not watch TV after dinner, except on weekends.

BOUNDARY: I will set an alarm for one hour, and when it goes off, the TV goes off.

BOUNDARY: I will only watch one episode of a show on weeknights.

BOUNDARY: I will set the TV timer to turn off at 9 P.M. every weeknight.

FREEDOM: If I uphold this boundary:

• I'll be free from negative self-talk ("I'm so lazy, all I did was watch TV again").
• I'll have more free time before bed.
• I'll get a better night's sleep.
• I'll start my day feeling more prepared and energetic.

CONSEQUENCE: If I don't hold this boundary:

• I'll feel rushed in the morning (or won't accomplish everything I want to that night).
• I'll go to bed stressed.
• I won't sleep as long.
• I'll wake up tired and cranky.

You could try a number of tactics here, but the key is giving yourself the space to do something more productive, restful, or fun. One thing I like to do is combine a reward with a task I've been procrastinating on, so another option is, "I'll only turn on Netflix as long as I'm cleaning or folding laundry." That's how I got through the first season of Love Is Blind—*my closet has never been so organized, and I didn't feel at all guilty for watching. (Embarrassed, maybe. Guilty, no.) The benefit is I watch far less, because my laundry or cleaning rarely takes more than an hour.*

I'm trying to establish a morning routine to help me start my day with less anxiety, but I can't seem to figure out how to make it stick. How can I create space for this routine?

BOUNDARY: I will not pick up my phone until my routine is done.

BOUNDARY: I will wake up fifteen minutes earlier every day, specifically for my routine.

BOUNDARY: I will ensure my journal, a pen, and a morning meditation are prepped each night.

BOUNDARY: To facilitate my routine, I will not hit snooze on weekdays.

FREEDOM: If I uphold this boundary:

• I'll be free from the anxiety that comes when I start my day reactive.
• I'll be free to pursue whatever self-care options feel good to me that morning.

CONSEQUENCE: Without my morning routine:

• I start my day feeling anxious and reactive.
• I will miss the self-care I know makes me feel so good.
• I will likely be disappointed that I didn't follow through.

Though I suspect the phone boundary alone might just solve this, the first step is to ask yourself, "What is holding up my routine?" Maybe you need to set a supporting boundary with your family, like "Please don't come in until 6:45 A.M.; I'll be journaling until then." But if a self-boundary is needed, figure out whether it's technology, your penchant for sleeping in, or your underpreparedness that is getting in the way, and set a boundary there.

Monday mornings are so stressful. I feel overwhelmed with un-read emails, early-morning Slack messages, and this "I'm already behind" feeling inside my head; I always end up spending an hour scrolling social media to avoid it all. Do you have any tips for me?

BOUNDARY: I will not check personal social media before noon on workdays.

BOUNDARY: I will spend the last ten minutes of every Friday making a to-do list for Monday morning.

BOUNDARY: I will arrive at work one hour early on Monday to settle in before everyone else.

BOUNDARY: I will reserve one hour on my calendar Monday mornings for email catch-up.

FREEDOM: If I uphold this boundary:

• I'll be free from the anxiety that accompanies Monday morning.
• I will be free from getting sucked into distracting and unful-filling social media scrolling.
• I will remain on task and therefore be more productive, which will grant me the freedom to set and manage my own priorities.

CONSEQUENCE: If I don't hold this boundary:

• I'll start my week feeling anxious and reactive.
• I'll feel mad at myself for not preparing more effectively.
• I'll feel less productive at work.
• I won't be able to respond as effectively to priorities, and perhaps I'll notice my job performance decline as a result.

Any one of these boundaries would likely help you start your week in a better way—and all of them would surely do the trick. Still, start with the one that you think would have the most impact. Once that becomes a habit, it'll be easier to layer another boundary on top of that, buying yourself even more capacity and freedom.

I'd like to drink less wine—coming home every night and opening a bottle feels like a habit now, and feeling out of control here has made my evenings stressful. This behavior makes me question my relationship with alcohol, and I know alcohol impacts my sleep, motivation, and productivity. What kind of boundary should I set here?

BOUNDARY: I will not drink any alcohol at all for thirty days.

BOUNDARY: I will not keep any alcohol at home, and I will only drink when I go out.

BOUNDARY: I will only buy one bottle of wine a week, and when it's gone, it's gone.

BOUNDARY: I will not drink during the week, only on weekends.

FREEDOM: If I uphold this boundary:

• I'll be free from the many negative impacts alcohol is having on my life (poor sleep, reduced motivation, diminished productivity).
• I'll be free to explore other ways to show myself love, relax, unwind, and be social.
• I'll be free from feeling enslaved to a habit that isn't serving me.
• I'll have more time in the evening for restorative, fulfilling practices.

CONSEQUENCE: If I don't uphold this boundary around wine:

- I'll feel tired, unproductive, and headachy throughout the week.
- I'll remain uneasy about the role alcohol has in my life.
- I'll feel embarrassed or ashamed of my habit; and perhaps I'll start hiding my behaviors from those close to me, which will be harmful for my mental health.

The first boundary of abstaining from alcohol for thirty days is the most effective, because habit research shows black-and-white rules (always or never versus sometimes) are the easiest for the brain to follow. Plus, it will force you to find other coping mechanisms to deal with stress, anxiety, or loneliness, which gives you the opportunity to discover healthier methods of handling adverse experiences—methods like journaling, walking, or taking cold showers. (That last one is my personal favorite—I have a whole podcast about how cold showers are an instant switch for my mood, energy, and mental health.)

With any of these boundaries, seek support from loved ones, online groups, and/or a counselor—you don't need to have a problem with alcohol to ask for help evaluating your relationship with it. And don't forget to set supporting boundaries with friends and family, like "Please don't pressure me to drink" or "Please don't bring wine when you come over for dinner tomorrow."

My bedroom is always a mess. The clutter stresses me out, especially before bed, but I never seem to have an hour to clean it, and on the weekends, I want to be out having fun, not stuck inside. There has to be a trick here.

BOUNDARY: I will spend ten minutes every night before I go to sleep tidying my bedroom.

BOUNDARY: I will practice the "one touch" rule for everything in my bedroom. (See the tip.)

BOUNDARY: I will spend one hour on Sunday night cleaning my bedroom while watching Netflix.

BOUNDARY: I will tackle one drawer or closet shelf a week until my room is organized.

FREEDOM: If I uphold this boundary:

• I'll be free from the stress of going to bed in a messy room.
• I'll be free to know where my belongings are and whether or not they're clean.
• I'll be free to move about my room with ease.
• I'll be free from the pressure to stop everything and clean.
• I'll wake up in the morning in a peaceful, calm space.

CONSEQUENCE: If I don't uphold this boundary:

• I'll go to bed every night stressed and anxious.
• I won't have easy access to exactly what I want to wear.
• My belongings might get dirty, wrinkled, or lost.
• I won't feel peaceful in my own space.

If cleaning off your entire chairdrobe (that one chair where you throw all your stuff) while watching Inventing Anna *isn't your idea of fun (can you tell I like to mix my reward with my chores?), commit to just a few minutes a night—those few minutes do add up. You could apply the Marie Kondo method of tidying by category (like folded items first, hanging items next), choose one area (like your nightstand or that chair) to tackle at a time, or start with one side of the room and make your way to the other. Choose whatever you think will have the biggest impact.*

THE "ONE TOUCH" PRINCIPLE

The "one touch" principle was created by Ann Gomez, a productivity consultant and the founder of the Toronto-based company Clear Concept. "One touch" was originally designed as a business organization tool to help executives better manage email, paperwork, texts, and voicemails, but it's also incredibly effective when applied to household organization. Essentially, once you touch something, it *has* to go directly where it belongs. That means when you take that T-shirt out of your gym bag, it can't be tossed on your chairdrobe for later; you have to fold it, hang it up, or toss it in the hamper. (Make this rule work for you—if you're cleaning the entire playroom and have ten things to bring to your child's bedroom, it's okay to stack them and take them up all at once, but you can't just let them sit there in a pile for another day.) It may feel like more work in the moment, but this practice will save you time in the long run, and it helps you not accumulate piles on surfaces for the "one day" that you'll put them back. Learn more about Gomez's "one touch" principle at clearconceptinc.ca.

SCRIPTS FOR SETTING BOUNDARIES WITH YOURSELF AROUND HABITS AND GOALS

In this section, we'll set some boundaries designed to help Future You achieve everything on your vision board. Focusing on the consequences here will be extra-important and can feel especially challenging, because the consequences of not upholding these boundaries are noticed in the future, not the present. In the face of temptation and reward, it can be easy to lose sight of what *really* happens (or what *will* happen) when you spend the money, skip the workout, or say yes to yet another project. Keep your "why" close to you and do your best to automate the boundary or make it as black-and-white as possible.

I'm working hard to pay off debt and I'd like to set some boundaries around how I'm spending money, particularly during shopping trips at Target or on Amazon, where I always end up with more than I need. Can you help?

BOUNDARY: I will buy only household and grocery necessities for the next thirty days.

BOUNDARY: I will only visit Target or Amazon with a detailed list, and buy only what's on that list.

BOUNDARY: I will review my budget every week and stay within that budget.

BOUNDARY: I will connect with my financial planner every week to report on my spending.

FREEDOM: If I uphold this boundary:

- I'll be free from debt faster.
- I'll be free from the anxiety and worry that debt brings.
- I'll be free to save for a big-picture goal like a car or a house.
- I'll be free to have more options because my credit scores will be better.
- I'll be free from stress about unplanned expenses.

CONSEQUENCE: If I do not uphold this boundary:

- I'll remain in debt for much longer.
- My home will be cluttered with things I don't need.
- I'll be stressed and anxious every time I open a bill or review my credit card statement.
- I won't be able to achieve my long-term goals.

Automate that boundary! Download an app like You Need a Budget (YNAB) or Goodbudget. These are geared toward smarter financial planning, rather than tracking expenses after the fact.

Apps can also provide external accountability, sending alerts when you're close to your limit in any one expense category.

I just joined a gym and I really want to be consistent, because I feel so good when I go. But I'm finding lots of reasons to skip "just this once." How can I keep this promise to myself?

BOUNDARY: I will not skip the gym for any reason for thirty straight days.

BOUNDARY: I will go to the gym and do just five minutes of activity five mornings a week.

BOUNDARY: I will go to bed and get up forty-five minutes earlier to start going to the gym in the morning.

BOUNDARY: I will sign up for a regularly scheduled class at the gym and not miss any of those sessions.

FREEDOM: If I uphold this boundary:

- I'll be free from the guilt and unhappiness that I feel when I skip the gym.
- I'll be free to move my body in a way that feels good.
- I'll be free to feel amazing and proud of myself afterward.
- I'll be free to enjoy being in my body more.

CONSEQUENCE: If I do not uphold this boundary:

- I'll continue to feel guilty about skipping.
- I'll continue to feel low-energy, tired, achy, and weak.
- I'll be distracted thinking about how I should have gone and frustrated that I can't seem to honor this commitment.
- I'll know I'm wasting money on this membership.

I have a ton of tricks that I used to create my gym habit, including going first thing in the morning, laying out all of my clothes the night before, and committing to just *putting them on in the morning (at which point, I felt so dumb standing around my house in workout clothes at 5:30 A.M. that I'd end up driving straight to the gym).*

I'm a new entrepreneur trying to meet a sales goal, but I'm quickly approaching burnout. I find myself taking on clients I know I'm too busy to handle because I really want to hit my target, but I realize that it's counterproductive if I'm too over-worked to make my clients happy. How can I set a limit here?

BOUNDARY: I will not take on another new client this month.

BOUNDARY: I will take on only two new clients a month for the next six months.

BOUNDARY: I will not allow myself to book more than four appointments a day.

BOUNDARY: I will not work more than eight hours a day and will not work at all on Sundays.

FREEDOM: If I uphold this boundary:

• I'll be free to spend more time with each client.
• I'll have more free time to recharge and rest.
• I'll be free from the stress of missing deadlines or working overtime.
• I'll be free to evaluate my goals against a realistic workload.
• I'll be free to structure the business any way I want, in alignment with my self-care.

CONSEQUENCE: If I do not uphold this boundary:

• I'll continue to feel overworked.
• I will stress about missing deadlines and deliverables.

- I will end each day feeling like I didn't do enough.
- I will feel unsuccessful because I'm neither meeting my goals nor taking good care of myself.
- My physical and mental health will suffer to the point that my business itself might not succeed.

This is also a limit you'd want to set with prospective clients. After committing to yourself that you won't take any new clients on this month, you'd also communicate that clearly and kindly: "I'm at capacity for the rest of the month. Would you be able to start with me in April?" The self-boundary here is the first step toward recognizing you also need a boundary with your clients, for the good of your future relationship.

I'm new to recovery and am committed to making it stick. I've set good boundaries with friends and family, but I haven't set any boundaries with myself yet. Do you have any tips for self-boundaries around recovery?

BOUNDARY: I will not drink alcohol or use drugs, under any circumstances.

BOUNDARY: I will attend meetings or therapy three times a week for one year.

BOUNDARY: I will not attend social gatherings with people I don't know.

BOUNDARY: If I am uncomfortable in a social setting, I will leave immediately.

FREEDOM: If I uphold this boundary:

- I'll continue to remain free of alcohol and drugs!
- I'll be free to expand my life to include fulfilling, uplifting, energizing pursuits.

- I'll be free to adopt healthy habits.
- I'll be free to meet like-minded, supportive people.
- I'll be free to restore good relationships with family and friends.
- I'll be free to pursue therapy to heal old wounds.
- I'll be free to find a new job, a new partner, and create a new life.

CONSEQUENCE: If I do not uphold this boundary:

- I'll fall back into drinking or using, and my entire life will fall apart again faster than I could ever imagine.

That first self-boundary is an often overlooked one, probably because it's so obvious, but unless you've explicitly made that promise to yourself, the other boundaries you set won't hold you up. This one is personal, yes, and I could write a whole chapter on the list of boundaries I set with myself around my recovery, but these are the ones I found the most important and helpful. The more you can layer these on top of one another, the more space you'll create between you and your addiction. Godspeed.

LOVING THE LIMITS THAT SET YOU FREE

Exploring the intersection of self-boundaries and habits is one of my favorite topics because habit research can help you support just about every boundary you set with yourself. Whether you want to keep your bedroom neater, drink less wine, or be more consistent with the gym, the tools and techniques from habit science can offer strategies to layer on top of your boundaries to really make them stick. Here are three bonus habit hacks that can apply almost universally to any self-boundary:

- **MAKE THE GOAL SHOWING UP.** Habits are built on consistency, and you build consistency by showing up again and again. It's not about the actual workout, how many shirts you hang up, or what you do after you turn off Netflix; the point is, you went to the gym, made it to the bedroom for tidying, and turned off the TV. If you just keep showing up, it will feel far more natural and effortless to do more—get into the workout, fold the rest of the laundry, or prep your lunch for the next day. Chase consistency.

- **DON'T RELY ON MOTIVATION.** When you're starting a new habit, it's easy to be motivated and excited. But nobody is motivated 24/7, and when motivation fails, you may feel lost—and revert right back to doom-scrolling, wine-drinking, or hitting "snooze." Motivation doesn't precede action; action precedes motivation. The key is just to do *something,* and trust that a body in motion tends to stay in motion. This is why "showing up" is so important—start with action, commit to consistency, and watch the habit groove itself.

- **PRACTICE, NOT PERFECT.** You may spend the next year reminding yourself, "Don't say yes to a client before you evaluate your capacity," then get excited about a project and agree to take it on immediately. The point isn't to hold boundaries perfectly every time, it's to hold them conscientiously. Demanding perfection can shift us into an unhealthy "all or nothing" mindset that says, "I messed up today, so screw it all." This may mean interrupting yourself to say, "Actually, can I give you a final answer tomorrow?" or telling your client, "I got excited about your project yesterday, but let's make sure we're aligned on scope and timeline before we sign a contract." It's okay if you forget, buckle under stress, or act without thinking—just recommit to showing up for yourself at the very next opportunity, no negative self-talk required.

Finally, a self-boundary is only as effective as the freedom that boundary grants you, so if you find a boundary isn't working the way you thought it would, pivot! Maybe you don't need to spend ten minutes a night cleaning your room—you actually need to budget for a cleaning service to come in every other week to help you maintain a baseline level of tidiness. There is no shame in changing a boundary. Self-boundaries are a gift from Present You to Future You, and if that gift isn't what Future You needs, exchange it for something better.

PART THREE

Boundary Benefits

Gifts to the World

How to Hold Your Boundaries, and Everyone Else's

In early January, a woman named Cheryl wrote to me to ask for help with a boundary gone bad. Over the holidays, her son Jason set a boundary with her about how they'd be spending Christmas. Cheryl wrote, "Our family holds a lot of get-togethers over the holidays. We make plans for Christmas Eve, open presents together on Christmas morning, invite the extended family over for Christmas dinner, then everyone comes back the next day for coffee and brunch. This year, my son and his partner decided they wanted to spend most of the holiday with their new baby, just the three of them." He told Cheryl they'd come over on Christmas Eve and they invited her to their house on Christmas morning to open presents, but they planned on spending the rest of their holidays at home alone.

Cheryl did not handle it well. "I took it quite personally," she wrote. "I felt like he was denying me my new grandbaby, and I told him in no uncertain terms it was selfish." Despite the pressure from his mom, Jason calmly held his boundary, explaining it was important to him that he and his partner create their own family traditions now that they have a child of their own. He gently said they'd talk about it again soon—and hung up. Cheryl reported, "We ended the call on a sour note, and I fumed about all of it for the rest of the morning."

Once you identify the need for a boundary and find the right words to establish it, it might still be that the hardest part is yet to come. Holding your boundary and dealing with the pushback, anger, or manipulation that might follow can challenge anyone's resolve, especially if boundaries are a new practice for you. Learning to hold the boundary requires its own set of scripts, and much like Jason, you may need to accept that not everyone will like or understand the limits you set. This chapter will prepare you for these situations and give you the words and strategies you need to effectively hold your carefully considered boundaries.

DEALING WITH BOUNDARY PUSHBACK

In a perfect world, you'd state your boundary and your conversation partner would immediately confirm their understanding of and respect for your limit. That actually does happen pretty often, which means you can and should approach boundary-making with a positive mindset. As I mentioned in Chapter 2, you should assume your conversation partner wants to respect your limits, and that they just need more information about where they are and how to do so.

However, there are instances where your conversation partner will respond poorly to your boundary, and I want you to be prepared. That doesn't mean heading into conversations ready for battle, sounding antagonistic, defensive, or attitude-y. None of that feels kind, and it's likely to generate the very response you're trying to avoid. This section is devoted to helping you navigate responses that might range from the gaslighting "You're being way too sensitive," to the passive-aggressive "We're just trying to help," to the just-plain-aggressive "How selfish can you be?"

The most common in-the-moment reaction to a boundary is defensiveness. Defensiveness can be a cover-up for embarrassment, guilt, disappointment, hurt feelings, or shock, as it was for Cheryl, who had no idea her son wanted to start his own family tradition at Christmas.

Someone who reacts defensively might see your boundary as a criticism of them, rather than a healthy limit you are setting for yourself. Perhaps Cheryl heard, "We don't want to spend Christmas Day with you," instead of, "We're excited to create new holiday traditions with our child." Or perhaps your boundary request directly or indirectly highlights how inconsiderate or rude their behavior has been, which can be very uncomfortable, especially if you're in a group setting (like calling out a co-worker for his sexist joke during happy hour). When people react defensively, they're trying to distract or deflect from their own discomfort or negative emotion by somehow shifting the blame back to you.

RE-PATTERNING STARTS WITH YOU

Many negative boundary reactions stem from a lack of witnessing healthy boundaries in action. If you never saw boundaries modeled by your family, friends, or co-workers and weren't explicitly taught that boundary-setting is a healthy practice, it might feel jarring or harsh to be on the receiving end of someone else's boundary. Cheryl acknowledged this when we were talking about Jason's holiday request. She said, "I was never able to set these kinds of boundaries with either side of the family when my kids were young, and frankly, I was resentful that Jason got to." Also, the same factors that make us feel guilty for setting a boundary (see page 44) make it equally hard for us to accept one. If we're taught that setting a limit and standing up for ourselves is arrogant, impolite, or greedy, it's only natural that we will apply those same negative labels to someone else when they set a boundary with us. The key is to reframe the boundaries *we* set as healthy acts of self-care, which makes it much easier to see everyone else's boundaries in that light. As with so many of my tips so far, your friendly neighborhood therapist can help you with re-patterning.

While defensiveness is often a subconscious reaction, other responses can feel more deliberate. Some people may try to convince you that the boundary you're setting is selfish, unreasonable, or rude as a means of avoiding accountability for their own actions. They'll argue that the issue isn't their behavior; it's that your boundary is unnecessary, overly dramatic, or punitive. If they can convince you that *you're* the one making unreasonable requests, then they have nothing to apologize for—and they may go to great lengths to gaslight you into believing you're in the wrong for asking them to respect your healthy limits.

People also get mad when it feels like you're taking something away from them, even if they never had a right to it in the first place. These folks may apply *all* the tactics—defensiveness, hostility, blaming, manipulation—because if they make you feel bad enough, maybe you'll drop this inconvenient (for them) boundary altogether, and then life can resume as it was. This is common when you've been letting someone overrun your limits for some time now, and they've become used to the ways you've allowed them to take advantage of you.

> *People reacting this badly to your boundaries means you're revoking a privilege they were never meant to have.*

And in many cases, how someone ultimately responds to your clear, kind boundary will tell you everything you need to know about whether or not the relationship can be salvaged.

That having been said . . . don't rush to judgment *too* fast. People's initial reactions aren't always how they want to show up, or how they'll continue to behave, as long as you're willing to extend them three small courtesies.

THE COURTESY OF SPACE, GRACE, AND FACE TIME

If you drop a boundary and it doesn't go over well, don't draw any conclusions just yet. People often respond poorly in the heat of the moment. The best thing to do when a boundary you've set is poorly received is to extend three small courtesies: space, grace, and face time.

SPACE: Give your conversation partner the space to process your boundary request on their own time. Pushing them in the moment to understand or accede isn't productive, especially if they're hurt, embarrassed, feeling guilty, or otherwise stuck in defensive mode. Jason shared his boundary with his mom, explained his desire to start his own family Christmas tradition, then kindly said goodbye, allowing Cheryl time to process her feelings and removing the potential that she'd vent more of her in-the-moment hurt or anger onto Jason, which could damage their relationship. This is especially important if you express your boundary in a group setting, like at work or a family gathering. Give the person a chance to save face by sharing your limit, then gracefully stepping away to allow them time to process their feelings without any pressure from you.

GRACE: Recognize that someone's initial response to your boundary may not be their final reaction. It's natural for someone to automatically react with hurt, anger, or frustration when presented with a boundary, but when you give them space, they will likely arrive at a different mindset all on their own. Don't judge someone based on how they react in the moment, and don't allow yourself to be swept up in their anger or irritation. Be compassionate if the initial reaction to your boundary was less than ideal; wait patiently for the right moment to revisit with your conversation partner; and see if you can empathize with their feelings of disappointment, confusion, or hurt. Remember, boundaries are a practice for everyone, including those receiving them, and you can hold your boundary and acknowledge the receiver's feelings at the same time.

FACE TIME: If the person receiving your boundary comes back to you with a different attitude, offer to share more about your boundary in an effort to deepen your relationship and smooth over their initial response. This isn't the same as justifying or overexplaining the boundary while you're setting it; in this situation, you've stated the boundary and the person has (reluctantly or otherwise) agreed to respect it. Now, in the spirit of good communication, feel free to share more about what this limit means to you, and how much you appreciate them upholding it for you. Jason might tell his mom that his favorite childhood memories from Christmas were the quiet times with just his mom and dad, and how much he's looking forward to re-creating those with his own family. He might also reassure his mom that she'll have plenty of time around the holidays with her new grandchild.

If you allow your conversation partner time to process and they come back, apologize, and initiate a healthy conversation around the issue, you've accomplished what you set out to do. You've established a healthy limit, preserved the relationship, and perhaps even deepened your connection by sharing from the heart and listening with grace and empathy.

WHEN ALL ELSE FAILS

But what if they double down and continue to push back, manipulate you, or refuse to respect your limit altogether? Here is a bit of life-changing boundary magic: Their anger, defensiveness, and manipulative tactics are not your problem. Remember:

> *The way other people respond to your boundary is not your business.*

You've identified a limit to keep yourself safe and healthy, and you've set it with someone in the spirit of improving your relationship with them. You've used clear, kind words. You've reminded yourself not to feel guilty, because you deserve to have your needs met and you are worthy of holding expectations around the way people treat you. And you've given them the space and grace to process your boundary on their own time. If they *still* refuse to respect your limit, then it's time to enact your boundary by enforcing the consequence—and walk away. *Your work is done.*

How other people choose to receive your words and respond to them is *their work*. It's their job to process your request and determine how to respond to it. It's their job to practice self-awareness, and decide whether or not to take it personally. It's their job to respond to you from a place of empathy and in the spirit of cooperation, rather than from a place of anger, defensiveness, or hurt. It's their job to decide that your limits are worthy of respect, whether they agree with them or not.

You can't do any of that work for anyone else. You also can't back down on your boundary, because that would hurt you *and* your relationship. So, what is left? Taking responsibility for your own boundaries; communicating them in clear, kind language; and understanding that how someone chooses to respond is not your business, or your problem. Write that down on a sticky note, Sharpie it on your palm, or otherwise burn it into your memory, because there's a chance you're going to need it.

Should you find yourself in a situation where someone responds poorly to your boundary in the moment, here are a few phrases you can use to express empathy without backing down:

- "I know this is hard to hear, but not speaking up was making me resentful, so it's better for our relationship that I do."
- "This is uncomfortable for me, too, but I'm committed to communicating better and expressing my needs more clearly."
- "I can see that you're disappointed, and I hope you'll respect that this is what's best for me."
- "I understand you're upset. I'll give you some time to process that—let's talk later."
- "I appreciate you wanting to help. The best way to do that right now is to be supportive of my decision."
- "I'm sorry this is how you're choosing to experience our conversation."

That last one is my favorite—you're not apologizing for the boundary, but you are sad that they're choosing to see it as a punishment or act of meanness. (And it's certainly nicer than saying, "Sorry, not sorry.")

The day after Jason first expressed his boundary around Christmas, he and Cheryl talked again—and she told me this conversation went much better. Cheryl said, "I kept replaying the 'selfish' comment in my head and felt really bad. I knew it wasn't about me, and I recognized that I couldn't project my feelings and insecurities about it back onto him. It was a real lesson, and if I hadn't had all of your advice on boundaries, I wouldn't have seen it for what it was."

Here's the other benefit of having a regular, healthy boundary practice—you'll be a much better relationship partner when someone sets a boundary with *you*.

ASK, AND YE SHALL RECEIVE: ACCEPTING BOUNDARIES GRACEFULLY

You might imagine that since I am "the Boundary Lady," I must be the *perfect* conversation partner when someone tries to set one with me, right? Eesh . . . not always. I can also get defensive, take things personally, and behave poorly in the face of someone else's boundary. Just ask my sister.

My son and I have been visiting my sister, Kelly, in San Diego every February since he was two years old. At this point, we have our routine down: Fly in Friday at noon; hit the beach early Saturday afternoon to look for shells, play in the surf, and build sand castles; and leave on Sunday afternoon. But the first year we visited, I assumed we'd get up early on Saturday and head to the beach right away—my sister is an early riser during the week so she can get to the gym before work, and I knew the time change would have my already-early-bird son up at 5 A.M.

When we arrived for that first visit on Friday, however, my sister told me, "I've had a super long week at work, and I'm exhausted. I'd like to sleep as long as I can tomorrow morning. We'll get ready for the beach as soon as I get up." I agreed, although I was disappointed she didn't want to maximize our short time together. "Still," I thought, "how late can she sleep?"

ELEVEN O'CLOCK, that's how late. Which was *six hours* after my toddler woke up demanding chicken sausage, blueberries, and the beach.

I was fuming. How could my sister not be more respectful of my time, knowing I was awake entertaining a two-year-old all by myself? Also, we were her *guests,* and she left us to fend for ourselves all morning—our mom raised us better than that. More than anything, though, I was hurt. Didn't she want to spend as much time with us as possible? We were only there for one weekend. I took her slumber personally—like she'd rather be in bed than hang out with us.

In essence, I did the exact *opposite* of what I'd want someone to do when I set a boundary with them—embarrassing, I know. But it's only natural that uncomfortable things provoke an initial defensive response, and you may notice this same double standard inside your head, too, when people set a boundary with you. You might feel like:

- *Your* boundary makes total sense, but *theirs* feels unreasonable.
- *Your* boundary is focused on your needs, but *theirs* feels personal to or critical of you.
- *Your* boundary will ultimately improve the relationship, but *theirs* feels kinda selfish.
- *Your* boundary was carefully thought out, but *theirs* feels impulsive or sudden.

It's normal and natural to apply this double standard when your boundary practice is new, but here are two truths: First, the more you set boundaries with others, the more others will feel empowered to do the same in their own lives. (Yay, you're a change-maker!) It's likely that as you further your own boundary practice, you'll find yourself on the receiving end of more boundaries, too, which is a good thing—it means that relationships in all areas of your life are getting to a more honest and healthy place. Second, the better you get at identifying a need for, communicating, and holding your own healthy boundaries, the more easily you'll be able to recognize when someone is doing that with you. This means that as your own boundary practice develops, you'll be able to more quickly switch from feeling defensive, hurt, or angry to responding in an empathetic and collaborative way to other people's boundaries.

Though I was frustrated, I did respect my sister's request to let her sleep in. I didn't passive-aggressively make a lot of noise so she'd wake up earlier, or barge in at 10 A.M. and say, "That's late enough." In the time and space I had to process how I was feeling, I recognized that her "selfishness" was probably a boundary. I knew her job had been stressful, and that she'd been working late many nights. We showed up during an especially busy season for her, but she insisted we come anyway because she really wanted to see us. She wasn't telling me I wasn't important or that she didn't care, she was saying, "I want to spend the weekend feeling refreshed and recharged, and if I can get one great night of sleep, I'll be right there with you." (Or at least that's what I told myself during an early-morning cruise through the local Target in an attempt to keep my kid entertained while we waited.)

Because I had so much practice with boundaries, it was easier for me to assume that my sister wasn't being selfish or callous, she was communicating her needs for the rest of our visit, and ultimately the good of our relationship. But discerning someone else's motivation for their "boundary" isn't always easy.

THEIR BOUNDARY, THEIR BUSINESS

The truth is, we can all get defensive, frustrated, or angry when someone sets a healthy boundary with us, and that might lead us to create stories in our head about what that boundary *really* means. Here are some examples:

The boundary they set with you: "I don't allow smoking inside."

Their healthy limit: Because it affects my health and breathing, and makes my house smell bad.

How you may experience it: They're trying to pressure me to quit by making it harder for me to smoke.

The boundary they set with you: "I don't have capacity for that conversation tonight."

Their healthy limit: Because I've had a hard day, and my mental health can't process this topic in a way that would be helpful.

How you may experience it: They're mad I brought it up, so they're teaching me a lesson by refusing to talk.

The boundary they set with you: "I'd like to sleep as long as I can tomorrow."

Their healthy limit: Because I'm exhausted and catching up on sleep will keep me energized and happy for the rest of our visit.

How you may experience it: I flew all the way out here, but they'd rather sleep than spend time with me.

If boundaries are new to you, be on the lookout for these knee-jerk reactions when someone sets one with *you*. In the spirit of the Relationship Golden Rule, I like to assume the best of others here—if it sounds like a boundary, I assume it *is* a healthy boundary, so I won't take it personally, and I will choose to respect it for the good of the relationship. Nine times out of ten, assuming the best leads to the best outcomes, stronger relationships, and more open conversations. But if you're still fighting the urge to know why they need to set this limit with you, remember:

The motivation behind their
request is not my business.

Your only responsibility is to respect other people's needs, in your integrity and for the sake of the relationship. My recommendation is to do that, unless or until their "boundaries" demand that you compromise your own integrity, values, health, or safety. That's not always easy to judge, and you may find yourself being more respectful than the situation deserves, in an effort to be a good relationship partner.

In my own life, I'm okay with that, to a degree. However, there *are* some warning signs that your conversation partner is avoiding, punishing, or manipulating you with their "boundaries." When I notice these red flags, they are an immediate sign to pay attention to how the relationship progresses, especially if they become a pattern:

- **Avoidance without follow-up:** It's one thing to say, "I need some time to process this, I'll call you next week" and another to give you the silent treatment without any warning, or to not respond to your requests to talk.
- **Enforcing a "rule" that has nothing to do with them:** If my sister had said, "I'll probably sleep until noon, but please don't go anywhere until I'm up," that's not a healthy limit, that's just her telling me how to spend my morning.
- **Only enacting "boundaries" in retaliation to yours:** If the only time someone tries to set a "limit" with you is after you've called them out on their bad behavior or tried to establish a boundary with them, that might indicate blame-shifting or a reluctance to be held accountable.
- **Sneakiness instead of clarity:** If someone else's "boundary" includes going behind your back, gossiping about you to others, or engaging in otherwise harmful behavior under the guise of "caring" or "trying to help," that's a red flag.
- **Making you responsible for their feelings:** If someone's "boundary" only involves you doing or not doing things to

preserve *their* emotional stability, that's controlling behavior, not a healthy limit they're prepared to enact.

As always, the only things you are responsible for are your own actions, and how you choose to respond. So, here's how to maintain a healthy relationship and stay in your integrity in the face of a request that may or may not be a healthy boundary.

FOLLOW THE RELATIONSHIP GOLDEN RULE. Remember on page 167 when you committed to saying what you mean and *trusting that your conversation partner will do the same*? Practice that here. If someone sets a boundary with you, assume it's coming from a healthy place and they are speaking their truth, and reflect that back to them. "I hear that you need extra sleep tonight. Thanks for letting me know. I'll be quiet in the morning so you can rest as long as you need." If they *were* being snarky, they'd likely expect you to be angry or snarky back. Being courteous and kind can be disarming—in a good way! Maybe they'll say, "Thank you, I really appreciate that," or maybe they'll say, "Wow, thanks—you know, I think I can set my alarm for 10:00 as a compromise. Would that be better?" Either way, it's in your interest to give your conversation partner the benefit of the doubt. By respecting their boundary, you'll demonstrate your commitment to the relationship.

SPEAK YOUR TRUTH, TOO. This is the part where you also need to consider your needs and speak your truth clearly and kindly, too. If you really wanted to head to the beach early, then say, "Cool, sleep as long as you want. We may head to the beach ahead of you, though—you know we wake up super early. Text when you get up so we can coordinate." This is a much better strategy than agreeing resentfully, then spending the morning grumpy (take it from me).

REINFORCE THE RELATIONSHIP GOLDEN RULE. If it comes out later that their request *wasn't* a healthy boundary but an expression of frustration or anger, call them on it. "I hear that you're upset. I wish I had known that last night, so we could have talked it through. It's hard for me to be respectful of your needs if you don't share them with me. Next time, I'd appreciate a more honest conversation."

LOOK FOR PATTERNS. If your conversation partner is repeatedly demonstrating any of the "red flag" behaviors, now might be a good time to initiate an honest conversation. Describe what you've observed, how this pattern makes you feel, and give them the opportunity to self-observe and course-correct.

TAKE RESPONSIBILITY. In the end, you are responsible for your own feelings and behaviors. If the way your conversation partner continues to behave doesn't work for you, then perhaps it's time to accept that this person isn't willing or capable of respecting your relationship, and set your own boundary around how you interact going forward, for your own self-care. Whatever you choose, make sure your action is in the best interest of your own health, and not about perpetuating the cycle of punishing or controlling each other and calling it a "boundary."

IT'S OKAY TO BE DISAPPOINTED

When my sister finally woke up that morning, I was committed to respecting her request as a healthy boundary while still sharing how I felt. I didn't want to pretend I wasn't disappointed, but I didn't want her to think I was guilt-tripping her, either. When she came out of her room, I first asked if she slept well and felt better. "I did!" she exclaimed. "That was the best night's sleep I've had all week, thanks for being so quiet." I told her what we had done that morning, and how excited my son was for the beach. Then I said, "At first I was bummed that we didn't get an earlier start, because we're only here until tomorrow. But I can see how much you needed the rest, and we'll still have plenty of beach time." She smiled and said, "I know you've been up since forever, but Auntie Kelly is ready to rock! I'm gonna run that kid ragged on the beach and let Mom relax for a change." In that moment, I was *so* glad I didn't give in to frustration or disappointment, accuse her of being selfish, or blow up at her in resentment. We ended up spending the whole afternoon at the beach, and I did get time to relax while she and my son went off and hunted for just the right rock.

When someone sets a boundary with you, it can be disappointing. You might feel hurt or sad, and you should express that. It's possible to acknowledge your feelings and convey your respect for someone's boundary at the same time, but there's a right way and a wrong way to do that. Let's go back to Cheryl's holiday scenario, and imagine you're her. You invite your son, his partner, and their new baby over for three full days of Christmas events. But your son says they're hoping to start their own tradition, so they won't be spending all of that time with you. How could you respond?

Option 1: "Wow, I didn't expect that. I'm really disappointed; I assumed you'd let me spend time with my new grandbaby. But I guess Christmas morning is better than nothing."

While you *are* honoring his boundary here, this feels more like a guilt-trip than kind acceptance. You lead with your disappointment, your "I assumed" comment is mildly passive-aggressive, and you only reluctantly acquiesce to his proposal to visit on Christmas morning. Yes, you're respecting his boundary. Yes, you're expressing how you really feel. But this isn't the kindest way to go about it, and your son probably feels like you're trying to pressure him into changing his plans.

Option 2: "I understand—it's your first Christmas together!

I'll miss spending the whole day with all of you, but having you here will make Christmas morning even more special."

In this response, you acknowledge and honor the boundary *first*. You're not pressuring him to change it, because the first thing you say is, "I hear your limit, and I respect that." You then go on to express how you feel, while taking responsibility for those feelings. You're not dumping your emotions into your son's lap, expecting him to fix it. Instead, you're acknowledging that your time together is special and committing to make the most of it. When you apply this framework, you honor the boundary and your relationship more directly.

To healthfully express your feelings *and* honor a boundary:

First, honor the boundary. Then express your feelings and take responsibility for them.

That's exactly what I did when my sister woke up—I asked her if she slept well and how she felt, expressed my very real feelings of sadness that we didn't have more time together, then took responsibility for my feelings by committing to making the most of the day we had left.

SCRIPTS FOR RESPONDING TO OTHER PEOPLE'S BOUNDARIES

Now, let's take some of the boundary scripts from this book and turn them around, demonstrating how you might respond if these boundaries were being set with *you*.

> **We have an infant and I'm going back to work. I need my partner (that's you) to start waking up earlier to share in the responsibilities of everything that needs to get done in the morning. How can we tackle this?** (See page 183.)

The boundary they set with you: "Next week, I need you on baby duty from 6 to 6:30 A.M. so I can get ready for work."

Your response: "I'm on it—I'll set my alarm fifteen minutes early just to be sure. I'm feeling a little stressed with this transition, so I'll tell work I need a lighter meeting schedule to help me adjust. How are you feeling?"

First, reassure your partner that you really do have this. Then share how you're feeling—nice touch asking your partner how they feel, too. Bonus: Follow this up with, "Let's sit down on Saturday so we can establish our minimum standard of care, and so you can fill in anything I'm forgetting. I want your first week back to be as stress-free as possible."

My partner (that's you) comes home from work and immediately starts to vent about the hardest parts of their day. Their job is stressful, I know, but I also just got home, and it makes me even more stressed when I should be trying to unwind. Help? (page 190)

The boundary they set with you: "I'm over capacity and can't handle a vent session. Can we take the night off from work talk?"

Your response: "Absolutely—why don't you take the night and do something that feels good. I'm really struggling here and need to get this off my chest, so I'm going to call my brother. I'll check in with you later."

Nice work validating their feelings—and sharing your own. If you really need someone to talk to, go find that person! If you still want to fill your partner in, wait a day, then say, "I'm feeling better about work stuff, but I'd still like to tell you what's been happening. Let me know when it's a good time."

My in-laws (that's you) are always inviting themselves on our family vacation. We're planning our next trip, and I'd like to head this off at the pass. How can I nicely say, "You're not invited?" (page 115)

The boundary they set with you: "No, you can't join us for this one. We're looking forward to having quality time with the kids, and we've promised them that this time, it's just the four of us."

Your response: "Totally understand—I'm sure you'll make some wonderful memories together. Can we FaceTime with the kids before you leave?"

Here, you're clearly respecting their vacation boundary with no pressure whatsoever to plan another trip or visit another time— well done! If you'd still like to plan a trip with them or the kids, bring it up at another time, but give them a proactive out, like, "If vacations just feel too hard with so many people in the mix, please say so and we'll stop asking."

The same strategy applies if you want to ask a clarifying question while honoring the boundary, like asking the person setting the boundary to share more about how they're feeling, what they're experiencing, or how you can further improve the dynamic going forward. You'll still want to explicitly honor the boundary first, then inquire if they're willing to share more in an effort to improve the relationship and your understanding. Here's an example from the Sensitive Subjects chapter:

I'm navigating a chronic health condition and am constantly receiving unsolicited advice about trying this treatment, that diet, or "positive thinking" my way to healing. People (that's

you) mean well, but they're just adding more stress. I need some words at the ready for the next time this happens. (Page 271)

The boundary they set with you: "Thanks, but I'm not looking for advice outside of my own healthcare team right now."

Your response: "Understood—I'm sorry I offered that unsolicited advice, it won't happen again. If you're willing at some point, I'd love for you to share what would make you feel supported. I could bring you meals, run errands for you, take the kids to a movie on Saturday, or just listen—if any of those sound good, I'm here."

Excellent work acknowledging the misstep and reassuring them they've been heard. Asking them to let you know how you can best support them is a lovely gesture, but even more lovely is offering them a few concrete suggestions on how you're willing to show up.

Another considerate tactic is to simply uphold the boundary in the moment, and save the follow-up questions for another time, when you're both calm and comfortable, and the other person may feel more receptive to opening up. Accepting the boundary and then immediately changing the subject can feel like a relief for the boundary-setter, making it extra-clear your only intention is to agree to their limit. If you sense your conversation partner is feeling defensive, shaken, or upset, save the clarifying conversation for another time, and be sure to preface it with "I'd like to ask a few questions about how I can be of support to you, so let me know if you have capacity for that."

PREEMPTIVE STRIKES

As you get more comfortable with setting boundaries, you may find your-self going out of your way to preemptively inquire about other people's capacity, time, or needs so they don't have to set a boundary with you. It might sound like:

- "I had a hard day at work—do you have capacity for a five-minute vent session?"
- "It's been a long weekend with the kids—do you want some quiet time to yourself tonight?"
- "I'd love to include your quote in my next article. I'd need it by Friday at the latest, so if your plate is full or it's not the right fit, just let me know."
- "I'll be in town for a week, but I'll spend three of those nights with my friend downtown to give each of us a bit of space. Does that work?"
- "Hey, we're having a party this Saturday. If the noise gets too loud, please call me at this number—we'll keep it down after 10 P.M."
- "Nice to meet you, finally! Do we hug or should we shake hands?"

My sister and I have become especially good at this. She'll often text me with "I need to vent about something. I don't need anything from you but to listen and occasionally agree that this situation is wild. Do you have time?" This kind of conscientiousness will likely feel like a natural extension of your boundary practice, and the habit of asking up front can quickly spill over into your social circles, too—bonus!

There's another Golden Rule (okay, I guess it's THE Golden Rule) that also applies beautifully here:

Treat others the way you'd want to be treated.

In thinking about how to respond to someone else's boundary, ask yourself, "How would I want this conversation to go if the shoe were on the other foot?" Would you hope the other person gave you the benefit of the doubt, honored your boundary, and expressed their feelings around it without attempting to guilt-trip you or pressure you to change your mind? I'm sure you would. So take a breath, think back to these lessons, and extend some grace.

LOVING THE LIMITS THAT SET YOU FREE

I recently polled my community on the subject of boundaries, asking, "Now that you're more comfortable setting and holding your own boundaries, how has that changed how you respond when someone sets a boundary with you?" The results were overwhelmingly positive, and remarkably similar.

- "I handle it completely differently! I listen to what they say and do it, rather than pushing or reacting defensively."
- "Now that I feel more confident setting my own boundaries, I recognize them faster when they're set with me, and I'm much better about respecting them."
- "It's helped me not take other people's boundaries personally. I recognize now it's about them and their needs, not about me."
- "I no longer see boundaries as selfish—mine or anyone else's."
- "Hearing someone set a boundary with me makes me value that relationship more, because they're telling me exactly what they need to feel supported and cared for."
- "When others set boundaries with me, it's reassuring. I know they're going to tell me what they need, where the line is, and if I unintentionally cross it."
- "I love it when someone sets a boundary with me now, because

it creates a safe space for the relationship and it's confirmation that this person wants to keep me in their life."

- "I've found myself asking up front, 'Do you need advice, or someone to listen?' I'm more conscientious about not offering unsolicited advice, which alleviates a lot of the need for others to set a boundary with me."
- "I now celebrate when I hear someone else set a boundary, even if they're setting it with me!"

Your practice of setting and holding boundaries is the pebble in the pond, setting off positive ripples that extend into every area of your life. When you establish your own boundaries through clear, kind communication; hold those boundaries; and respect others', you feel more confident identifying your own needs and asking others to respect them. This improves all of your relationships, and helps you reclaim your energy, time, and health. Your boundary practice empowers others to realize *they* can set and hold their own boundaries, modeling the same kind of clear, kind language they've heard from you. Now their relationships are better, and they're feeling all of the same benefits. As a result, everyone in your circle gets better at preventing a boundary overstep in the first place, or at the very least, recognizing a boundary when one is set with them. This makes you all quicker to respect a boundary, and less likely to take it personally or get defensive. Now *all* of you are setting healthy limits, respecting one another's healthy limits, and enjoying the freedom that comes with your newfound commitment to *boundaries*.

You've made the Boundary Lady proud.

CHAPTER 12

The Magic
of Boundaries

I've told a lot of my own stories throughout this book, and I thought it fitting that I close with another. I want to share what happened last week, but not because it was exciting or un-usual—in fact, it was completely typical, and therein lies the magic.

Our week with my son began Monday after school. I knew I had a pretty full week ahead of me at work, too, so I decided to go to bed extra-early that night. My husband and I are super into *Top Chef* reruns and I was excited to see what happened in Res-taurant Wars, but I really wanted to work out before my day started, so I went to bed on Monday right after my son went down at 8 P.M. I call this going to bed "toddler early," and you should try it once in a while because it's *glorious*.

I hit the gym early Tuesday morning, and started the day feel-ing energized. Later that afternoon, a friend and colleague emailed, asking if I would share her new project's Kickstarter on my Instagram channel. I shot her an excited note back, telling her that I've been hearing about this project for years and was thrilled to see it coming to life, and of course I would help. I explained that I don't share fundraisers on social media, but I offered to schedule an Instagram Live with her to promote the venture, and

I made a contribution personally. We booked the Live for the following week to give me enough time to comfortably prepare.

On Wednesday, I received an unexpected invitation to guest lecture at a prestigious university's Food, Health, and Technology class. (It was *Stanford;* I won't even try to be coy about it.) I knew the course instructor and was flattered she wanted me to present, but I was already richly scheduled at work and couldn't prepare a lecture and PowerPoint in time. I told her I'd love to accept, explained my work capacity was at its limit, then offered a few ways that I *could* fit this into my schedule. We settled on a free-form discussion with students submitting questions ahead of time, no slides needed—a format they'd successfully used in class before. (Spoiler: It went so well that I barely resisted the urge to add "Stanford professor" to my LinkedIn bio.)

On Thursday, my nail technician (who I've been seeing for years) texted me to say she was running unexpectedly ahead of schedule, and could I come in a half hour early for my noon appointment? She knows I have a flexible work schedule, and I've often said yes to these requests to make her day easier. That day, I technically could have come in early, but that half hour was blocked out for lunch, as the rest of my day was back-to-back with Zoom calls. I quickly replied that I could not, but confirmed I'd be there promptly at noon with a color in mind so we wouldn't waste any time.

That weekend, my son had his first rock-climbing competition. We went to cheer him on, but during a break in the action, I stepped outside to share some scheduled sponsored content on Instagram. An hour later, I got a text from the sponsor, asking a few questions about how the content was performing. I immediately replied, "I'm with my family this weekend—let's touch base on Monday." He sent me back a quick "have a good weekend" and I returned to the event, where we spent four hours waiting to watch four minutes of climbing—sports mom life in a nutshell.

Sunday morning, my ex-husband sent me a text asking to have a conversation about one particular aspect of our son's day-to-day life at my house. To be honest, I wasn't sure if it was a reasonable conversation for us to have; we don't micromanage what happens at the other parent's house, and this felt more than a little micromanage-y. After thinking about it for a few hours, I typed back, "I want to be a good co-parent and hear your concerns, while reminding you that we don't micromanage what happens at each other's houses. Why don't you send your thoughts over via email, and I'll take them into consideration." That felt like a reasonable compromise to me.

By Sunday evening, I found myself mindlessly refreshing my email and checking my Instagram DMs, which was starting to stress me out, so I decided to put my phone away so I could enjoy our last night with my son. We finished our week strong with a walk with our dog, Henry, a gluten-free pizza with extra pepperoni, and a *Star Wars* movie.

The following Monday morning, I dropped my son off at school and went home to dig right in, knowing I had the week "off" from mom duty to catch up on work, sleep, writing, and of course, Restaurant Wars. We're rooting for you, Gregory! (No spoilers, please.)

LIFE WITH BOUNDARIES

Did you catch all of the boundaries I set throughout the course of this very normal week? I bet you did—or at least, most of them. (Bonus if you caught the boundaries with myself!) But first, let's walk through how my week would have gone *without* those boundaries in place:

- I stay up late watching *Top Chef* with my husband, then skip the gym because I'm too tired to get up early. My week starts off on the wrong foot, and I'm super cranky about it.

- I spend three days ignoring my friend's request because I don't *want* to say no, but I know if I share her Kickstarter, I'll be deluged with requests from others. She emails me again and now I feel so guilty that I share it anyway, but secretly get mad at her for putting me in that position. I don't follow up to see how it went, which I also feel terrible about.

- I say yes to Stanford ("whatever you want, I can make it happen!") and bust my butt to add a lecture and slides to my already full week, leading to more burnout, less sleep, and far more crankiness. The lecture goes okay, but I know I could have done better.

- I skip my lunch to accommodate my nail tech's schedule, then spend the rest of the day mad at her, mad at myself, and hangry because the rest of my afternoon is jam-packed. Why do I do this to myself?

- I miss my son's two best climbing routes because I'm drilling into Instagram stats answering my sponsor's questions on a Saturday, because maybe they won't work with me again if I don't reply right away. (I don't stop to ask myself if that's the kind of company I'd even *want* to work with.) I feel like a terrible mother and I'm frustrated that work always seems to creep into my personal time.

- I stew all day on my ex's request. Because I'm so overtired and triggered, I reply with something snotty, which understandably leaves him confused and upset. I spend the rest of the night venting to anyone who will listen about how tired, burned out, and annoyed I am this week. The pizza arrives cold.

- I stay up too late refreshing email, scrolling Instagram, and watching Netflix, and start the week off by skipping the gym (again) because I'm just too dang tired.

Is the pizza just a coincidence, or do boundaries make *everything* better? I'll leave you to be the judge. I won't make any assumptions about how close this scenario is to your life right now, but if this sounds all too familiar, I'm so glad you found your way to this book and your new boundary practice. You don't have to live like this! By now, you know that a few kindly spoken, clearly outlined limits can help you preserve your energy, time, and mental health, and reduce or eliminate all of these sources of frustration, anger, resentment, and burnout.

Are you ready to peek into your future? Here's what my week looked like after I confidently applied those clear, kind boundaries in the way that served my health, happiness, and capacity:

- I was able to fulfill my health commitments by setting an "early bedtime" boundary with myself, getting enough sleep to keep me healthy, and starting my week feeling proactive and energized.
- I supported my friend's project without compromising my integrity or violating my own social media boundaries, which helped her succeed and made our relationship stronger.
- I got to guest-lecture at STANFORD without burning myself out or dropping the ball with other work projects. Because of the way I handled that request, the course instructor knows she can count on me to say what I mean and follow through, which bodes well for future collaborations.
- I practiced self-care by eating lunch instead of feeling pressure to give up that block of time to accommodate someone else's schedule, leaving me energized and focused for the rest of my day and reaffirming that I am worthy of taking care of me.
- I stayed in the present and was able to enjoy watching my son compete instead of getting pulled into a work conversation on a Saturday. The whole boundary took ten seconds to set, and I didn't even think about it again until Monday morning—and the way this partner responded reaffirmed that they were a good brand to work with.

- I co-parented in the healthiest way possible (for me) by setting a boundary with myself not to reply until I knew how I felt about my ex-husband's request, and I was later able to reply in a way that felt aligned with my integrity and still supported my son's best interests.

- I recognized my behavior with my phone was taking away from the quality of my evening, and set a boundary with myself to put it away, allowing me to relax and enjoy the night and get to bed early . . . again.

This could be you! This *will* be you, if you take everything you've learned about boundaries and start applying it in the real world. You don't have to do it all at once. You don't have to do it perfectly right away. You don't even have to tackle the hardest boundaries first—although kudos to those of you ready to wade right in. All you need to do is recognize the need for a limit, take a deep breath, and use those clear, kind words we've been practicing to hold that space for yourself.

I've helped thousands of people do just that throughout the years, and I've heard about the ways their boundary practice has changed their lives in unexpected ways. When you successfully set a boundary in one area of your life, it gives you the confidence to set limits in other areas, too. When you see your relationships improve, it reaffirms that boundaries aren't selfish—they're acts of kindness, designed with love for them *and* you. When you move through your day feeling more closely connected to yourself and your needs, you start to believe that you *are* worthy of putting yourself first. And when you start showing up everywhere with more confidence, energy, capacity, and grace . . . there is nothing in your life that won't change for the better.

Because *you've* changed it for the better, with boundaries.

Bonus
Chapter

Mom Prefers to Pee Alone

Setting Boundaries with Children

I have a general rule of thumb that I don't offer advice unless I have personal experience in the area—which is why the section on boundaries with children (pages 130–32) is brief. My son was only eight years old when I was writing this book, and honoring kids' developing brains while creating family rules and boundaries is really a job for a child therapist or educator.

So I invited Dr. Chelsey Hauge Zavaleta into the chat.

Dr. Chelsey has a PhD in education and specializes in applied educational neuroscience, social emotional learning, and building calm, cooperative family relationships. In this bonus chapter, Dr. Chelsey will help you recognize the benefits of a healthy, boundaried relationship with your own kids, and offer language you can use to set and hold boundaries with children of all ages.

MELISSA URBAN: Why is it so important to set and hold boundaries with and around our kids?

DR. CHELSEY: When our babies are first born, there are no boundaries. As their parents, we use our intuition and our bodies to soothe them—from feeding them to bouncing and rocking them to holding them. We are the body and nervous system that help them to regulate, calm, and know that they are safe and secure. As our children grow into toddlers who push bound-aries, then into school-age children who push the edge of what is acceptable, then into teenagers who roll their eyes and yearn for independence, what should boundaries look like?

You [Melissa] define boundaries as limits that don't tell other people what to do. Instead, they tell other people what *you* will do, and so they don't require the other person's ap-proval or cooperation. This is true when it comes to boundaries with your children as well. However, because you are responsi-ble for teaching your children how to work with and navigate boundaries, you are also tasked with providing them both with the rules and with positive guidance that supports their par-ticipation in your family unit.

This is the main difference in setting boundaries with your children versus with other adults: You don't need to support your mother to cooperate with your boundary around elimi-nating body-shaming talk, but you *do* need to support your child to cooperate inside your family ethos of maintaining a body-positive culture. And when a child pushes up against a boundary you've set, you must respond with both firmness and compassion—and, most important, with the frame that there is still some learning that they need (and that you can facilitate!) in order to cooperate. When we assume our chil-dren are doing the best they can—even when they're eye-rolling tweens—we position ourselves to be their supporters, and we continue to be the nervous system that helps our children to regulate even in the face of boundaries that require stretching and growth.

Children's first experience of what it is like to rub up against a boundary will happen within the family unit. It is with their parents that children are first able to experience what it feels like when others hold boundaries, and, later, to hold their own boundaries. It's important that our children know they can have boundaries too, and that they experience having those boundaries respected—just as they need to experience other people setting and holding boundaries with them.

MU: All of this makes sense. When my son turned five, I started telling him, "Please let me sleep until 6:30 A.M. If you wake up earlier than that you can read, build LEGO, or play with your cars." While I recognized this was a perfectly reasonable request, I still felt like the meanest mom in the world! Why do we feel so guilty about setting boundaries with our kids, and how can we shift our mindset around this?

DR. CHELSEY: There does not need to be guilt around boundary-setting, as long as it's done well. However, when we set boundaries without giving the appropriate support to allow our children to be successful upholding those boundaries, we may struggle.

Boundaries can be hard for us to hold as grownups, and sometimes we might want to offer lots of reasons and explanations. This often comes from a place of needing to justify boundaries that should be completely neutral. With our kids, this often shows up with worries like, "If I don't offer other activities for my child to do in the morning, or give him a way to track the time, or explain that when Mom gets a good night's sleep, she's more energetic and patient, he may not understand why I'm setting this boundary or he may struggle to maintain it."

Here's the thing: Your child is likely to get lost in all those words. Your child just needs the simple, compassionate boundary, *plus* easy, age-appropriate support for them to be successful with the boundary. If you notice this feeling of guilt around setting boundaries, it's worth asking yourself how you might support your child to meet them. It's likely that all that is needed is a shift in how you approach the boundary, and your child will benefit from the positive support that enables all of you to thrive *with* your boundary. To be clear, rules are only one of the positive supports that will help your child to thrive within your boundaries.

Children are likely to be more successful with something like, "Hey, sweetie, Mom needs to sleep until 6:30 A.M. Can you believe what a sleepyhead I am? This light will help us track the time. When the light is blue, that means it's time to stay in our own bedrooms. When the light is green, that means it's time to wake up sleepyhead Mom! Let's try it tonight!"

MU: Let's talk about rules, then. What's the difference between a boundary and a family rule? I'd like to cover three examples that parents often share with me. First, "No hitting." That's a big one with toddlers. I know parents also struggle with "No phones at the table," especially with teens. Finally, telling your preschooler, "Please don't come into our room until 7 A.M." Are these boundaries, rules, or both?

DR. CHELSEY: A *boundary* is something that an individual person or a family unit needs in order to function in wholehearted ways that support all family members. A *rule* typically supports a family or individual boundary, for the parent or the child. Let's walk through some examples to consider whether they are boundaries or rules, and also how to hold them in ways that support cooperation.

No hitting: No hitting is *neither* a family boundary nor a functional rule. It is a negative desire—something you don't want in your family culture. While I understand why you don't want your children to hit—frankly, nor do I—this language doesn't support children not hitting. Importantly, it also does not tell them what to do *instead* of hitting.

The boundary here might be something like "All bodies are safe," a boundary that all families should have! When children are hitting, the rule to support that is, "In our family, we keep our hands on our own body." Is that going to solve all the hitting? No, it is not. In order to support this rule, which upholds the boundary on safety, parents will need to employ multiple positive supports. For example, "Hands on your own body" should be stated the same way, with the same intonation, by all parents. "Hands on your own body" may also need to be accompanied by or followed by the parents who are in physical proximity to the child who is hitting doing one or all of the following: noticing and/or mapping what happens before the child hits, reducing sensory input ahead of the hitting, sitting behind the child and offering physical support to reduce frustration, giving praise for small moments of cooperation, or offering another option that helps the child get their needs met before the hitting begins.

No phones at the table: This is the same as *no hitting*, a negative statement that is neither a boundary nor a rule. Boundaries state what individuals need. In this situation, from the parents' perspective, that might be "I need our family to connect during dinner." A rule that supports this boundary could be something like "All phones at the charging station after 4 P.M."

What's tricky about this boundary and its upholding rule is that it implicates *all* family members, including the parents. Most of us who are setting a phone boundary at the table are parenting teens, but we might as well extend this rule to "No screens at the table," so that it includes children with tablets *and* grownups with phones!

What is important here is that boundaries and rules should state the desired outcome. Instead of saying "No phones at the table," try saying what you *do want* at the table, and focus on supporting the desired engagement. If you want all phones in the charging basket during dinner, you should build a charging shelf or provide a basket with space for all phones. If you want to connect with your family over dinner, you could purchase a series of question cards or create a structure to talk about the day. And when your children or teens resist, hold your family boundary and the rule, but offer support for their frustration: "Wow, you really want your phone. This is hard, I know. It's dinner, though, so all phones go in the charging basket."

A FRAMEWORK FOR DINNER TABLE CONVERSATION

We have a deck of cards called "Table Talk" that invites different conversation topics around the table, but Dr. Chelsey offered an even easier way to share about your day. You could talk about "rainbows [something amazing that happened] and raindrops [something tough that happened]." Or you could use the structure of "rose [something amazing], thorn [something tricky], bud [something you hope for tomorrow], and watering can [something you helped with today]." Simple metaphors like this—whether it's Table Talk or something a parent suggests as a framework for conversation—can help kids stay engaged and attentive during meals, which in and of itself is a big win for the whole family. All of these tools will help you spark the kind of meaningful connection you hope to have with your kids over dinner (or any other meal you have together).

Please don't come into our room until 7 A.M.: This one comes closer to being an effective boundary or rule, but is still negatively stated. The boundary underneath this statement is something like, "We parents need alone/sleep time until 7."

Assuming this boundary is appropriate for your child's age and profile, we can teach the vast majority of children to respect this boundary—but it does require teaching. You will need to incorporate multiple parenting regimens into this boundary. For example:

1. Employ a consistent bedtime and nighttime routine for the child (and ideally the parents, especially when it comes to mornings).
2. Create a way for the child to understand time. This could be night/wake light, an alarm/story/song on auto-play, or other auditory/visual/physical stimuli that signal the child that it is okay to be in communication with the parents.
3. Praise the child when they are able to cooperate, as well as showing compassion for the child when they "miss it." Praise should be immediate, specific, and incredibly frequent. If the child only partially meets the rule, make sure to praise the fragments of what they've done well, and use these moments to prime them forward. That might sound like, "Wow, you knew it was *almost* time to come into our room, and you tiptoed in to be quiet. So considerate! I bet sometime soon you'll look at your wake light and think, 'Hmm, today I'm an early riser. I'll read two more books and then check my light again.'" Your vote of confidence shores up the relationship *and* moves your child closer to cooperating with your boundary.

MU: Okay, I'm getting it—the language you're recommending here is a huge lightbulb moment. What about something more benign, like, "Place your dirty clothes in the hamper, not on the floor?"

DR. CHELSEY: More than our other examples, "Place your dirty clothes in the hamper, not on the floor" comes close to setting a boundary (and rule!) that children and teens can cooperate with. However, the latter half of the statement—"not the floor"—undoes every positive intention of the first part of the statement.

MU: Ah no! Just when I thought I was getting there! [laughing]

DR. CHELSEY: It's so complicated, right? We get into all these extremely mundane moments with our kids that also just crack us wide open (who would have thought we'd spend so much time figuring out the rules of where the dirty socks go?!). Remember, this is a judgment-free zone! You'll get the hang of it. If we want our children to cooperate with boundaries, those boundaries must be stated in the *positive*. This nurtures both understanding and cooperation, as well as the felt sense of "I know you can do it!" This last part is a critical and often-missing assumption in the parent-child relationship.

MU: This has been a wonderful conversation—I feel like I have a brand-new toolbox to keep working on boundaries with my son! What is one last thing you want all parents to know about boundaries and kids?

DR. CHELSEY: It is *absolutely all right* for you to hold boundaries with your children. Knowing how to meet boundaries is a critical life lesson for our kids. Your boundaries enable your children to be better humans right now, as part of your family unit, *and* in all of their future relationships.

We can best teach them this skill when we meet them with empathy, recognize their developmental stage, and help them figure out how to cooperate. Children need to feel respected; they need their parents to understand their experience of the world. Sometimes that means we have to work on our relationship with our kids before we can set boundaries for them. The things that are going to allow children to flourish inside of your boundary are your positive regard and the support you show them as human beings. Nurturing our children to express their feelings and be curious about our boundaries—while at the same time helping them to respect our limits—are some of the biggest gifts we can offer them. So go forth, create boundaries that enable you to be a better parent, and set your children up to thrive inside those boundaries.

LEARN MORE FROM DR. CHELSEY

Dr. Chelsey Hauge Zavaleta, PhD, offers parenting advice, tools, and programs that combine educational neuroscience and social emotional learning. She and her mother, Dr. Robin Hauge, PhD, have decades of experience in relationship-based parenting and behavior management. You can learn more from Dr. Chelsey at guidingcooperation.org, or on Instagram and TikTok @drchelsey_parenting.

Acknowledgments

Two years ago, I woke up in the middle of the night with a fully formed book proposal in my head. I shot a note to my agent the next morning: "Listen, I had this wild idea in the middle of the night, so I thought I should send it to you . . . I want to write this book about boundaries." Today, I have a lot of people to thank.

To my agent, Christy Fletcher, you have always been in my corner, and your support with this project as it morphed and grew made all the difference. Thank you isn't enough.

To Sarah Fuentes, Melissa Chinchillo, and Yona Levin at Fletcher & Co., I am so grateful to all of you, and excited for every project we still have to come.

To my editor at the Dial Press, Whitney Frick, you saw the vision for this book so clearly, and your motivation and guidance enabled me to carve it out. Writing this was way harder than I thought it would be, but I knew we'd get there because you told me we would. It's been a pleasure and a joy and I count my lucky stars that you picked me.

To my associate editor at the Dial Press, Rose Fox, I met you through your edits and immediately knew you were for me. Direct AF and smart as hell—I'm so glad you're on my team.

To the Dial Press team: Avideh Bashirrad, Brianne Sperber,

Debbie Aroff, Sarah Breivogel, Maria Braeckel, Loren Noveck, Debbie Glasserman, Chris Brand, and Donna Cheng, I am honored and thrilled to be one of your authors now. Thank you for believing in me, and working so hard to bring this book to life so beautifully.

To Andrea Magyar and Suzanne Dunbar at Penguin Canada, thank you for your continued support of and faith in me. I am so proud to bring this book to life in Canada with you behind me.

To Victoria Hobbs at A. M. Heath and Susanna Abbott at Ebury Press, I am thrilled to begin this relationship with you. Thank you for believing in me.

To Leslie Goldman, I adore working with you. You straighten out my messes, inject humor into just the right places, and polish it all up with grace and precision. Bless you forever.

To Allyson Bird, Nora McInerny, Dr. Dolly Jaye Jenkins, Olivia Myers, and Romaissaa Benzizoune, thank you for lending me your talents and expertise for this book. These pages are stronger for your collaboration, and I am grateful.

To Brené Brown, you inspire me in all things, and the impact you have had on my life and work is immeasurable. Thank you for your words and gifts.

To Gretchen Rubin, you were one of just a few people on my vision board a decade ago—and now we're friends, which makes me pinch myself regularly. Thank you for your support, generosity, and kindness.

To my Whole30 HQ team, thank you for taking the reins and giving me the time and space I needed to write this book. I am blessed to work with such a talented, hardworking, and passionate group.

To Erica, especially, you've been my biggest cheerleader throughout this entire process, and crafted the vision we needed so all of us could realize our potential and dreams. Thank you for being my person.

To my husband, who so generously lets me share whatever story I want, as long as it's in the interest of helping people . . . we are the luckiest, I am always on your team.

To my sister, who laughed with me over so many of our shared stories, and who has helped me practice my boundaries for longer than anyone, I love you.

To Nate, you will always be my favorite ex-boyfriend.

To James, you still hold a special place in my heart, even if I'm terrible at texting.

To my son, everything is for you, always.

To each and every person who shared their boundary story or asked a question in my DMs, comments, and email: this is for you. I have never had a good idea in my whole life that didn't start with my community, and your generosity, support, and encouragement are why this book exists. I will forever be grateful to you, and I will never stop supporting you in any way I can. Thank you.

Notes

CHAPTER 1: A CRASH COURSE ON BOUNDARIES

33 **"Clear is kind"** Brené Brown, *Dare to Lead: Brave Work. Tough Conversations. Whole Hearts.* (New York: Random House, 2018).

CHAPTER 3: THE REAL WORK/LIFE BALANCE:
SETTING BOUNDARIES IN THE WORKPLACE

64 **"Job-hunting"** Joshua A. Luna, "The Toxic Effects of Branding Your Workplace a 'Family,'" *Harvard Business Review,* October 27, 2021. hbr .org/2021/10/the-toxic-effects-of-branding-your-workplace-a-family.

CHAPTER 6: LOVE, MARRIAGE, SEX, AND DISHES:
SETTING BOUNDARIES IN ROMANTIC RELATIONSHIPS

180 **"a 2020 report by Oxfam and the Institute for Women's Policy Research"** Cynthia Hess, Tanima Ahmed, M. Phil, and Jeff Hayes, "Providing Unpaid Household and Care Work in the United States: Uncovering Inequality," Institute for Women's Policy Research, January 2020. iwpr.org/wp -content/uploads/2020/01/IWPR-Providing-Unpaid-Household-and-Care -Work-in-the-United-States-Uncovering-Inequality.pdf.

180 **"same-sex couples manage this division"** Reina Gattuso, "Why LGBTQ Couples Split Household Tasks More Equally," BBC, March 10, 2021. www.bbc.com/worklife/article/20210309-why-lgbtq-couples-split -household-tasks-more-equally.

181 **"Resource: *Fair Play*"** Eve Rodsky, *Fair Play: A Game-Changing Solution*

for When You Have Too Much to Do (And More Life to Live) (London: Quercus Books, 2019).

188 **"Resource: *Nonviolent Communication*"** Marshall B. Rosenberg, *Nonviolent Communication: A Language of Life* (Encinitas, Calif.: Puddle-Dancer Press, 2015).

203 **"orgasm achievement"** David A. Frederick, H. Kate St. John, Justin R. Garcia, Elisabeth A. Lloyd, "Differences in Orgasm Frequency Among Gay, Lesbian, Bisexual, and Heterosexual Men and Women in a U.S. National Sample," *Archives of Sexual Behavior* 47, no. 1 (2018): 273–88.

204 **"Resource: *Come As You Are*"** Emily Nagoski, *Come As You Are: The Surprising New Science that Will Transform Your Sex Life* (New York: Simon & Schuster, 2015).

CHAPTER 8: CLEARING THE TABLE:
SETTING BOUNDARIES AROUND FOOD, ALCOHOL, AND TABLE TALK

234 **"food, beverage, and restaurant companies spent $13.4 billion"** Jennifer L. Harris, Willie Frazier III, Shiriki Kumanyika, and Amelie G. Ramirez, "Increasing Disparities in Unhealthy Food Advertising Targeted to Hispanic and Black Youth," UConn Rudd Center for Food Policy and Health, January 2019, uconnruddcenter.org/wp-content/uploads/sites/2909/2020/09/TargetedMarketingReport2019.pdf.

234 **"Alcohol spends between $1 and 2 billion"** "Advertising Spending of the Distilled Spirits Industry in the United States in 2019, by Medium," Statista, November 2, 2021. statista.com/statistics/259642/advertising-spending-of-the-distilled-spirit-industry-in-the-us-by-medium/; "Advertising Spending of Selected Beer Manufacturers in the United States in 2020," Statista, November 8, 2021. statista.com/statistics/264998/ad-spend-of-selected-beer-manufacturers-in-the-us/.

235 **"eating behaviors are transmitted socially"** Eric Robinson, Jason Thomas, Paul Aveyard, and Suzanne Higgs, "What Everyone Else Is Eating: A Systematic Review and Meta-Analysis of the Effect of Informational Eating Norms on Eating Behavior," *Journal of the Academy of Nutrition and Dietetics*, 114, no. 3 (2014): 414–29.

235 **"social media plays a role in influencing your choices"** Lily K. Hawkins, Claire Farrow, and Jason M. Thomas, "Do Perceived Norms of Social Media Users' Eating Habits and Preferences Predict Our Own Food Consumption and BMI?" *Appetite,* 149 (2020): 104611.

CHAPTER 9: HANDLE WITH CARE:
SETTING BOUNDARIES AROUND SENSITIVE SUBJECTS

281 **"Bystander Intervention"** Right to Be, "The 5Ds of Bystander Intervention." righttobe.org/guides/bystander-intervention-training/.

CHAPTER 10: GIFTS TO FUTURE YOU:
SETTING AND HOLDING BOUNDARIES WITH YOURSELF

292 **"Resource: *The Four Tendencies*"** Gretchen Rubin, *The Four Tendencies: The Indispensable Personality Profiles That Reveal How to Make Your Life Better (And Other People's Lives Better, Too)* (New York: Harmony Books, 2017).

295 **"Resource: *Tiny Habits*"** BJ Fogg, PhD, *Tiny Habits: The Small Changes That Change Everything* (New York: Houghton Mifflin Harcourt, 2019).

Melissa Urban is the co-founder and CEO of Whole30 and an authority on helping people create lifelong healthy habits. She is a six-time *New York Times* bestselling author (including the #1 bestseller *The Whole30*); and has been featured by *Today, Good Morning America, The New York Times, The Wall Street Journal,* and CNBC. She lives with her husband, son, and a poodle named Henry in Salt Lake City, Utah.

melissau.com
Instagram: @melissau
Twitter: @melissa_urban
TikTok: @melissa_u

To inquire about booking Melissa Urban for a speaking engagement, please contact the Penguin Random House Speakers Bureau at speakers@penguinrandomhouse.com.

The Dial Press, an imprint of Random House,
publishes books driven by the heart.

Follow us on Instagram:
@THEDIALPRESS

Discover other Dial Press books and
sign up for our e-newsletter:

thedialpress.com

Your personal information will be processed in
accordance with our privacy policy, located here:
penguinrandomhouse.com/privacy